Serendipity

A Journey with Joe Larter

The Life and Times of the Man who created
Pleasurewood Hills American Theme Park

An environmentally friendly book printed and bound in England by
www.printondemand-worldwide.com

Mixed Sources
Product group from well-managed
forests, and other controlled sources
www.fsc.org Cert no. TT-COC-002641
FSC © 1996 Forest Stewardship Council

PEFC
PEFC/16-33-415

PEFC Certified
This product is
from sustainably
managed forests
and controlled
sources
www.pefc.org

This book is made entirely of chain-of-custody materials

First published 2013 by FASTPRINT PUBLISHING
of Peterborough, England.

www.fast-print.net/store.php

SERENDIPITY: A JOURNEY WITH JOE LARTER

The Life and Times of the Man who created Pleasurewood Hills American Theme Park

A catalogue record for this book is available from the British Library

ISBN 978-178035-679-2

Acknowledgements

Charles F Carrodus – *The Horning Story* Soman Wherry Press 1949

A Norfolk Village in Wartime – R H Clarke (London) Ltd 1946

Keith Skipper – *A Fresh Delivery of The Boy John letters* Mousehold Press 2003

Sydney Grapes – *The Boy John letters* – Wensum Books 1974

John Wardley – *Creating my own Nemesis* – Amazon Books 2013

Alfred Hedges – *The Gunton Story* Weathercock Press 1977

Ida Fenn – *Tales of Norfolk* Geo. R Reeve Wymondham 1976 illustrated by her son-in-law Colin Grapes

Bill Bryson – *Down Under* - Random House 2000

The Archant Group – Eastern Daily Press, *Lowestoft Journal* and *Great Yarmouth Mercury*. Various photographs and press cuttings quoted.

Ron Bagely, photographer, for the *Pleasurewood* and current pictures

I have had enormous help from my family and
friends in putting together these memories of my life
and the times in which we have all lived.

I cannot mention you all by name but I have appreciated your
comments and suggestions. In particular, David Porter, my editor, has
given me some good guidance along the way, with a long-suffering
wife, Betty, showing how good she is at playing patience as well as
bridge by the time she had read the 6th and final draft.

Introduction

*S*erendipity – *happy and unexpected discoveries by accident'* and that, I think, has been the thread through my life.

Opportunities occur for all of us, but it is the individual who chooses to say 'yes' or 'no'. Those decisions shape our future and, when they turn out well, people often say 'that was lucky'; but it is no such thing, just that one had the courage to make the decision at the time and it turned out to be a good one.

A trait I have is always to be positive and want to say 'yes' to any new and exciting-looking experience. I am pretty sure the early death of my father caused that attitude – say 'yes' if you can today, because tomorrow you may not be here to have the choice.

The book is not so much an account of what I have done because, in the scale of things, it is very little, but the memories I have of a unique period and stories of some unusual and interesting people I have met along the way. It is the memories, the anecdotes and my love of living in Norfolk that I hope my family and friends will appreciate and find interesting.

In the same way as Ronnie Corbett, in his end-of programme monologues, you will often find me 'digressing' – going off track for a paragraph or two or an anecdote.

A chance meeting in a broken-down taxi in Antigua led to winters in Freeport, Bahamas, and 35 years or so of experiences and involvement in Florida, and to the investments in the USA. That tiny event altered the whole course of my life.

You will see that 'by chance', following the takeover of our building companies, I was able to regain immediately the leisure developments in Norfolk and Wales, and thereby hang a few of the major tales including *Pleasurewood Hills* and the disastrous sale to *RKF Group*.

'By chance' a Dutch family turned up in the very early days of *Pleasurewood Hills,* and the resulting involvement secured the success of *Pleasurewood.* Helping a friend of Betty with a travel business was just that – help, but led to another Dutch involvement and eventual takeover of her company.

I was delighted, when I went back to Great Yarmouth in 2009, to be asked to speak at so many occasions. It was the answering of so many questions and the telling of various anecdotes there which helped convince me I should record it all in a book.

I have tried to keep to a rough chronological record so that you see my people and events in the context of the world in general, but sometimes I have to mention things out of order to make sense – my 'digressions' – so my apologies in advance if I occasionally confuse you. Blame my editor! As you will read, at one time I was the subject of a fraud and it was no consolation for me to read in 2012 that a far better Norfolk businessman than me, Graham Dacre, was also defrauded. I wrote to him and we met for lunch, but I don't think either of us could explain how these things happen to perfectly sensible, honest businessmen, except that we trust people too much. Enough of that – let's get this show on the road.

Chapter One
1939–1944 – Early Memories,
and Martham in Wartime

As the man said: 'Let's start at the very beginning.'

In the early hours of 27 July 1939, with the Second World War in the offing, the Larter family's own life-changing event was about to take place. Oswald (Ossie) and Helen (Rhoda May) were about to receive an invasion of their household in the form of me (5lbs 12 oz) and my twin sister, Mary (6bs 2oz) - twenty minutes behind me, although you would never guess that from knowing her.

Mary tells me Dad was in a panic when Mother woke him up to say the birth had started. He ran across the road, trousers in his hand, to alert a Mrs Turner to help whilst he fetched the local midwife, Nurse Greenacre, such was the system for home births at that time.

Various stories circulate in the family as to how we got our names. However, I am assured by my twin that Father was given names on a piece of paper by Mother and went off to register our births. Unfortunately, by the time he got to the Registry Office, he had lost the paper and could not remember the names he'd been given!

Father had to think fast and could only come up with Mary and Joseph – so that is what we got! Not sure what the original couple would say about us, but I have settled down as Joe and Mary is, well - Mary. Whilst it makes a nice story that has been repeated in the family over the years, as I have examined the genealogy material assembled by Marjorie Terrill (sister of my wife, Betty) I realize that, even back into the 1700s, the names Mary and Joseph, or Joe, were appearing in the family tree and maybe Father had more 'guidance' than we knew about – but it seems we even got our names 'by chance'.

I am sure Mother was looked after well by various family and friends at her father-in-law's house and The Limes, which he built next door – and Granny Blanche (Storey Smith) came and stayed as Mother needed help for a time. As Betty has pointed out to me, a total birth weight of 12lbs was no mean feat for our delicately-framed mother.

Obtaining a rented home just as the war was starting was extremely difficult, but Father knew a Mrs Tullock from Lerwick, in the Shetland Islands, who owned a house in Repps Road, Martham. Mrs T lived in London and she rented out the house on condition the family kept one room available for her, should she wish to stay for holidays. I think we must have stayed at Repps Road for just over two years, but then Mrs T found London too dangerous, or perhaps had been bombed-out, and wanted the house back.

I think she must have been a very good friend, because I have found a couple of postcards from her, one addressed later to Moregrove Farm, our next home, and wishing me a happy third birthday. I recall being taken to the bottom of the Repps Road garden to watch the enormous steam trains rushing through and, when the film *The Railway Children* came out in the '60s, I certainly already knew the experience and the magic of steam. Did that affect me in later life? We shall see.

I just remember from an early age being in a huge, double *Mary Poppins*-style pram with Mary and that, as we were taken for a 'promenade', we were a curiosity because twins born in Martham were a great rarity. To obtain such a pram in wartime was no mean feat for Father and when, three years later, we had 'competition' in the form of Peter and Paul Randell – there we go again with names, maybe we should have started a church – Mother gave them the pram, our cots and other baby gear to use as well.

There is also an embarrassing studio photo portrait of Mary and me in curls. How beautiful we were! Alongside that I have printed you a picture of my own first children, Andrew and Rebecca, to show the extraordinary likeness between Andrew and me at the same age.

There is also a comparison of myself and my father at about 25 years.

Andrew has also inherited my own brand of humour. Just recently, when clearing our house to move, I emailed him that I was really doing the job he and his three siblings would otherwise have to do on my death. There would be a charge, and I had decided on two cases of good red wine – each. He immediately replied that he would pay when I completed my side of the bargain.

Mary tells me the photo studio had a request from Caleys, the local chocolate factory, to use our portrait for the front of a chocolate box. Apparently, Father would not allow that, but think of the chocolates we missed, and with wartime rationing too!

War was by now well under way and, with Mrs T back in possession of Repps Road, Father had to find another home urgently. It was very difficult and, in the end Billy Chapman, a local farmer and Father's cricketing friend, asked the Jones family, who lived in a rambling farmhouse he also owned at Martham, if they would let us share their house. Moregrove Farm became our new base, and a more idyllic home for children of our age could not be imagined.

Sadly, Moregrove is no more, but we happily shared with the Jones family – for us, one big room downstairs, plus a scullery/kitchen and just one big bedroom upstairs, we twins at one end with Mother and Father at the other. No indoor facilities at all, with a 'thunder-box' toilet in the backyard and a hand-pump for washing water from the pond nearby. All this was quite normal for the day, with a weekly 'nightsoil' cart calling at each house to empty the outside toilets.

Mrs Jones, for ever known as 'Joney', helped Mother in her part of the house and we realise, looking back, that giving birth to us really had made her very weak. In addition Mary and I caught measles, and Mother followed by catching it from us. Not a problem these days, but then for an adult to get measles was very dangerous. Mother was seriously unwell and Granny Blanche had to come and stay again, this time with very limited sleeping conditions. She got allocated a large cupboard into which was placed a small, temporary bed.

Imagine the effort required of a mother in those days, with two babies and a husband: cleaning, washing, laundry, cooking and looking after an old farmhouse – all without vacuum cleaners and the electrical aids we take for granted today. Washday was always a Monday and for drying there was an area near the orchard called 'The Bleach' with wires, strings and props to help. Some laundry was simply laid on the crop of stinging nettles to dry out. 'Joney' was to remain a very close friend and help Mother for many years even after we had moved away.

Another 'aid' that did not yet exist was, of course, the washing machine but, also, we had no washing powder. The lady doing her weekly laundry had to manage with a boiler and large blocks of yellow or green 'carbolic' soap, rubbing out stains by hand on a corrugated 'washing board'. 'Dashing away with a smoothing iron', literally.

A silly thing I remember is of soap being quite expensive and all the small pieces carefully saved, to be put into a small, wire container on the end of a handle, so they could be whisked in water to provide the 'soap' for washing dishes, rather like we add a squirt of liquid detergent today. Such were the times.

Still on sickness; rather like today, where one might give a child a vitamin C tablet or suchlike to ward off a cold, the thought then was that cod liver oil was the cure-all. The song *A Spoonful of Sugar Helps the Medicine Go Down* says it all – except we did not get the sugar. Each night we were given one CLO capsule to swallow. I hated it intensely. Mary tells me that in one year, when Mother and Joney were spring-cleaning, they lifted the stair carpet and were puzzled to find a considerable number of small, clear, egg-like cases. Only later did it dawn on them that I might not have been taking my CLO capsules.

Situated in the centre of a real working farm, still with carthorses to plough and steam traction engines to thresh the harvest, the house had neither running water nor heating, other than one coal fire. A portable oil stove was in the scullery for Mother to cook on, but there was no electricity for lights or anything, and I remember pump-up paraffin lamps hissing away and forever burning out their globe-type 'wicks'. I believe that, in the last years at Moregrove, we did have a battery wireless set on which Father and Mother could follow the progress of the war. Weekly bath-time on a Friday was a tin bath in front of the fire, filled from a coal-heated water boiler in the kitchen, and the water carefully shared.

But for us as children? We were oblivious to any wartime problems, having a pond outside, an orchard with every fruit- and nut-tree you could think of, and mysterious barns and farm buildings to explore and play in. It was just perfection. Although we helped ourselves freely, all fruit, nuts and anything edible would be gathered carefully and sent or sold for the war effort, as quite severe food shortages were building up.

If people had chickens, a goat or any farm animal that needed feeding, then they had to agree to send away a certain percentage of their 'produce' in order to get a permit for farm foodstuffs but it still meant that, living in the country on a farm, we ate considerably better than in the average town.

Candles, with all the shadows they cast, creaky twisting staircase (Alfred Hitchcock would have been in his element), then an odd gale blowing in the rafters of the house; we were not always happy to go up to bed! For Mother, the lack of the basics we have today must have made life very difficult.

When I tell my own children and grandchildren that on winter mornings we would scratch our names in the frost on the *inside* of our bedroom windows, they find it hard to believe. Except that my son Andrew has told me it was just the same boarding at his Glebe House School in Hunstanton and, as he put it: 'you were paying for that!' My children would also not understand how important the word 'bedsocks' was! A very different world from the centrally-heated, insulation-obsessed one of today, with electric blankets and duvets.

We also had a scruffy mongrel of a family dog called Jiggs, whose best trick was to escape to the village pond by the church, get as filthy as he could, and then come home to show us.

The Jones family – father Leslie worked on the farm and had a marvellous team of horses – had three children, Douglas, Barry and Jennifer, the latter two being about our age, so plenty of adventures around the farm. Not quite *The Famous Five* but a lot of fun, and we were allowed a freedom to roam and play we would never have been given today. Ponds, farm machinery, haystacks and straw stacks, and dykes, all not then seen as "'elf and safety' dangers. I just think they taught us a lot of common sense.

Harvesting was the fun time, still carried out with a steam 'set', I think they were called, with a gang moving from one farm to another. Usually the team, with a big traction engine, would arrive at the next farm in line in the early evening, to be ready to steam up early next morning. The excitement and attention they got on arrival and set-up was very much like I saw later, when a travelling circus would arrive in a village to erect its 'big top'.

As soon as either cutting or stacking was under way we were allowed to take our own 'elevens' or 'fourses'

(the refreshment breaks taken by farm workers at 11am and 4pm), which usually consisted of homemade lemonade, egg sandwiches and the great homemade delight (for me) of ice-cream wafers stuck together with a chocolate sauce spread. We would make a proper drinking 'straw' from a piece of straw from the field, and sit ourselves against some sheaves of corn to watch progress.

Unlike today, where combine harvesters take all the romance away and cut acres in hours, there were two stages to harvest. First, a horse-drawn 'binder' (this cut down the corn and bound it into sheaves) would slowly circle the field, ending with an ever-decreasing centrepiece into which all the rabbits, hares and vermin would have been forced to hide. There would be great excitement amongst the farm workers and followers (mostly teenage village boys) when the cutting came to the end and they spread themselves around the remaining section to tackle the rabbits and hares that appeared – certainly one for the pot THAT night…

On the cutting day the sheaves would be 'stooked', three or four stood up against each other to dry a little later. When ready, in the second stage the sheaves would be collected by horse and cart and brought to an 'elevator', powered by the steam engine, which would slowly drop them so another team could arrange them as a base on which to build a stack. It was amazing to watch the stack 'master' build a perfect 'house' of a thousand sheaves or so, all absolutely symmetrical and ready to be straw-thatched and kept dry for later threshing, to produce the corn itself as the farmer required it.

The farm had a goodly herd of cows, and milking took place each day in the 'parlour' at the entrance to our garden. Milking was very early in the morning and I recall one Christmas morning being convinced that the pattern caused by the light from the parlour window on to snow was, in fact, the sleigh indicating Father Christmas had arrived!

The whole farm was based around the horse. Every day, carthorses would be brought out for whatever tasks and were lined up at the edge of our pond, which was their 'watering hole'. Leslie Jones seemed to be the main horse man and it was a wonder to see him and his team plough a field with dead accuracy. Each horse responded to its own name, Rosie, Betsy and so on and, with just his eye, Leslie ploughed the furrows as if they were drawn with a ruler.

It was not until many years later, when staying with a school friend in Barnoldby le Beck in Lincolnshire, that I saw a competitive ploughing-match, and understood how much entertainment and rivalry there must have been in the real village ploughing days.

Although we were well out in the country, with Father working on the wartime boats that came into Great Yarmouth for repair, Moregrove nevertheless always reacted to the numerous air-raid warnings that came on a lot of evenings. A complete blackout (no light whatsoever) was mandatory. It seems not too serious looking back, but we would be woken up by Mother as soon as the siren went off and taken to 'safety', which in our case was deemed to be below the old farmhouse wooden staircase!

The main advantage for me was that Mary would always sleep through but I would be awake, and there were various goodies on offer to keep us quiet and peaceful, of which I am sure I got more than my share. Our dog, Jiggs, came too and Mary remembers him as being more nervous than the family. Even in a thunderstorm, he would rush to hide under the stairs.

Aged about 3, one of my first and vivid memories is of a disabled plane crash-landing in the field next to the farmhouse, with a team from the RAF coming to dismantle it. Before they did so, I was lifted into the cockpit and must have been one of the youngest-ever 'temporary' pilots in the wartime RAF. The recovery people camped on the Jones' kitchen floor for a few nights and, after they had departed, there was an amazing collection of nuts, bolts and screws left on the ground which were gathered for Father and the farm to use.

War certainly did not seem serious to us children, but the fact is it was deadly serious, of course. Only years later did I read about the terrible carnage in Great Yarmouth, Lowestoft and lower down the coast, when those areas were deemed 'soft' targets by the Germans. On 7 May 1943 (me just 3 years and 10 months) seven bombers swooped in, strafing Winterton and Hemsby on their way to the Vauxhall and Southtown railway stations at Great Yarmouth. In four minutes, before they then flew out over Newport (where they lost one plane, which clipped a telegraph pole), that attack inflicted more than 60 casualties, with 13 deaths. But worse was to follow.

On 11 May, as Great Yarmouth had barely recovered from the first raid, another lightning strike by 18 FW 190 bombers caused devastation. 49 service personnel and civilians were killed, the majority being ATS girls billeted at Sefton House. The town took years to recover from that raid, and so Mother hiding us below the stairs at

Moregrove, however ineffective that might have turned out, was not so silly after all.

Another memory I have of that time is of Douglas Jones taking us all down onto the marshes to gather insects and sticklebacks in jam-jars, no doubt to bring home for Mother eventually to dispose of in our own pond when we had grown tired of them. I still love the Norfolk marshes and their calm wilderness with an old windmill in the distance, and maybe that stems from our time at Moregrove and those trips. In later days I did actually buy a windmill at Horsey, but getting power, water and drainage sorted really proved too time-consuming and other matters took precedence.

In the early 2000s I went back to look at the old Moregrove site (I so wish they had not pulled it down) and found that a new owner of the old barns we had played in had converted them into a beautiful house. He was curious about my visit and readily sent to me by email a collection of aerial photographs of the old Moregrove farmhouse he had discovered and which I did not have.

Did we suffer at all in the war? I think not, and especially not as far as food was concerned, and neither did most country people because there was always someone who happened to have killed or shot one animal or another and shared the spoils. We had our abundant fruit trees and nut trees, a large vegetable garden we shared with the Joneses and, of course, chickens for eggs and the occasional Sunday lunch.

Strange items would appear now and then. I remember 'pork cheese' from a Mrs Bailey, which then did not appeal at all! Hedgerow fruits and things like blackberries, bullace plums and wild horseradish were all important. We later collected rose hips (to make syrup) at school to help the war effort. Not quite sure what they did with them, but that is what we were told.

Another activity we all joined in was the making of butter. I guess because the farm had the dairy there was always a good supply of milk for both the Jones family and ourselves. We would two-thirds fill a Kilner jar with full-cream milk (that was a jar of about 1½ pints where you could seal the lid, and which was normally used for preserving fruit) and shake it until the cream consolidated and you could skim off very soft butter. Delicious!

I think the rationing of sweets and sugar we would have noticed, but then we started to get food parcels sent over from the USA by 'Aunt

Nora', my maternal grandmother's sister, who had emigrated there in the early 1930s. Mary remembers Mother being very annoyed that every food parcel arrived having been opened by Customs. That would not have been too bad, but if there was a tin of *Golden Syrup* they would not be too careful about putting the lid back on securely. Many years later, on a USA trip with Mother, I was able to personally thank Nora for what she had sent over.

By the end of the war Father, as a skilled tradesman, mainly plumbing, was working in places like Trimingham where the USA forces were active, and I recall him bringing home the very first bananas we had ever seen. We shared them with the Joneses and Jennifer it was, I think, who insisted we should be eating the skin and not the inside. The strange things one remembers from so long ago!

Father was a great shot and, working amongst all the farms and their owners, was frequently invited to a 'shoot'. We have a favourite photograph of him standing on the Martham Ferry road with his yellow labrador, Jimmy, his ever-present 'Norfolk' hat and looking as content as any man could. I think his most enjoyable shooting was duck 'flighting', which involved late-night decoy arrangements using wooden duck 'look-alikes' to persuade the birds to come down and join their 'family' already feeding. Father and his gang would be there ready to give them a welcome.

To get to the village of Martham itself, we had to take a footpath through the centre of a ploughed field. Being at our age and tiny size, standing alone in the middle of a large, ploughed field was daunting. I remember looking towards what was Somerton in the distance and being convinced I was looking at Africa. I must have seen a book or heard about Africa at school because, of course, there was no television or cinema and we just had the war-time radio. I believe the BBC started television programmes just before the war, but stopped when war commenced.

We started school aged about 4½ years, and walked the footpath each day. At Martham our teacher was Miss Bates, and I have a vivid recollection of outdoor lessons in the sun in summer, where we had to be very quiet because the playground adjoined the local churchyard. Maybe it was because of the war, but there seemed to be an amazing number of funerals, in which of course we children took a morbid interest.

Prior to Martham School I also recall that Mary and I spent time with a Mrs Dyble at West Somerton School whilst Dad did some repair or other. From Mary's notes she recalls us being curiosities as twins at school and always being placed together which, apparently, I hated, making sure we were split up for the following term.

In those very early days transport for Father's business was a motor cycle and side-car, which also took all of us around as well when needed, together with a trailer for his builders' gear. There was a lot of walking, but Martham had a railway station, the stationmaster being Mr Bill Temple. In those times the stationmaster was a VERY important and respected member of the community, and he was a great friend of Father's through the cricket club.

By the time we moved from Moregrove Father had a small Austin, affectionately known to the family as 'The DoodleBug' after the German rocket with the same nick-name. The Germans invented the unmanned missile with a bomb on the end of it, directed it fairly inaccurately to a particular UK city and, at the end of a predetermined time, the power would stop and it would drop wherever it was at that moment. The rocket might be directed at Birmingham, but drop down in Leicester. The only certainty was that if you heard its familiar drone, like a motorbike without a silencer, and then silence, you knew you were pretty near an enormous explosion about to come. Terrifying. It could happen just anywhere as they were so inaccurate. I don't think Father's driving was as bad as that but, as Mary reminded me, no safety-belts of course, and doors that tended to open by themselves as you rounded a corner.

The other lovely memories of that time are that it was still the early days of the motor car, and of the old-fashioned 'Are you being served?' type of shop. Milk was from a pony and trap carrying churns, into which the milkman dipped his measure and poured what you wanted into your own container.

Groceries in Martham were from Clowes or AA Francis' store (Francis was also the local photographer), where your goods would be delivered by the shop assistant on his bicycle with the carrier at the front. Shoes could be bought or repaired at Cobbs, meat was from Chapman's (cousin of our landlord) or Geary, and all on the lovely village green which remains today. When later, as a builder, I got the first approvals to expand Martham, I was really pleased to be able to place trees on the rather bare village green. They enhance it so well today.

The first garages were being opened, one by a real character, Chairman of, and umpire for, the Cricket Club and, later, local Councillor, Jimmy Bensley. He not only started a garage, but also had the first public bus in Martham – a 'charabanc', it was called - to take groups to foreign places like Great Yarmouth, Clacton-on-Sea and Felixstowe! Latterly he also ran a secondhand and antiques shop; I have a beautiful oil lamp I converted to electric, and for which I paid him 5 shillings (25p).

One thing Father had (and I have certainly inherited) was a tremendous sense of humour. The village green was the place where, on a Sunday, the local Home Guard (Dad's Army of the so-accurate TV series) would meet to parade and get some very basic training. The Home Guard was made up of those men who, for one reason or another, were held back from active service to look after the population and vital services, or had reserved occupations, I believe they were called. In Father's case it was as a plumber working on or repairing the damaged boats coming in to Great Yarmouth.

The arrangement was that the men would meet in the *Kings Arms* public house by the green, have a pint and then parade. On the occasion I am told about, the General Commanding Home Guard for East Anglia was coming to inspect the Martham Home Guard. In the *Kings Arms*, ahead of the inspection, Father bet all the others a pint that the only person the General would speak to would be himself, which they all thought nonsense and took on the wager.

Sure enough, walking up and down the lines, the only person he stopped to speak to was Father. Back in the pub, shelling out the pints he had won, no one could understand how this could have happened, and asked Father what was said. 'Well, he asked for my name and number, to which I replied: "42347598 Larter, sir". He then asked me how long I had been in the Home Guard and I replied: "Three years, sir". He then said: "Well, Larter, if you have been in the Home Guard for three years, it is about time you learned to put your cap badge on the right way up."' That was Father to a 'T'.

Come 1945, and the war was over. I think Father did quite well working all over Norfolk and, as a number of tradesmen returned from the war safely, he started to build a small team which formed the basis of his future building business. In particular the Myhill brothers – Stanley, a plumber and decorator who had also worked his apprenticeship alongside Father, with Grandfather John, and George, a very skilled carpenter who, along with Herbert Powley, became the mainstay of the firm at Winterton when I had to take over so much later.

Mary remembers Stanley Myhill coming home on leave from the war and sharing his ration of coupons for sweets. He would buy us a large slab of Cadbury's chocolate and we would very carefully make sure we ate no more than one square at a time.

I do not recall money ever being short, but it was also never plentiful. Mother, who had trained in Norwich as a dressmaker, made most of our clothes, at which she was very gifted. I know supplies of used parachute silk, which Father obtained from his Trimingham contacts, were very important to her. No doubt other items, like occasional nylon stockings from America, were passing around as well, but I was too young to understand that.

Father built up his small business and Mother did dressmaking for various clients. Each week they would pay their bills and, if anything was left over, they would buy another tool or whatever Father needed to improve his business. I know in those days Frank Cooper, the head of Cooper's builders' merchants in Great Yarmouth, was an enormous help with advice and, more importantly, credit, as he was to be to me so much later.

As we got older, Mary and I would go into town with Father who, I think, was immensely proud to show off his twins and, whilst he saw Frank for help with pricing some job or other, Frank's secretary would 'entertain' us in the outer office – not much typing on those afternoons. Even in the late 1990s I would still occasionally see Frank's secretary at the shop, which had moved to Harfrey's Estate in Southtown in Great Yarmouth, although Frank himself was long gone. His son, Brian, and I became great friends in the days of Round Table and the Young Conservatives, but all that much later.

In the back of my mind, there is a vague memory of meeting at this time a 'Captain Mainwaring' bank manager type – a Mr Lord, I think, then followed by Jimmy Parslow - who may have helped, but somehow Father got together the funds to buy an old house right on the edge of the sand dunes and sea at Winterton, 5 miles from Martham. In 1936 the house was recorded as 'Town Hill House' but when we arrived it had been re-named 'Broad View', no doubt for the enormous expanse of dunes you could see from the property. This was a very different world from Moregrove but again, for children, absolutely idyllic living by the sea and the huge marram grass areas of sand dunes on the doorstep.

So, at my age about 6 or 7 years, we all decamped from Moregrove to 'Broad View', and were there for the rest of our childhood and beyond, with Mother living there until she died. Mrs Jones and Mother had become very close, and for many years 'Joney' came over to Winterton once a week to help her.

Later I have devoted some space to my twin, Mary, because although quite different from me, she has always had that Larter energy and enthusiasm but used it in a different way. Before we move on to Winterton, let me fill you in with what I know about the earlier members of our family on both sides.

Chapter Two
The Family History

What we had was the bringing together of the Larter family (thought to be from Martham when I first started looking at this book, but see later) and the Storey Smith family from Horning and that area. Mother's Storey Smith side first, and why 'Storey' Smith? Sometimes it is very interesting to ask questions, so here's the 'Storey!' with help from Betty's sister Marjorie, who did the research.

In 1843 William Smith, a 'husbandman', married Elizabeth Willis, and one of their children was Hannah, baptized in April 1838. In 1859 Hannah Smith is recorded as a 'single woman' and she has a son baptized William, the father given as one William Storey of Ludham. Hanky-panky here, then, and worse to follow.

According to the 1861 census the son, William, lived with his grandparents and was known as William Storey Smith, taking both parents' names, but Hannah, who lived next door and was still unmarried, later had another son, George, whose father was recorded as James Alcock. Obviously she did not want to get tied down! –it must have been quite a serious matter in a small village in those days, or perhaps not.

Young William Storey Smith was a labourer and married (that's better) Sarah (?) from Dereham circa 1883. They had a family of 14 children and Herbert, my grandfather, was the eldest and baptized circa July 1882 - the year before they were married – hmmm!. Well 'circa' in those days could be a year out so we will give them the benefit of the doubt; then Herbert married Blanche Myhill London of Smallburgh in 1906. Thus you have the 'story' of our Storey Smith ancestors, Blanche and Herbert being my grandparents on my mother's side.

The London side was also the branch of the family that went to the USA in 1932, but is another part of the story.

My mother, Helen, was the only child of Blanche and Herbert; for a time, Mother was a pupil teacher in the Horning School at Upper Street. The family could not afford the cost of her training to be a full teacher, so she then went to train as a 'court' (I think that means 'formal') dressmaker in Norwich, at which she became very skilled. Mother was born in Horning on 19 March 1910 and died at Winterton in 1981.

In Potter Heigham (more or less midway between Martham and Horning) there is a public house called the *Bridge Inn*, and next door was what may have at that time been looked on by parents as a den of iniquity (if they were told) – Drake's Dance Hall! - And that is where my father, Oswald, and Helen met.

Two more different characters you could not imagine - but I think, all considered, it was a successful marriage; a man's man and a very gentle lady. Father was a great cricketer and, on occasion, did not turn up for the Saturday dance, but Mother said she would always get a note during the week to offer an excuse, no doubt late cricketing celebrations if they had won.

Although from farm labourer stock, Herbert was a real gent, as was his father, also William, and who died in 1939 just as my sister and I were born. Herbert was the man who would help everyone; he was the Churchwarden and Sexton at Horning and seems to have been much relied upon.

At the christening of my daughter, Rebecca, from my first marriage to Susan Baker, our doctor friend Tommy Stuttaford, whose family had lived in Horning, was Godfather. He told the story that, as a small boy, he saw Grandfather Herbert as the Churchwarden and was convinced, because of his white hair and distinguished looks, that this was Jesus!

I am grateful to Frank Carrodus, a local writer who wrote both *The Horning Story* and *Horning in War Time* for his story and the photograph of my great grandfather, William Storey Smith, which I otherwise would never have known or seen.

Great Grandfather William, his father and his grandfather, all worked on the farms in the Horning area, and William had a great gift of being able to talk to and calm down any animal in distress, but particularly horses. Carrodus describes him as one who was scarcely ever known to raise his voice in anger.

William set up a record of working 65 years at Grove Farm and had many awards at agricultural shows and at a later Norfolk County Show where, in their archives, they have a picture of him with the President.

The photograph Carrodus provides of GG William is of a very distinguished-looking gentleman in a Homburg hat – and there is a fabulous picture of his horse, Prince, as well.

William claimed that he never went to school more than a couple of days and went to work at the age of seven, most likely scaring crows off the crops at Horning Hall farm, where his father and grandfather worked. Although he could neither read nor write, he had a natural talent for mathematics and was a first-class ready-reckoner, particularly in calculating the acreage of land and so on, in his head.

Carrodus tells a story which he claims had never before appeared in print – quite rightly, I suspect, because apart from the *National Enquirer* in the USA or *Private Eye* in the UK, I doubt he would have found a newspaper to print it or an audience to believe it.

William would always be accompanied by his horse, Prince, and on the occasion Carrodus tells of at Neatishead, he was outstanding in dealing with a very difficult horse – the farmer's favourite - which it was feared would have to be put down. William having completely calmed the animal, to the amazement of farm hands, the farmer wanted to show his gratitude and took him into the house for what was known then as a 'refresher'.

William was a plain man, no doubt used to drinking beer in the local public houses, and was not accustomed to spirits. The black bottle was produced and his grateful host poured a stiff glass or three! When William departed, feeling more than a bit overwhelmed, he rode his horse the last part of the way home, but in attempting to dismount fell in a heap in the farmyard. Prince apparently looked around, saw the problem and promptly grabbed William by his coat collar and carried him to his door. As I say in one of my later tourist attraction developments – Believe it or Not!

Another story Carrodus relates is that of Sarah Smith working at the Rectory at Horning for the Revd Augustus Pyne. In the garden was a mulberry tree and, when she was pregnant with my grandfather, Herbert, she was sent to collect some mulberries for the kitchen and, as she did so, a mulberry splattered itself on her head. She cleaned it off but, when Herbert was born, he had a birthmark in that exact position and it grew to look like – a mulberry. I can vouch for that, as we always wondered what it was and did not know the story.

Both Mary and I spent holidays at Horning, but I seem to remember myself there more than Mary, and she reminds me that it was church twice on a Sunday when we were staying there. Blanche and Herbert lived in a council-owned property, with a large, long garden where Grandad Herbert grew pretty well everything they needed, and they also had a prolific white peach tree near the back door. I was very fond of Grandmother Blanche and would call in on the trips from school which came later. Blanche died on 13 May 1962, aged 82 years.

As Father grew his building business he got Herbert to come over to look after gardens and, later in their life, Father built them a small bungalow to live in at Winterton. I also recall that, on his way back to Horning from Martham or Winterton when he had been working there, Herbert would get off the bus at the Horning Upper Street stop so that he could visit the *Half Moon* public house and then walk the mile or so to his house. Not something you would ever risk doing on that road after a pint or two today.

For information on the Larter side of the family we have notes from Aunt Eileen, my father's sister. Those notes came from Derek Blois, one of the sons of Eileen's sister, Ethel (May), and who I made a point of meeting in 2012.

Eileen tells us that her grandmother had 22 children, many of whom she knew, and the last died at age 91 years in 1969. Her grandfather, Joe Larter, lived for 90 years and, on her mother's side, there was Grandfather John Gallant. He seems to have been quite wealthy, with stories of gold sovereigns being showered into aprons when he came home – a horse-dealer in Wales and a pork butcher in Norfolk and who died at 65. What I would give to have been able to interview him – Wales was like a foreign country in those days, and maybe still is.

John Larter, my grandfather, was born in 1868, surprisingly also at Horning, and married Edith Mary Cubbit Gallant, who was born in 1873 and died in 1933. Grandfather John's mother was Blithe Lincoln, who died in 1950 aged 82. Eileen records that her mother, Edith Mary, was born in the old farmhouse on the green and married at 19 years, with the fascinating piece of information that she had an 18-inch (46cm) waist. John and Edith had eight children, three of whom died very young.

One of those who died was an Oswald George, the same names as my father, but born on Christmas Eve 1897; he lived for just 4½ months. Eileen records that they all died 'after vaccinations', which maybe indicates how risky medical attention was in those days.

My father, born 10 years later in March 1907, was given the same names (which I think was quite common in those days), and he always joked that he did not mind dying because he was already buried in the churchyard. The five surviving children were my father, Oswald (Ossie), Harry, May (grandmother of Derek Blois), Jack, and Eileen. Jack was killed in World War 1.

We also see my father, Oswald George, recorded as born at Horning, as was his father, John, so I think there was already a Horning connection we do not know about and that led in some way to the meeting with Helen – maybe his grandparents lived there. Disappointingly, I have not found any royal or ducal connections, or even an Australian transportation, but we are all very happy as we are.

What I have seen in the records is just an amazing repetition of all those Christian names we have, by chance, used in our later generations, when we did know of their past connections – Mary, Rose, Alice, Alice Rebecca even!, a previous Joseph (aged 12 'a servant of all work' – you can say that again!), an Elizabeth and a Mary Ann.

Perhaps the most interesting story on the Larter side concerns where we lived a few hundred years back. Because of the large number of siblings around Martham and Ludham, and the now several mentions of Horning, we all thought that the East Norfolk area was the Larter base and origin of the family. However, research by my daughter, Alice, found that we are recorded in about 1735 as living at Mulbarton in Norfolk.

The reason we know this is that a William Larter (1735 to 1797) was recorded as the landlord of the *World's End* public house at Mulbarton, which stands to this day. We can then trace the family from William, all the way down to the birth of John Larter (my grandfather) in 1868 and who died in 1951.

As you progress through the book you will find that, in 1997, my own family will be living at Hapton, just a few miles from Mulbarton, long before we knew any of this history. When we later visited the *World's End* to have a drink in great-great-great grandfather's pub (and to literally stand in his footsteps, as the original doorway is there), we met the local historian.

He confirmed (as we have done since) that the churchyard is full of the graves of Larters down the years. Not knowing who I was, the historian amusingly told me there were now no Larters in Mulbarton and the only one they had heard of recently was 'a little chap called Joe Larter, who built Pleasurewood Hills'.

My personal recollections of Grandfather John are only of him as an old man. He died, aged 83 years, when I was just 12 years old. He had been apprenticed as a decorator, sign-writer and plumber, and that was his business. Both my father and my Uncle Harry took after him – Harry building up a very good decorating business at Hemsby, and my father developing as an all-round builder, first at Martham and then at Winterton. One story Father and Harry told was of not being very well-paid by their father, so they were always on the lookout to earn a bit extra.

They took on one 'private client', for whom they did a very good job. However, before they could get paid, the client met their father John by chance and complimented him on how well his boys had worked – and paid him! They got nothing other than a raging tell-off, and no money because he claimed they had used his materials.

I remember Grandfather with a large garden full of fruit trees, and his growing vegetables. His wife, Edith, predeceased him by 18 years, but he seemed very self-sufficient. He did his own cooking and had a large workshop next to his bungalow, which was next to the Limes in Black Street, and which Eileen Dack says Grandfather had built for the family in 1914. He was still sign-writing when I knew him, but was a 'frugal' man – if he offered you an apple, of which his trees produced thousands, it would always be a windfall and never a nice fresh one.

Father told me he was the same way with the family over food – if a chicken was cooked for Sunday lunch, he would have one breast for lunch, and have the other put away for his supper, with the rest of the family sharing what was left.

Betty's sister has kindly produced a family tree to link us all in together, for which I thank her, as it has brought information of which we had no idea. In the meantime, I am going to bring together here all the current Larter family members so you can see how they fit into my story as we go along.

Oswald George Larter – my Father b 1907 – d 1963

Helen Rhoda May Larter – my Mother b 1910 – d 1981. They were married in 1938.

Joseph Larter (obviously me!) – b 27.7.1939. First married to Susan Baker (married 1961, divorced 1969) and we had two children:

Andrew Larter (b 28.4.63). On 30.3.93 he married Janice Jawarskyj but they have no children and live in Limpenhoe, Norfolk.

Rebecca Jane Larter (b 25.7.65). Married Mark Tassie on 30.8.86; they have 3 children: Benjamin and Imogen, who are twins (b 28.9.87) (another gene following through), and Abigail (b 2.11.92).

Joseph Larter secondly married Betty Ann Hayward (nee Rudling; b 7.5.36) on 27.4.73, and we have two children:

Alice Emma Helen (b 21.11.74)

Rose Sarah Ann (b 30.12.77). Rose married James Hindle 13.8.11.

Portrait of grandmother Edith May Larter, wife of John at Martham

Joe's mother Helen (nee Storey Smith) age 21

William's horse Prince

Great grandfather William Storey Smith the horse whisperer.

*Helen Larter with her mother Blanche Storey Smith
on boat to USA in 1932 to see Aunt Nora*

Nora with Helen and Betty on revisit in California 1976

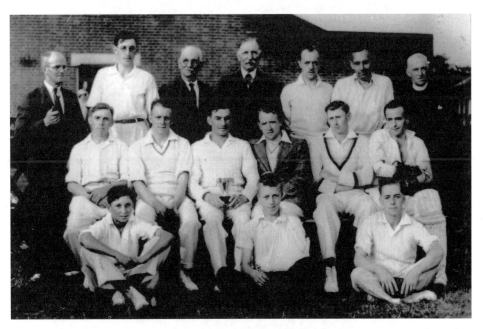

Martham Cricket team in about 1938. Father 'Ossie' Larter centre row far right and George Beck President centre back row

Helen and Ossie wedding party with Blanche and Herbert Storey Smith,
John Larter and sister Eileen.

Joe's father Ossie with dog Jimmy on Ferry Road Martham

Moregrove farmhouse from air about 1940

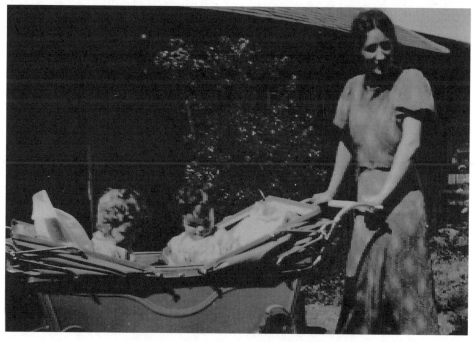

Joe and twin Mary in pram with their mother

Joe and twin Mary studio portrait at about 4 years

Joe's first children Andrew and Rebecca at about same age

Joe at age about 25 years

Father Ossie at about 25 years

*Mary and Susan Larter with
their father at Winterton against
one of his walls*

*Joe on first day
going to
Duncan Hall
School at Scratby*

*The Larter children Mary,
Joe and Susan Larter
at Winterton*

Chapter Three
1944–1955 New Horizons, Growing Up and School

Moving on to live at Winterton, Mary and I were now aged about five and, if you think of the *Famous Five* books, you again have the atmosphere and excitement we felt. Almost a foreign country compared to Martham, where of course we had done little except spend our time on the farm and latterly start school, with the biggest adventure walking across a field or down on the marshes.

Suddenly, as a family we not only had our own house and each with our own bedroom, but a large garden and thousands of acres of sand dunes, marram grass, beach and sea next door and stretching for as far as we could imagine, all undeveloped. We might have been on the Scottish island in the *Whisky Galore* film – not a bad comparison, actually, as you will see later.

The first thing I did when I was 'helping' Father renovate the house for us to move in, was to fall down some very steep stairs. Bruises, but no other damage we could see – so far! The house when bought was very basic so, with the experience of Moregrove, the first priority, especially for Mother, was to get plumbing and drainage and a Raeburn-type coal-fired oven for the kitchen. Electricity! This was luxury beyond our dreams.

The house was literally on the edge of the sand dunes and had belonged to a Mrs Ackland – a lady whose husband had been someone of importance (maybe a diplomat); when her husband died she had been left wealthy, owning several houses in Winterton and other places. I think Father did building work for her at her own home and in the old lighthouse, which had been converted, and she obviously liked and trusted him – hence the sale of Broad View to us.

That lighthouse later collected an amusing trio of charmingly eccentric elderly sisters as owners, the Misses Newbound. Broad View really was on the sand, which was also half-way up two of the house walls, and making a garden was a challenge.

Life in Winterton then was very simple in almost *Huckleberry Finn* style, except that we had the sea and not the river. No restrictions – just take the dog, a sandwich and a drink and you were gone for the day. Does anyone now look for sand bees hiding their honey in the dunes, or lay on their back in the sunshine and complete silence, except for the trilling of a skylark as it disappears higher and higher into the sky?

The skylark is one of the few birds to do that, and in such a boisterous way, providing the meaning of the word 'skylarking' – larking around. In the same way, I don't now see children buying silkworms and then getting mulberry leaves for them to eat and spin their silk. Maybe that was a war effort as well, like the rose hips.

From reclaim areas, Father gathered second-hand bricks and was a dab hand at building brick retaining walls to make a boundary for Broad View – a hobby in his spare time. When I read the wartime books on Winston Churchill, I could see a certain similarity (Father was a dyed-in-the-wool Conservative) and, in true Churchill style, not all of the walls he built were either perfect or remained standing for very long. I don't think he would have been a candidate for Prime Minister and he would agree with that, but he did turn Broad View into an attractive property with a lot of walls which kept the sand away.

We now had a younger sister, Susan, born September 1946, and Mother seems to have been well this time. What Mary and I now had to face was school! First this was at Winterton, with Mr Redvers Playford as Headmaster of the buildings, which remain there today.

I think there were only three school classes at most, and teaching was general and basic. Heating was one very large coal fire, and every day each child was given a 1/3-pint glass bottle of full-cream milk with a cardboard top. In winter, on arrival at school we were allowed to place these by the fire to heat up during the morning, and could bring flavouring (*Ovaltine*, I think we had) to mix in at break time to make a chocolate drink. It was lovely drinking the cream off the top first as, in those days, it was thought to be good for you.

At lunch time we would all go home, and return for another session in the afternoon. I remember Mr P trying hard to get me interested in football but then, as now, I really just don't have any inclination towards sport, the exception later being that I did love skiing. Susan being a baby just as we started real school at Winterton, meant Mother had at least the daytime to attend to her without the two of us under her feet as well.

Winterton had a real Lord of the Manor in the form of a Rolls-Royce-driving, very mustachioed and distinguished gent by the name of Mr George Beck, who lived at the Manor. Mr Toad of Toad Hall very much comes to mind when I think of him. The highly-respected Mr Beck was very 'old money' and quality and, once a year, would appear at school to hand out oranges and, maybe, sixpences to the children. I think after the war he fell on poorer times, and seems to have disappeared from the scene very quickly, but you can see him in the Martham cricket team photograph, where he was President.

Winterton village was very fishing orientated, even though it had no harbour and, with rationing still continuing, there would often be a furtive knock on the door, with someone selling a sea trout or something else they had caught, with Matthew ('Matty') Shields being the chief vendor of those. I have another Norfolk book, *Tales of Norfolk*, a collection of articles published in the *Eastern Daily Press* and written by Ida Fenn. She spent a lot of her younger life in Weston Longville (Parson Woodforde country), but when she was married she ended up living with her farming husband at the Mill Farm at Winterton, the mill itself long since destroyed in a gale. She was a very observant writer and teacher, and I was delighted to find in her book a chapter entitled 'Shrimps', all about Winterton and its people at the very time we lived there.

She tells of Willie (Goffin – otherwise known as Casey – Kezzie in Norfolk!), a local character who was a whizz at catching shrimps and who taught Mary and me. A home-made 'funnel' net on the end of a long stick, with a piece of timber at the broad end of the funnel to make the shrimps 'jump' as you pushed it along in the sand. The ideal place for us children to catch them was in the 'lows' – shallow areas of water left behind as the tide receded, with the adults catching theirs in the same way out in the deeper water. For us children, catching something which we could then take home, cook and EAT, was very exciting.

Casey had two wonderful parents, Roger and Mandy, and we would all either take the whole catch to them for boiling or, if Mary and I had gone alone, we would take them home to Mother, where I seem to remember our joint expectation of catch size never seemed to match the size of the large pot she had ready and boiling for us. As Ida says, at first when you caught these grey 'insects', you did not imagine they would turn into the delicious pink shellfish they are.

Ida also mentions the real Winterton *Whisky Galore* moment I have referred to, which came in the winter of 1948, when the whole country had been told there would be no oranges in Britain for the Christmas period. The following weekend a boat passing near the Scroby Sands, and loaded with boxes of oranges headed for Europe, was wrecked - Scroby Sands are just off Winterton, and are a wind-farm base today. I don't suppose the ship owner would agree, but we called it justice then, and certainly I call it serendipity today.

The beaches of Winterton, Somerton and Horsey were awash with boxes of oranges. The local police (PC Lovell) and Customs forbade anyone to collect them and of course, just like the whisky bottles of *Whisky Galore*, the boxes of oranges mysteriously all disappeared every night soon after they floated in. Happy Christmas, indeed.

Tales of Norfolk also gave me some history of terrible times at Winterton about which I did not know. The shifting Scroby (Scrotby in older times) sandbank was a notorious hazard for sailing vessels. Daniel Defoe called by Winterton in 1726 and commented that nearly every house there was built partially from marine wreckage- materials collected from the constant loss of ships.

The most terrible disaster off Winterton had been in 1692, when a combination of events occurred in the one night. A fleet of 200 sailing ships had left the Yarmouth Roads in good weather but, a few leagues past the Scroby sands, near Winterton Ness, they encountered a freak wind from the northwest. The boats took various evasive actions, but few got to safety. At this moment, another fleet laden with goods was coming in from the north and they too got caught.

From the west, and making their way to Holland, was yet another group of vessels, heavily laden with corn. In all there were some 400 boats, 200 of which were lost on that one night, all manned by families from the Norfolk area. I believe there are memorials in various Norfolk churchyards recording the disaster, but the horror of losing so many lives from what must have been quite a small total population anyway, and in a few hours, must have been unbearable.

My thanks to Ida Fenn for all this knowledge, but let's cheer up a bit! Father continued his shooting hobby, and Mother was good with the chickens again, so no shortages of food at Winterton. Later, Father taught me how to fish with a line off the beach and, however much or little we caught, it was always an excitement and nice to be out with him and take our catch home.

Later, when I started raising funds for the local village hall, or whatever was going on in the village at the time, I arranged fishing competitions on the beach and was astonished at how popular they were. For a modest cash prize I would find myself very early in the morning, setting out 30 or more fishing positions which, when you gave each one 100 yards or so of space, was a very long line – with often some fine fish caught. I learned that there is definitely a skill to fishing; it is a very competitive sport – and fish are delicious!

Mother absolutely loved Winterton and, of course, the 'luxury' of Broad View compared to Moregrove farm. She was the most gentle person you could ever want to meet, and a very loving mother. She just let you get on with what you wanted to do, always there when you needed her and was – well the best word I can think of is 'contented'. I treasure a small photograph I recently found, showing Mary and me on the beach at Winterton. Wanting to record on the reverse just where and when it was taken, Mother had charmingly written (in her beautiful handwriting): 'Mary and Joe on the beach, the year before last.'

Another very late find by Mary is a delightful letter written by Father to Mother when she had gone to the USA with Blanche. That trip, for a couple of very ordinary people from Horning in the 1930s, must have been almost epic and, clearly, Father is in love with Mother and missing her. We remember Father as being not a very 'demonstrative' person, with not too many hugs and kisses around, so the letter was a charming surprise. He writes in part of his letter:

'I miss you very much and am looking forward to your homecoming. If I could hear you just once, that would help a lot. I went to Potter (that's Potter Heigham and Drakes Dance Hall) *last night but did not dance. The old dear with glasses was there and dancing with some fellow and making quite a 'fuss' of him, as I will of you when you come back.*

'How is your mother? I hope she is quite well. This afternoon I am going on the river fishing. Will you come? I don't suppose we would do much fishing. Well dear, I can't write any more now but shall have lots to tell you when we meet.'

It is lovely that we have the original and its envelope addressed to New York and dated 2 August 1936. They were married in 1938.

A note about Winterton at our time would not be complete without a mention of 'Kitty' George, who ran the *Fisherman's Return* for Steward and Patteson, the local brewers. I knew all this later, of course, but Kitty was again just what you would expect in a *Whisky Galore* village, and she ran a legendary hostelry for what must have been 30 years or so.

The local policeman for many years was PC Lovell, a real character in the *Dixon of Dock Green* style – a TV series after the war for those of you who don't recognize the name. He used the 'clip round the ear' remedy for any slightly wayward youngster, which would certainly not be allowed to do today. I think he was also a bit flexible on opening and closing times at Kitty's bar – so long as he was there to keep an eye on what the customers were doing late at night. All harmless stuff, but maybe Winterton is where they first got in practice for occasional 24-hour drinking.

Kitty also had on her premises 'The Tinno', which was where any serious meeting took place, or a wedding, or local variety concert. The premises remain there today and *The Fisherman's Return* has always attracted tenants of the style and quality needed to carry on her tradition.

Now developing a solid building-and-contracting business, Father established his base in some old net-repairing sheds on Low Road, which he first rented and then bought. Several of his workmen lived in Winterton - particularly George Myhill, the carpenter, and Tom Crafer, his chief plumbing and heating man. The problem builders had after the war was in obtaining construction materials, with so much having to be reclaimed, and I think this is where Father came into his own – he was a natural 'dealer'.

One had to get a permit to buy new materials, but you could freely use anything you reclaimed. There was also then no such thing as 'planning permission', which helped him to buy some land on which to build bungalows for George Myhill to rent and then later, next door, for grandparents Herbert and Blanche. Later still he built another bungalow, although the rules quickly changed, and I think he later regretted he did not make claim to more uncontrolled land whilst he could have done.

The local 'reclaim' area was on Caister Road, Great Yarmouth, where all the materials recovered from bomb damage sites were gathered together. I used to join Father and his men sorting whatever they had found, and was always particularly pleased to be sent with the appointed person to collect the newspaper-wrapped fish and chips for our lunch, with mine washed down with a bottle of *Tizer*. So-called health and safety regulations today mean that few people will now experience the sheer pleasure of eating out of real newspaper without the plastic inserts and styrene boxes they are served in today.

Everything and anything was reclaimed and the waste that occurs on building sites today would have George Myhill – our 'master reclaimer' – pulling his hair out. He would extract nails from used timber and straighten them for reuse – of great value too in those days. Timber in 2012 is so cheap per metre that I have seen contracts where, because of the labour cost, it is not even worth extracting nails to reuse the timber itself.

One 'coup' of Father's was to be at Caister Road when bricks from some of the bombed-out old houses in the Great Yarmouth Rows came in. He quickly bought them up, and the main fireplace at Broad View is built of narrow Dutch bricks many hundreds of years old – although I doubt the current owner knows that. He was also able to do the same for some of his other customers, including the Whartons at Winsford Hall.

That dealing gene in Father's nature led him to auction sales all over the county, and he had a talent for spotting the most beautiful antiques. He had no great funds to spare, so the antiques he could buy would most likely be flawed in some way – chipped or cracked - and cheap, but still very beautiful. I got that collecting habit from him as well, and we would often be in the old Corn Hall in Norwich (then just below *Jarrolds* store further down Exchange Street) bidding for the most unusual things. He acquired a group of 'cronies' he met there, all experts in various fields, who really guided him, and made a great fuss of me.

I got attracted to old drinking glasses, and used my own money to start a small collection which I still have today. I could not afford the beautiful glasses with twisted stems (worth hundreds of pounds today), but the old man who guided my father taught me how to identify glasses from the 1800s and before. If the glass has a base where you can feel it has been 'broken' off where it was moulded, then it is very early whereas, if it has a 'ground' bottom it is around the Victorian period. Just a piece of useless information for you!

In those days masses of silverware would be sold at more or less scrap price. Sorting Broad View after Mother and Father had both died, we found an amazing number of silver candlesticks, dishes and the like, which we have retained.

For years, not only was there the Great Yarmouth reclaim site, but also the sea continued to deliver up wreckage on the various beaches. Many a night local men would 'reclaim' timber in particular and if it was, say, a large beam, they would be round at the door the following morning to negotiate a price for delivering it to the workshop on Low Road to be sawn up.

'Matty' Shields was there again, leading reclamation as he did with the sea trout, and some pretty massive timber appeared from time to time. There also came a time when various wartime beach defence constructions were being dismantled and these were in the form of steel poles – rather like scaffolding poles today. Father realized the poles were available just for the effort of clearing them away, so his next acquisition was a donkey we called Rosie.

Also to become a great family pet, Rosie was tethered outside Broad View to graze in daytime, and she became quite a tourist attraction at times. I can hear her braying to this day, and Father made a simple harness for her so she happily went into the sand dunes with him to drag home his free scaffolding.

Matty's father (also a Matthew, I think), a very charming, old-fashioned gent, was the local bookies' runner – that means he took bets on behalf of bookmakers in Great Yarmouth and passed them on, keeping a small commission; all slightly illegal at the time, but carefully supervised (i.e. overlooked) by PC Lovell.

In those days in a small village, children were always welcome everywhere, and Mother made great friends with 'Aunt Myrtle and Uncle Jim' who were a childless couple living on the corner opposite Broad View. They were also very kind to Father when he was ill, and kept an eye on him as he went around the village. Jim worked for the local Drainage Board, and often we children would be called in as we passed by, for a slice of cake or a drink.

We were very lucky and they were like part of the family. Later, as he became more successful and before he was ill, Father bought their little, rented cottage so they would never have to worry about moving out. I think he saw Myrtle as a great friend of Mother's, and maybe he was thinking of the future if he should not be around.

As a family we were not into religion in any serious way. Uncle Harry was a lay Methodist preacher and Eileen was a Methodist supporter, but not us. Mother had played the organ at Horning church, but at Winterton at our age we were expected to attend 'somewhere', so most Sundays would see Mary and me at the local Methodist Sunday School. Not very serious, and going on the various children's outings was a big incentive! A very old and kindly spinster lady, Aunt Zaida, was in charge and, after Sunday School, we would often queue at a small fish-and-chip shop which also had an ice-cream concession.

Remember, rationing was still very much in place in the early years after the war, so one normally needed ration book coupons to buy ice cream, but here, if you took a plate, you would be allocated a slice of ice cream from a large block. The trick then was to get it home to share out before it melted but, with no deep-freeze-type refrigeration, it meant we had ice cream before Sunday lunch!

Another aspect of rationing was how it taught us as children to be very careful with our purchases. My 'coupons' might run to a *Mars Bar* one week and then the skill would be to cut it carefully into as many slices as possible, and you might swap one slice for, say, two toffees from someone else. I still like *Mars Bars*!

We also had the excitement of this being the early days of telephones being expanded into the countryside; a great innovation and help for business and in emergencies. We had the number Winterton 230, all calls going through the exchange with an operator to put you through to your intended contact – and maybe listen in. It was normal to ask for a number and for the operator to say, maybe: 'Well, I don't think he is in at the moment, as I heard him arranging to meet someone.' How strange in 2013 to think of Alexander Graham Bell, the inventor of the telephone, saying, rather optimistically, on being awarded his patent in 1876: 'I foresee that within a few years there will be a telephone in every town in America.'

Now life had to get a bit more serious. Mary had a place in the St Mary's Convent School (all girls) at Great Yarmouth, where she did very well over the years and developed her dressmaking, design and craft skills she had most certainly inherited from Mother. I got a place at Duncan Hall School (all boys), which had just removed from Great

Yarmouth to a lovely old country house at Scratby, a few miles from Winterton.

Mary went with her friends into Great Yarmouth by bus, but I linked up with a boy named Tony Bush living in the 'highlands' area of Winterton - for Norfolk that's about 50 feet above sea level. His father was also a builder, and Tony and I would cycle the 6 or 7 miles each morning and back in the evening – maybe having tea and sometimes doing homework at his house on my way home. A big adventure at aged about 8 or 9 years – but, again, we thought nothing of it and sometimes took a small detour past the amusement and ice-cream parlour area of Hemsby on the way home.

I enjoyed Duncan Hall where the Headmaster, Mr Morgan Hughes, ran the show like a big family – with his wife in charge of all the admin. There were lovely grounds, good teachers (a Mr O'Brien I remember as living in Winterton and helping me enormously) and I do not recall the work as very hard.

Particular friends were Tony Bush and a Lynn Thomas, who was a very gifted, artistic type and led the school theatrical productions, as did his mother, who was involved in amateur dramatics in Great Yarmouth. In those days, school at age 9 and 10 years was very much about taking your 'eleven plus' which, at that time, was the exam to get you to the next stage of your education.

It was a pretty important stage and, although I passed the exam, I think it was not a sufficiently high mark to automatically get me into the local Great Yarmouth Grammar School. Alternatives were discussed and I was offered a place boarding at King Edward VII Grammar School at King's Lynn – KES as it was known - and Mother and Father obviously thought it was a good idea for me to go there.

The then-headmaster, Mr Wagstaff, interviewed me, must have approved, and I was allocated a place. I liked Wagstaff, but soon after I arrived he retired and we had a Mr Sleigh take over, but still with very nice family. A Mr Cuthbertson was our live-in housemaster but for me, never having been away from home, sixty miles was a long distance.

It was a whole new experience, and one I did not particularly look forward to after holidays at home – and actually never really took to in spite of all sorts of interesting angles over the years. We were still in the days of steam trains and the line ran from Great Yarmouth to King's Lynn via Melton Constable, Corpusty, and all those old pre-Dr

Beeching stations. My father collected me at either Hemsby or Martham stations. In the later years with telephones, if we ran late when I was to return to school we could call his cricketing friend Bill Temple, the Stationmaster at Martham, and he would hold the train for a few minutes. Nowadays, of course, virtually every train from Norwich to London has its own built-in auto-delay system!

I recall that the only boy similarly coming in from 'outside' King's Lynn from my direction was Ian Angell who had, I think, lost his father in the war, and came in from Sheringham. It was mainly a day school and the boarding house was a bit spartan (that means pretty cold on winter nights and not much furniture!) and, although the food was adequate, we all looked forward to food parcels arriving from home once a fortnight.

I don't think anyone who did not live through the age of steam trains can EVER imagine the feelings one got when on board and hearing the whistle, the gentle hiss of steam and *the smell* of steam as the brakes were released and the train moved off. Often it would be a dark and damp, late-winter afternoon with very few people travelling and, even if it was a bit lonely for an 11 or 12 year-old boy, I certainly always felt I was on an adventure. Noel Coward and his *Brief Encounter* come to mind.

For the benefit of those who never had that steam experience, I have tried to think of how to describe the melodic sounds, the clickety-click, clickety-click that the passengers got as the train gathered speed; and then I remembered the start of the TS Eliot poem *Skimbleshanks: The Railway Cat*:

> *'There's a whisper down the line at 11.39*
> *When the Night Mail's ready to depart*
> *Saying "Skimble, where is Skimble has he gone to hunt the thimble?*
> *We must find him or the train can't start."'*

If you say that in a 'sing-song' way you get the perfect rhythm of the train. Look it up on Google; it is well worth the read and it is easy to understand why JK Rowling started the Hogwarts journeys by steam from King's Cross. A boat-train journey must have been fabulous.

On reading the first draft of this book, my daughter Rebecca told me that, at school in Suffolk, she was one of the first girls to be diagnosed with dyslexia and they took it very seriously. She had wonderful attention and the results were remarkable – so much so that at a full assembly of the school later, they got her to read a poem, which she did perfectly – *Skimbleshanks*!

As I have said, I was not sporty but, having settled into boarding, much of weekend life for me was about ' How do I get out of this place' until Monday? There was, of course, no television and our radio entertainment was listening to *Dick Barton – Special Agent*. For those who never heard that programme, it was as important as any one of the current TV soaps or *The Archers* on radio are today and, of course, far more exciting to us boys.

Cricket teams travelling to other schools needed a scorer, and no one learned how to score faster than 'non-cricketing Joe'. It meant a trip, a nice tea, and late night back. The school played against other local schools and I particularly remember a private school at Ingoldisthorpe in West Norfolk, run by the eccentric Reverend Potts. If I meet someone at a party and find they originate from that area of Norfolk, I only have to say: "Potts' Circus!" which was the highly irreverent 'nickname' for the school, and they are immediately greatly amused that I know of it. We all thought the Reverend Potts was a bit unusual, but I think the pupils there had a rather more relaxed time than we did. I have no idea what effect that had on their education.

The local Gaywood Church needed choirboys. Now no one then or now, including me, knew if I could sing, but choirboys were paid! I have forgotten how much, but it got you out of school for choir practice, you had to go to church on Sunday anyway, and at the end of each term a very useful sum of money had accumulated for the coming holidays. Weddings were paid extra, but I do not recall ever having to attend a funeral – no doubt because they would likely have been on a weekday.

In holiday time, another way Mary and I used to accumulate pocket money – and very lucrative indeed – was to go with 'Joney' of Moregrove Farm fame, to pick blackcurrants on the Bracey farms between Martham and Somerton. Regrettably only for a short summer season but, in a week of quite hard work, £15 or £20 could be earned quite easily. That was a huge sum, the equivalent of £300 to £400 in today's money and, for a young teenager, certainly financed the holidays. Pay was by picked weight and not related to the age of an individual.

In spite of what you might think from the way recycling is put forward as a new phenomenon today, it will never match the re-using and reclaiming materials in the early days after the war as I have already indicated – the country was desperately short of cash to buy raw materials, and reclaim was vital. Father, in his business, would slowly accumulate odd bits of scrap metal - brass, lead and so on - over the course of the year from the building contracts he had, and that would be taken to King's scrapyard in Great Yarmouth to exchange for cash.

Mary and I thought we should open a waste-paper depot to complement the metal collection (in the old stable after Rosie had departed) and over a period we would buy in quite a large quantity, for later taking to King's when Father took his metal.

We got skilled at buying in for less than we would sell, but somehow we always seemed not to have enough cash to pay people, so had to take a 'loan' from Mother to pay out. I think our finances sometimes got mixed up to our advantage on settlement day, but I believe Mother was quite pleased to see us being enterprising. We were also allocated a small amount of the metal cash 'for helping' when it was paid out. Earning that cash from blackcurrants, paper-collecting or whatever was so much more satisfying than any pocket money a parent could hand out.

At school, the KES Combined Cadet Force occupied some weekends and meant going to ranges to fire guns, and once a year to a summer camp and so, of course, Private Larter was there. One summer camp (Major Kenyon in charge) was down near the Romney Marshes, and there I rode on the Romney, Hythe and Dymchurch miniature steam railway for the first time – another serendipitous moment when you consider what I tell you in the future. What I do remember at camp was the most awful food and, after a week, none of us could wait to get to a café for a proper meal. The appalling washing-up facility after each meal (which we did ourselves, of course) meant various bugs were picked up quickly and without fail, but we all survived.

The school debating society was another way of getting out of school, and I recall at one time my leading a debate defending the spider that sat down beside Miss Muffet. Don't ask how I got there! I don't think I could ever have been an actor, but today I do not dislike being the 'lead' on any event and am happy to talk, if anyone wants to listen, and often come up with a polar opposite idea. This is sometimes because I believe in it, and sometimes just to make people think and talk, but I usually take the attitude of: Got a problem? Let's get a blank piece of paper and set it all out to find a solution.

Our History master, Mr Stittle, was a great cyclist and offered in summer that on a Sunday we could get a packed lunch and then cycle with him as guide to a specific church or historic building where (genuinely) we did learn a lot of history. It is likely that's why I have a strong interest in history and tradition today.

We cycled through a lot of West Norfolk and I think the boys slightly older than me were very occasionally allowed a beer shandy with him. A bit of common sense that would be frowned upon today, no doubt, but he always knew of a tea room or a place to get refreshment, and I have great memories of the trips.

In 1951, Mother and Aunt Eileen decided to take us all to the Festival of Britain in London, which was the first time since the war that Britain had felt able to 'celebrate' itself. For Mary and me it was the first time ever to London, and a great excitement. I think we stayed with a bed-and-breakfast couple Mother and Father had met on a holiday, and were taken to meet a 'famous' relative.

It seems that a not-too-close relative of Father's was the Chief Registrar of Births and Deaths at Somerset House, and I remember being in awe of the amazing building when we visited. Father took us to meet this relative and we had a great time with Cousin Paul in tow. There is a lovely photograph of Eileen with the Skylon (the tall, symbolic Festival steel structure) appearing to be balanced on her head.

In January 1953 the Norfolk east coast had the most terrible floods, which were most severe around Sea Palling, the Norfolk coast and North Suffolk. I recall walking only a few hundred yards from school in King's Lynn and finding flood water in the streets. Father was involved in the recovery work, and there were some hair-raising stories of bravery during that time – people being rowed to safety during the storms and a postman delivering letters in spite of all obstacles.

At KES we also had the most wonderful countryman as chief groundsman, Bill Leggett. He was a bachelor but, if I recall correctly, very keen on the lady in charge of our canteen. He had a small fisherman's 'hut' on the beach at Heacham and, on occasion, would take two or three of us there for fishing. We picked samphire (now a very popular seaside vegetable, but I had never heard of it then), lit a wood fire in the evening to cook the fish we had caught, and slept in bunk-beds. *Famous Five* again, but I'm not sure what a school today would think of a single male employee taking two or three lads to stay the night with him in a hut on the beach! All was always well, and the school obviously approved.

There were all the usual pranks – lifting Mr Cuthbertson's car into the centre of the main cricket pitch in the middle of the night, and so on, and at weekends we had the whole run of the school, which was like an Edwardian castle inside.

Mr Cuthbertson, our housemaster, was a very good 'stand-in' father, but I think the man who had more influence on me than any other was Walter Rowe, a dry old stick with no nonsense. He taught mathematics. I remember his way of teaching taught me a discipline – an order of doing things - and logic. I loved the theorems of geometry, where we looked first at one solution and then another, and from which final conclusions were then assembled.

To this day I love to have a complex problem, setting it all down on paper and coming to what one always hopes is the logical and correct conclusion. If I am planning something, I like to write to myself about it first. Ken Sims reminds me that Walter had an MC from the war, as did Tom Bromhead who had lost an arm – all great teachers, and who could forget 'Pop' Freestone, later Mayor of King's Lynn? Pop was the original fitness expert and had more energy that the rest of King's Lynn put together. Always available to talk and just had a 'natural' way with himself. A very popular Mayor.

I also particularly liked English Literature (Mr Beaumont and Mr Price) and at that time we studied *The Pilgrim's Progress* for our 'O'-level exams. These were exams like today's GCSEs, and needed if one was going to move on to 'A'-levels and then university. I did well in Mathematics and English Literature, but not in English Language, which I took again when I was, by then, at home – with Mr O'Brien of Duncan Hall days coaching me.

On occasion, a highlight at KES would be Father coming to take me to watch Lynn Town team play football; not really an interest of mine, but anything to get out of the boarding house and, of course, always a nice teashop afterwards! He would often bring with him a great pal of his, Sydney Grapes, from Potter Heigham. Sydney was a tremendous character, speaker and comedian on the after-dinner entertainment circuit in those days, and dressed up either as the farm-boy 'Boy John' or as a country washerwoman.

His characters were taken from his regular writings in the *Eastern Daily Press*, and both writings and entertainment were in his very own Norfolk dialect style, unsurpassed to this day. Later, he was acknowledged by Peter Trudgill – a Norfolk boy as well, Professor of English Linguistics and an international expert in the field of dialects – who described the *Grapes* writings as 'work of not a little genius'. How absolutely true.

I have the book, published after his death, where many of his letters to the *Eastern Daily Press* (EDP) were put together. Absolutely wonderful stuff and not TOO much dialect, so it makes easy reading. *The Boy John Letters* – go on *Amazon*, find a copy and buy it.

Sydney wrote in the *EDP* every two or three weeks about his imaginary farming family: Aunt Agatha, Granfar and Oul Mrs W, and he had a fabulous insight into how country people thought, lived and behaved. Keith Skipper and the Friends of The Norfolk Dialect will never let Sydney be forgotten, and there is an enormous amount of memorabilia at the Broads Museum, now at Stalham. In 2003 Keith published the letters again, with his own comments, as 'A fresh delivery'.

Sydney's letters, for example, would always end with a PS. 'Aunt Agatha she say... "Tha's no good a putten yar fut down if yow hearnt got a leg to stan' on"' – and the like. Another was ' Granfar he say... "sorlt is wot meark tearters tearst narsty if yow dornt put it in".' The Norfolk dialect is wonderful at the 'put down', or 'reverse' humour I call it.

From one of Sydney's entertainments, Keith gives another quote, of the two local yokels seeing a plane in the sky and one asks the other: 'How would you like to be up in that plane?' To which the reply was: 'Well, I shouldn't want to be up there without it.' Or the two farm labourers told to get a muck-spreading job done between them – not the nicest of farm jobs – and one says to the other: 'Well , I'm a gorn ter drive – what are yew gorn ter dew?' All wonderful Norfolk.

At Potter Heigham, Sydney ran one of the first garages and lived in Up Top, the first-floor apartment above his garage and shop. He absolutely loved the countryside and just after the war was one of a gang of people, including my father, who met at the *Bridge Hotel* (next to that dancehall where he met Mother) where Frank Eaton, an ex-shoemaker from Northampton, held court as Mine Host. George Formby of ukulele fame, and his wife Beryl, were two others who used to frequent the bar. I was very fond of Sydney and he is much missed.

At KES, as well as our all-male annual theatrical productions, there were joint musical and theatrical ventures with the High School for girls, with us all performing in the *St George's Guildhall*, now better-known as the *Fermoy Centre* (theatre) near the Tuesday Market Place. I got to know and love *Gilbert and Sullivan* there, but I was never a performer, being always on the side with scenery, sound effects, or whatever.

Mr Bone (the Queen's music honcho at Sandringham) was our music teacher at KES but, although I love music, and opera in particular, I simply don't have the skill to play anything much, although I did try the piano. Mother played the piano well and had played the organ at Horning church, but her skill did not come down to us. Alice can play the saxophone and flute, and maybe grandson Benjamin, studying composing and conducting, is going to be the one to show us all how to do it.

In 1954 Fred Calvert, who was the local police superintendent (and also a wonderful baritone), organized the King's Lynn Pageant, a huge affair with a cast of a thousand actors and fifty horses, and for which he was much criticized for gross overspending. We, as the KES Cadet Force, were given the job of radio communications between the various (and far-flung) sections that Fred put together. As you may imagine, assembling and then controlling such a number and maybe 10,000 spectators on any one day, was a formidable task.

The pageant was to celebrate the 750 years since the granting of the King's Lynn Charter in 1204. You can actually Google 'King's Lynn Pageant' and watch a very good film made of it at the time. The cast included full-costume knights, monks, medieval folk and dignitaries, acting out the history of the town. Very grand, and we felt very important taking part.

As to the cycling, having reached 14 years or so, we were allowed to have our own bicycles and to go out on our own down town if we could give a good reason. An elderly spinster lady called Ethel, from a local farming family (as I discovered later), worked as a supervisor in the KES boarding-house dining-room. For some reason she took a liking to me, and I was duly invited to the farm, in the first instance I think to pick strawberries. The farm was about 10 miles out of town at Clenchwarton, to where I cycled, and found she lived in a large, old, family house with her other spinster sister and bachelor brother.

After the first visit, where they made a great fuss of me, I had obviously behaved myself and was invited back from time to time for proper afternoon tea at weekends. This also happened with another older couple living in nearby Gaywood who, from time to time, invited to tea another boy, Philip Neal, who had lost his mother. They were friends of his family and he was asked to take a pal with him and, once again, I fitted the bill. Another bit of serendipity in a way, but maybe I just recognized and took an opportunity when I saw one. Anything to get out for a day.

I don't think it was anything to do with the boys at the boarding house, but we woke up one day to find that our Matron (who went by the nickname of Bisqui – don't ask me why) had committed suicide. As Arthur Marshall might have said: 'All part of life's rich pageant', but it certainly shook us all at the time.

Another event for me was going down with chicken pox and, to my delight, all concerned decided I should recuperate at home. Mary tells me she was sent off to stay in Horning, so I had the house to myself. A bed was brought downstairs, I think to save Mother having to go up and down all the time, but even then I can remember thinking: 'when is this school thing going to be over so I can get one with doing something real back here?' However, back it was after a week or two, and on with that part of my life.

So now I had a cycle available and it was a racing type. I asked the school: 'Could I please cycle home for the weekend?' I don't recall making any detailed plans, anyone minding very much, or even my parents being asked, so there I was one Friday afternoon at about 3pm setting off from King's Lynn to Winterton - 60 miles and on my own. I had a map and a rain cover, some money, and that was it. Excitement was not the word for it and I had just given no thought to distance and time.

The journey took me six hours or so, right through the centre of Norfolk. I was able to stop off at Horning to see my grandparents (and get refreshment) and duly arrived at Winterton at about 10pm. There was no such thing as a mobile phone, Grandma had no telephone, but there were red boxes here and there, although I never recall needing to use one on a trip. So, Saturday at home and then, on the Sunday, slightly earlier, I set off on the reverse journey back to school and made it quite comfortably, that becoming an occasional trip from then on. No one even commented on what I had done.

On one occasion I persuaded Chris Sims, the brother of my great friend, Ken Sims, of Thrigby Wildlife Park, to come with me and I noticed afterwards that he did not offer to do it again. Strangely, I found it an easier journey alone than with someone else.

All those things made boarding life more bearable but I was never really comfortable, feeling a bit of an 'odd man out' – maybe, as I have said, because school then was always so much about sport. I got my 8 'O'-levels but did not want to stay longer. No 'A'-levels or university (and with hindsight I am sure, for me, that was right); I just wanted to get out into the real world – but as I had no training for anything, the question was *what* was I going to do?

Gunton Hall
advertising balloon

Aerial view of Gunton Hall and Pleasurewood 1983

Opening of miniature steam railway by John Mountford 1982

Joe driving CP Huntingdon train on arrival

Some 1982 attractions before the theme park

First entry ticket for theme park 1983

*Keith Sparks, Geoffrey Thompson
of Blackpool Pleasure Beach,
Kalle Justander of Linnemaki
Park in Finland*

Keith Sparks with Rupert Bear

*Malcolm Griffin architect and Mike Wilson
electrical contractor at first barbecues*

Helicopter landing part of chairlift

Visit of Duchess of Gloucester 1987

Woody with Queen on her visit to Lowestoft 1.8.85

Woody with Jim Prior Waveney MP and now Lord Prior

Woody in London

1,000,000th visitor 1985

Joe's 50th birthday and the staff gather together

Advertising on power boat racing on Oulton Broad

1983 family picture re posed June 2013 for 30th anniversary of the Park

Hey, Mr Larter! Whatever happened to section 3, clause 5b in my contract:
'Just stroll around, look cuddly and wave to the kiddies...?'

Tony Hall cartoon on 30th anniversary

Chapter Four
School's Out! - My World Turns Upside-Down
with a Steep Learning Curve

It was very strange returning home from boarding school in 1955 aged 16 years, with actually no plan of what I wanted to do with my life. Those were still the days of steam trains and the world was very parochial - no gap years, work experience or pushing off to go round the world with a back-pack. In fact it would be the early 1960s before I even went abroad for the first time. I was back at Winterton, and what was missing was any basic group of friends one would normally have built up over school and teenage years, with whom one might have fun and make plans for the future.

Winterton was a very small village and I was the only person who had been away at school, so the friends and contacts were not there. For that reason, and the way my life developed, I can see, looking back, that I became a bit of a loner – well, independent anyway, and often happy to be on my own making decisions.

So let's first put our feet on the ground – where was the world in 1955?

Disney opened in California, Steve Jobs and Bill Gates were both born, Eisenhower was USA President and, in the UK, Anthony Eden took over as Prime Minister from Winston Churchill. The hovercraft was invented at Somerleyton, Suffolk, Birds Eye invented fish fingers, McDonalds opened in the USA and *Play-Doh*, the *Frisbee*, *Lego* and *Velcro* were all invented. Beer was under a shilling (5p) a pint, petrol 54 old pence (22p) for a gallon, car tax £15.00 a year and 10 Woodbines (the worst cigarettes) 6p – too expensive to sell in 20s!

You could rent a 2-bedroom house for 8/6d (42p) a week, rates and water were £3.50 a year, and pocket money for children would be 3d (1.25p) to 6d (2.5p), for which you could buy an awful lot of sweets. The first atomic power station was opened in the US, as was the first commercial radio station and, finally (you learn something every day), the TV programme *$64,000 Question* grew out of a radio show called *$64 Question*, so-called because $64 was the top prize money at the time. I always wondered where that expression came from. What is so easily forgotten now is that only on 4 July 1954 did food rationing, which the war had brought to Britain, finally end.

Back home, nothing was really discussed about my future but, for a few months, I fell into going around with my father as he weighed-up jobs, meeting customers and sorting out his almost non-existent office. I was paid what in those days I thought was a magnificent sum of £5.00 a week, which bought a lot as you can see above. Actually, if you look at comparative tables, £5.00 was the equivalent of about £98.00 in 2012 terms. The Minimum Wage now is more so, although I had comparatively excellent buying power, it certainly illustrates what inflation does for values.

To try to get me into a building 'mode' I enrolled at the Great Yarmouth School of Further Education, going to night classes to learn the basics of building and architecture. I am not sure I was there long enough actually to learn very much, but I did get sufficient drawing experience to later make my own applications for planning approval. By coincidence Philip Liversidge, an architect, was the one who taught me, and it was his wife who was eventually to become a secretary and PA to me in the early years on my own in business.

At home we all realized that, even though it was coming to its end, in the very near future I would have to do the mandatory National Service – 2 years of basic army training, and that would be the time for me to decide my future direction. Two years in a completely new environment really would be different, and I had already concluded that I wanted to be something more than a small contracting builder. I was sure I had the confidence to expand my horizons beyond Norfolk.

National Service for the 2 years was (I had heard) pretty awful and boring. 10 years after the war ended, we were unlikely to have another one any time soon, and NS participants were treated very poorly, by not-very-intelligent sergeant majors. In Norwich one day, I went into the Recruiting Office to find out what it all involved, and came out having learned that, if I wanted to take a different route, I could sign up for 3 years and go for a Short Service Commission, if I could pass the War Office Selection Board - WOSB.

If I could pass, I would at least decide where and what I wanted to do for the three years. Like singing in the choir at Gaywood Church in

King's Lynn, if I am unlikely to beat them I might as well join them. Captain Larter would sound nice.

I duly went for a WOSB at Barton Stacey in Hampshire, passed, and found myself a few weeks later with a mixed, but very pleasant, group of similar people near Aldershot. We first went through 10 weeks of 'get fit' basic training, after which we were to choose the branch of the services to which we and they thought we were most suited. I enjoyed the training and getting fit (only time in your life you were fit, I hear Betty saying) and met some very interesting and (dare I say it?) quite educated and intelligent people, the odd one of which I would run into again in later years.

I remember our sergeant major (who actually was not a bad chap), explaining when we all first met him just what the rules of the game were. 'I shall call you all "Sir" (as we were officers in training), and you will call me "Sir". The only difference between us is that you will mean it, and I will not.' That's us in our place then but a very old joke from over the years of service. The Mons Officer Cadet School at Aldershot, where we were based, was very good, with food excellent and a great 'camaraderie' in the NAAFI (officer cadet branch!) after hours. For those too young, NAAFI stands for Navy, Army and Air Force Institutes, who provided catering establishments, and bars in the various forces recreational areas both during and after the war.

We were actually paid quite well – more than I was getting at home, I remember - and, of course, there was very little to spend it on. One ex-inmate came out of an audience I was addressing about our Sealife Centre in Great Yarmouth some 32 years later, and introduced himself to me. He was Evan Ozanne from Guernsey, who had joined the local authority there on the tourism side after completing his officer training.

After the ten weeks' basic training, and some interesting officer training stuff, we were given a week off to travel home, and that was my first true experience of disaster – and what a disaster it was.

The family, in writing to me at the camp in those first few weeks, had made no mention whatsoever that Father had, whilst hands-on digging a drainage trench for a farmer customer, Col Molineux at Ashby, suffered a massive stroke and was confined to bed. Worse, Mary tells me he partially recovered at one time, but then had a relapse, lost his power of speech and was never able to speak or be very mobile again.

Mother, Mary and Susan of course hoped Father would recover, but the Doc made it clear to me that, whilst he might improve, he was unlikely to recover more, or ever speak or work again. I was so angry on behalf of my Father and Mother – he was 50 years old, in the prime of his life and, to all intents and purposes, that life was now over. So, so unfair for such a good man, but he took it far better than I think I would have done and, in his way, as you will see later in this chapter, just got on with life as best he could.

Mother looked after him wonderfully well, and with great patience and love. Today he would have been rushed to a specialist stroke unit and no doubt recovered, if not to be the same, at least to have a decent life for many years – such awful timing of such a thing to happen.

I do not think the enormous decisions I was going to have to make really sank in, maybe because there was no alternative, but this was an absolutely life-changing moment of staggering proportions for the whole family, and I had to make out where we would all go from here. The workmen, and in particular the Myhill brothers, were doing their best to complete jobs Father had, but what about the future? – where was the family income to come from?

Father had no life insurance, pension policy, or savings. His 'savings' were in the two bungalows he had built at Winterton for George Myhill and then my grandparents, plus another one for Stanley Myhill in Martham. None of them was built with the idea of producing income – and it would not have been much in those days anyway. Catastrophic is a big word, but this was absolute disaster on a giant scale.

I returned to the Army with a very heavy heart, as a worried boy/man, and discussed my situation with the major who was allocated to look after us. To my amazement he was as concerned as I was, and told me that in such circumstances, and as National Service was anyway coming to an end, a letter from Father's doctor would likely see me discharged from the Army to go home and sort the family out.

Maybe the Army had also spotted that the entrepreneurial person I was to become was already showing through, and not really suited to the regimentation of Army life. Whatever, other than the reason for me being placed in this position, I was not disappointed to be leaving. 11 weeks after setting out I was back home again – and any idea of what job I was to do was settled. Aged just 19 I was going to have to be a builder, if I could hold the firm together.

One person who was appalled at what I had been landed with was Ken Temple, our next door neighbour and someone I admired. A real entrepreneur himself, he was building up a property and hotel group, having come out of the Royal Air Force. Mary and I were close to the whole family of his wife Val, Ken, and his children, Christine and Peter. Huge support from them in a difficult time.

What Ken taught me (and of course I had just recently had a hint of) was that a way of life existed which was different from that of our (up to then) very parochial existence in the village. I saw him develop some unique ideas; he was a very widely-travelled man and the *Hermanus Hotel* at Winterton was created by him in South African style out of really nothing, but all based on his recent visits to South Africa itself.

He had such charisma (powers of persuasion) that he even got the County Council to rename the village with '-on-Sea' added so as to improve his business chances in the holiday season. There is another village called Winterton in Lincolnshire, where he claimed much of his mail was being delivered.

The other thing we much admired Ken for was the way he looked after his wife, who had caught polio in a public swimming-pool when they were just married. She was forever after in a wheelchair and Ken just took her everywhere and would carry her around. Betty and I remained friends with them until their deaths.

Father had been a very popular man with his workmen and customers, and I can never thank them all enough for the support they gave this young 'lad' who had to take over. As I explained to his wonderful tradesmen: 'I can read, I can write and I can add up – but you will have to teach me to build.' And that is what we then all did together.

Father's farming and other customers, the Molineux, Whartons, Kittles, Chapmans and many, many others gave me support 'beyond the call of duty'. I have mentioned before Frank Cooper, who had the builders' merchants store in Great Yarmouth. He gave me enormous help working out prices, extending credit to me when I needed it and dispensing sound, common-sense advice. Father later recovered enough to get around with me sometimes, and would listen in on discussions we had – nodding or writing his approval, or not, from time to time, so I could get a sense from him that what I was doing was right.

Whatever job came up – and there were plenty thrown at us - I would take with me the main craftsmen to be involved and they would tell me about materials and the time it would take. I would then sit in the office (with various figures and details I built up as my own reference book over time, so I did not have to start from scratch on every job) and come to a figure which we rounded up or down according to how it looked.

We would then return to the customer, tell him the price and, in many cases – literally – watch his face. If he looked surprised – like it was more than he expected – we would say something like: 'Well, we have tried to cover everything, and we may be able to make some savings along the way. If we do, they are yours.'

If, on the other hand, the customer looked pleasantly surprised – like it was a lot less than expected – we would say: 'Well, we really have tried to keep it as low as we can. If we discover extra work as we go along we will tell you, and it may cost a bit more.' From such complicated formulae are great companies made! A slow learning curve it was not.

Thinking on how precise and petty building regulations are today, construction when I was learning from our workmen was still based on old-fashioned, tried and tested methods of calculation. What size piece of timber to span 8 feet? –2 inches x 4 inches.

For 10 feet – 2 inches x 5 inches. Not very scientific, but it was a pretty good guide.

When I was 16 years old I had obtained a provisional licence to drive a motor scooter, a Lambretta, of which I was very proud, even going alone down to Kent to stay with my Aunt Eileen a couple of times – big adventure in those days, crossing the ferry at Dartford – akin to Calais to Dover in my mind. It took me two attempts to get a full motor-cycle licence, because the test then was at Lowestoft – unfamiliar territory for me. I was told to drive a certain route round the town; I would be watched and, at some point, the examiner would jump out in front of me to test my emergency stopping skills.

After some time of driving around and seeing no one, I returned to the start to be told I had failed, because I had taken the second left instead of the first and, of course, had never driven past the man. Still, better than for a previous examiner there, who jumped out in front of the wrong motorbike.

I got my own back when the time for a full motor vehicle licence came up and it coincided with the 26 July 1956 Suez Canal crisis. For reasons only the Government will ever know, supposedly to save fuel, they allowed learner drivers to drive unaccompanied! At the end of the crisis and back to normality, drivers with certain birth dates were then given a pass without taking a test – and that included me. Betty will no doubt say it has been very obvious ever since.

Accountants got me to change the firm into a Limited Company, *O. Larter Ltd*, and we had the base at Winterton (a plumbing workshop at Broad View and the wood workshops at Low Road) and a small base in a building at Martham which Father had hired from Chapman's the butchers. In my early years as a builder and, I suppose, following in the trend Father had set, we decided to try to give the family an alternative income.

When possible we would build the odd property to retain and let, and thus we created 'Ambleside' and 'Windermere' – one at Hemsby and one at Winterton. That was the first slight change of direction for me and, later, we would build and keep a number of small holiday bungalows on land next to the Larter workshops at Winterton.

Father being ill caused me to meet Jim and Barbara Crampton, who ran *Travel Centre* at Castle Hill in Norwich when, with Mother, I was trying to find various cruise-type holidays for them to go on. Father would be well looked-after and Mother could have more of a holiday. They also hired houses at Sheringham, which was another of Father's favourites. Jim Crampton, who was a pilot in the war and had his own small business flying tourists from the beach at Clacton, also introduced me to Jimmy Hoseason of the Oulton Broad Hoseason's letting agency he had taken over from his father.

Jimmy was also a flying buff in the war, and later wrote a book on the various air squadrons based in East Anglia. He was just moving on to letting holiday homes as well as their traditional Broads hire boats, and we gave him the two new bungalows to let. Thus began a three-decade-long association with them and Eric Humphries, the joint Managing Director when my business moved on to holiday chalet developments.

Father was very good to his workmen, allowing both George and Stanley Myhill to rent the properties I have mentioned very cheaply, and we kept up that tradition until the deaths of both their wives in the 1990s. I owed the Myhill family more than you could calculate, for the guidance they had given me and, later in my life, I also employed George's son, Trevor, who had also become a carpenter.

Father left the Myhill bungalows to me and the Storey Smith grandparents' property to Mary, with another smaller bungalow let-out which he left to Susan. Father really was a very kind man, always doing what he thought right. In winter it would be: 'Let's just drop a load of waste firewood off to that old lady, as I know she does not have a lot' and, as a family, I think we all have that trait to a greater or lesser extent – goes with being too trusting, I think.

Not at first being certain that building was my 'for-ever' future, I also got involved with a company supplying some of the first vending machines, selling cold milk and drinks to tourists around the Norfolk Broads. We set up a small plant in Alfred Hedges' (see below) outbuildings, where we heat-sealed cartons; it was also a holiday job for Mary's first husband, Gordon Chapman, before they were married. Gordon was also a very skilled wood-turner and they later had a great craft shop in my old offices at Winterton when we moved over to Great Yarmouth.

For the vending machines we had a delivery van exotically decorated with a reclining cow, and called ourselves 'Val Vendos'. It meant arranging fresh bulk milk deliveries from *Collett's Dairy* each day (Collett Sr was a very solid fixture in the hierarchy of the Great Yarmouth business and political world, and quite amused at what I was trying to do) and then early morning filling of small, 1/3-pint cartons for delivery to our machines. We also produced orange drink so, all in all, quite a complicated business.

Today I don't think there would be a remote chance of such an amateur set-up being allowed (health and safety again). In fact, after two or three years, it was just too time-consuming, very seasonal and not very profitable, and we had to abandon it.

I mentioned the hobby Father had of collecting, and a lovely antiques story came about after he was ill, but still going to auctions, where the auctioneers all knew 'Ossie' and his having had a stroke. Stanley Myhill would drive him – often much to my irritation later, when there was urgent decorating work to be done. When Father had recovered a little from his stroke and could get around quite well, he took up a hobby (no one knows why) of restoring and re-gilding antique picture-frames – cheap because no one wanted them.

On the occasion in question, Father and Stanley were at an auction in a house in Southtown Road, Great Yarmouth, where a fire had badly damaged the property and the contents were being sold. At the sale he spotted a pile of burnt frames in the corner of the room and bought them for ten shillings – 50p in today's money.

On getting them home, he saw that one frame contained an oil painting which the fire had not destroyed – the fire had badly damaged the varnished surface, but his instinct told him it might be good, because of the quality of the frame perhaps. I was sent to take it to Arthur Davies, a renowned artist and restorer friend of his in Norwich. A year later, our having forgotten about it, Arthur called me to collect it and said: 'Father may be quite pleased.'

What we now had was a beautiful oil painting by E. R. Smythe (1810 – 1899), one of the two famous brothers who painted great landscapes and animals in Suffolk. That picture is now held by me as a family heirloom, with the legend pasted on the back, and I hope it will remain in the family for many years to come as a memory. Serendipity? Absolutely, and it obviously runs in the family. Mary has a T.Smythe (the other brother) painting, also bought by Father, but just in the normal way.

Stanley was the more amusing of the two Myhill brothers and, having worked as a decorator as a young man with my Father for my Grandfather Larter, they had great fun together as young men. He was very fond of Father and so sad to see what had happened to the energetic 'life and soul of the party' man he knew. He had the driest sense of humour and, when my sister Susan was born, remarked immediately: 'Another mouth to feed', in the nicest possible way.

When the building team was working at one time for the Misses Newbound at the lighthouse, a film was being made of *Unusual Houses in England*, and the film crew appeared without notice at Winterton. We were decorating the lighthouse at the time and the film crew needed an 'extra'. Stanley very quickly smartened up and was filmed as the professional gardener working on the property, with great success. I would love to be able to find that film in someone's archive today.

Father, when he was ill, could no longer drive, but was still ever the practical man he had been previously – such as when, on a hot summer's day, he thought he ought to have shorts, so simply took a pair of grey trousers and, without Mother knowing, just cut off half of each leg.

He now bought a tricycle to travel each day to see Shields Sr and place a bet or two, and to generally get round the village. At one time I was receiving telephone calls at home from a military gent who claimed to be a racing expert, and would always be asking if Father had taken his tip to back such-and-such a horse.

I asked Father what he was paying this man and he said he paid nothing at all, so I enquired how on earth the man could make a living. Father told me: 'Very simple – if there are 4 likely winners, he rings four clients and gives each one a different horse to back. When the race is over he just calls the man he gave the correct horse name to and, if he has backed it and won, he likely sends him a percentage of his winnings. If he didn't, then he likely feels guilty and sends him something anyway.' What a way to make a living!

Family genes and skills pass down from one generation to another and I think this applies to Alice. She absolutely loves placing the odd small bet on a horse; so much so that, for a day out as a treat for Betty and me on one occasion, her choice was to take us for a day at Newmarket Races – where we actually did quite well. Even now she is at university, we will be speaking on Skype or phone and she will tell me how, sadly, a horse she put £1 on has been withdrawn or has some problem.

1961 had crept up upon me with Father deteriorating slowly and now, at age 22 years, I had the good fortune to have a 'mentor' turn up on the scene. A good customer was Robert Ludkin, who lived at Somerton Hall, West Somerton. A London city company secretary, he and his wife, Elsie, had been very fond of Mother and Father. After completing a job for him at one time, he sat me down and asked: 'What do you *really* want to do?'

I told him that now I had experienced a year or so of the contracting side of building and had built the two holiday bungalows, I thought I would like to build houses on a small scale. For me, not knowing where men would be working each day and what to do with them when there was a lack of continuity of work, or when the weather was bad, was simply not comfortable. My problem was that I had no capital with which to buy land. He asked me if he could help in a small way, and told me to find a piece of land for a few houses and he would lend me the money. Just like that!

Wild horses would not have stopped me finding a piece of land, which I did, buying a piece my Uncle Harry Larter was selling in Martham. I don't really know how my Father and Harry got on in later years, but I think there was some animosity somewhere. Harry knew his brother was very ill and his son was trying to make a success of his business, but the fact that Mother was not surprised when I approached Harry to buy the land privately and he refused to have anything to do with me, told me a lot.

He made me go to the auction to buy the land – which I did. Such are families! I signed a cheque with the auctioneer for the deposit, which would not be met at the bank unless Ludkin came good. Next door to the land being sold was a large house, now owned by the same Billy Chapman who, in 1940, had allowed us to share the Moregrove Farm house with the Jones family. Billy wanted a small part of the land to extend his garden and I was delighted to be able to agree that, and in my mind to repay some of the kindness he had shown the family all those years ago. What do they say? 'What goes around, comes around', and I think that applies both ways.

In trying to paint you a picture of life around these times, I have said that the rationing of food came to an end in 1954 and so, by the late 1950s, the idea of actually finding a good restaurant to go to for a meal was catching on. I recall Father and Mother going sometimes to a restaurant above *Arnold's* department store in Great Yarmouth just after the war, but the idea of cordon bleu, Ramsey, or Jamie Oliver was in the far distance.

As restaurants started up, we would think nothing of driving 30 or 40 miles and then back, for an evening meal. Famous from those days was *Gasche's Swiss Restaurant* at Weybourne run by the Gasche nephew, Edmond - the very word 'Swiss' was magic and the food superb. Also in North Norfolk was the *Northrepps Cottage* and, a bit nearer home, the famous *Petersfield Hotel* at Horning. The *Carlton Hotel* at Great Yarmouth, with the charming and gracious Dick Chettleburgh as mine host, was where everyone met for a Saturday dinner-dance. Going south, we had the *Sherriff House* at Brockdish, where the very eccentric

Pichel Juan (PJ) was chef and host, but my favourite was *The Fox and Goose* at Fressingfield.

PJ had the *Fox and Goose* first and was famous for getting very irritated if you turned up late. Known for once having thrown the meal of a party out of the window and making them wait again – or so the story goes. When he left to go to the *Sherriff House*, Mr and Mrs Clark took over, with Mrs C to cook and Mr C as mine host. Excellent, but a much more English style of cooking, with Mr C having previously been a butcher. He was a real character, of whom I became very fond. More of Mr C later.

I cannot express adequately the excitement for me, at 22 years old, of buying my first piece of land and already planning the development. I was a developer! I rushed to see Ludkin with the news on the way home, collected a cheque from him and the rest, as they say, is history. A real life-changing moment which set the pattern of my business life for the next 30 years. Donald Maltman was my architect and with his guidance we were off.

The most difficult thing was that I had no management or office experience, or help – I just did everything myself at first; early mornings and late nights. Father did not even have a proper office. Alfie Rouse, a local rent collector, would do the wages one evening each week, followed later by a delightful gent, Bill Cacutt, who had retired to Winterton; Father then distributed the brown packets every Friday as he toured the jobs. That's what I inherited, but now I had to build an office and start on some sort of management organization, of which I had no experience at all.

Various young ladies came to help me deal with letters and answer phones, ending with Maureen Liversidge, the wife of the architect I have mentioned. Maureen later came with me to Great Yarmouth and on to Gunton Hall. I did my own drawing where needed and, as we developed, various council officials helped me with advice. Finally one of the *Blofield and Flegg* building inspectors, Michael King, agreed to join me to help with some of the estimating, design, planning and management.

That did not really work out, because he was on too high a level and too soon for me. Finally, Geoff Balls joined me (he chose me out of two jobs he was offered on the same day, he tells me!) and we never looked back. He went on to be with the building company *Asta Properties* after the *Hills* and *RKF* buyouts of later.

Geoff got stuck into buying materials, selling the bungalows and chalets, ordering, valuations, and stock-taking – a real jack of all trades and, I am sure he will say, greatly underpaid! He says he wondered what the rest of us did. The holiday chalets were furnished from Sheffield, and he reminds me of weekends when we were unpacking and placing furniture and planting grass seed to make lawns – using an old-fashioned 'fiddle' loaned by a local farmer.

Because I would like their families to know I appreciated them all, as many of our workmen as Geoff Balls (who I called on to help) and I can recall are named as follows. Obviously the Myhill brothers (and later, Trevor, son of George), Herbert Powley, Tom Crafer and Harry Futter were all prominent. Others were: Arthur Brown, Mervyn Postle, Harry 'Shopney' Utting, John Pembleton, Biff Harding, Stanley Ransome and later, son Keith, Harry 'Gilo' Nichols, Alec Green, Brian Warnes, Neville Wacey, John Grimmer, John Dyble, Richard Green, Tommy Harrison, Willie Carver, Robin Medlar, Geoff Jary and Richard Smith. I hope that covers the real 'old' firm, and apologise if I have left you out.

On the personal and 'social' front, such as it was, in the late 1950s Mary and I had joined the Young Conservatives (YCs, as they were known) in Great Yarmouth and for me, eventually, also Round Table – that being what you did in those days. It did not bring a very wide circle of friends but, through them, I met Susan Baker and, in September 1961, we married. I was able to get away from the family and set up my own home, first by taking over our 'Windermere' holiday bungalow at Winterton, more-or-less opposite to what was my office.

Susan suffered a miscarriage first, which had us worried; but then, light of our life, our first child, Andrew, was born on 28 March 1963. An absolute delight and, of course, great excitement for grandparents, both Larter and Baker. Mother, living opposite, was able to make all the fuss she wished, and I now had a great spur to find us a home of our own. Later that year, we decamped for our own spot on that first development at Martham, which I named 'Willows End' – living on the job, I think it is called.

Andrew was born just after one of the worst winters in history – only 1683/4 being recorded as worse. Our 1962 /3 winter brought blizzards, 20ft snowdrifts and temperatures as low as -19°C. In places, the sea itself froze up to a mile from shore. Not the best start for my first housing development or new family, but an innovative heating system by *Husqvarna*, a Swedish company that I had adopted for the estate, kept us warm.

Husqvarna invited me and other builders to Sweden to visit their factory, and again I was opening my eyes to the worlds outside. I made quite a friend of the Sales Manager, who later came to stay at Somerton Hall, but his main skill appeared to be in his ability to consume alcohol.

The other person I had become close to in Winterton after leaving school, and when Father was first ill, was Alfred Hedges, the librarian at Great Yarmouth. His wife, Mel, would later become my right-hand lady, looking after the office and holiday bookings. Alfred was always there to talk to before I was married, and he got Mary and me to join the Winterton Tennis Club to get us socializing a bit more – yes, me playing tennis!

It came to the club's annual dinner and we were not more than 18 or so, my hardly having seen a glass of wine, let alone having any knowledge. We were on Alfred's table at dinner and, when the wine waiter asked him what wine he would like for the table, he said: 'Joe will choose that.'

I was not going to say I was not able to choose, so took the list, which meant nothing to me; but I must have recognized a name and so was able to order something. That would have been fine except that, after the wine waiter had gone, Alfred asked if we were having red or white. Again, I was not going to admit I had no idea, so said 'red'. Needless to say, when it arrived it was white and, from that moment on, I determined to know at least a little about wine – more about which later.

The person in the family who had the most traumatic time with Father being ill was my younger sister, Susan, as she was very close to him, being only 14 years old when he became ill, and at home more than Mary and me. Father lived until 1964 and I know that at 18 it was very difficult for her. She felt isolated in the village and, as soon as she could, she was with girlfriends in Great Yarmouth – and not always the correct ones.

Father desperately wanted her to be happy and, on leaving school (with I think very little in qualifications), she first went to try nursing.

One telling-off from Matron and she walked out! Next, still only 16, she wanted to have a small boarding-house in Great Yarmouth, a home of her own and independence, but really at much too early an age.

Father gave her the support to do that but, like a lot of things with Susan, it lasted a very short time. Mother and Mary had a lot to do that first year to look after guests who had booked in and, at 19, Susan married Aleks Szymanski, son of a Polish family and a skilled jeweller. Sadly that did not last, but produced Aleks Jr, of whom a lot more later.

Father died in 1964, and I remember being very moved by the number of workmen, customers and friends who turned out for his funeral. George Myhill lovingly made his coffin from an oak tree he and father had cut down some years previously, and he was carried from Broad View to the church on the back of the Larter builders' truck. An end to an era.

Willows End Estate at Martham was first about 20 houses, and later extended by us with more land purchases to what it is today. Susan and I 'booked' the first £2800 bungalow as I had promised her, but it was sold before we got anywhere near moving in, and then the same again with the second one, with us eventually buying and moving in to No 3. Good for business.

Digressing as I will do all the way through this book, a writer I absolutely admire and love to read is Bill Bryson – now living in Norfolk and doing all sorts of good stuff for us. Telling you of building my first houses reminds me of a story he told in his book *Down Under*. Bill is American, but spent some time in Australia and, when he came to the UK, kept in touch with an old lady in Australia who from time to time would write to him with an update on the area in which he used to live. She wrote to say that a friend of hers had moved house next to a vacant lot where they were now building a new house. The 3-year-old daughter of the friend hung around the builders and they sort of adopted her, giving her little jobs and so on.

When, at the end of the week, the boss man came to pay the team their wages, he gave the little girl a wage packet with maybe a dollar in it. She rushed home proudly to show Mummy, who said they must straight away go to the bank and open a savings account for her. At the bank the teller was most impressed and, to be encouraging, asked the little girl if this was to be a regular occurrence and if she would be

working there next week. To which her reply was: 'Yes, if the f******
bricks arrive!' So innocent and lovely.

There was now a very hectic period of expansion for me as I created
various developments and, with the help of an old Norfolk farmer,
Tom Bammant, at Newport Hemsby, started the first of what would be
many holiday chalet developments on the coast.

Tom was a charming if somewhat irascible 'son of the earth', whose
real pleasure was going to Acle cattle market to buy or sell a small
number of animals that he kept. He first asked me to build him a toilet
block for a caravan site on some of his farmland, for which he had
obtained planning approval. Then, as he trusted me, he and his wife
would ask me to write letters or deal with officials for him, and we got
on well.

When I told him about holiday chalets, which were the thing of the
moment in Lincolnshire at that time, he said that, if I could obtain
approval on an 8-acre field of his near the beach at Newport, I could
build there and he would take ground rents for the land, which we duly
did, and called the development Hawaii Beach.

Where I was able to start to build myself a capital base was with the
use of heavy plant and machinery, and learning the benefits of
prefabrication, which one of our carpenters, Harry Futter, taught me,
he having worked at *George Mixer and Co* in Catfield on Government
contracts during the war. Also, the Dinkum Digger had arrived,
followed by the JCBs we all know today. However, at that time, the
majority of earth work was still done by hand.

Literally, if you wanted a drainage trench and the soil was hard, you
started to dig it and then overnight let the trench fill with water to
soften for hand-digging again the next day. Much work was measured –
priced by the cubic yard or metre and, if you got a contract where you
were paid to do the job by hand and then used machinery instead, you
were obviously in a very profitable position.

For a year or two people thought that the financial burden of buying
plant equated to labour cost, and I bought a second-hand Dinkum
Digger to find out that it was certainly better. When it came to the
holiday chalet developments, I chose cedar cladding and wood
construction for prefabrication, so we could make jigs and turn out a
series of each section one after the other.

It took a lot of planning, but we could manufacture everything in the Winterton workshop and then erect the whole thing in a couple of days, thus minimizing any delays from weather in the winter. At Newport, £798.00 all-in was our price for a chalet with two small bedrooms, and we made very good money indeed – plus a price of about £100.00 for carpets and complete furnishing, all bought in by us from a wholesaler in Sheffield.

In 1967 land at Kessingland, followed by Edmonds land at Scratby and then land at Heacham belonging to Mr Parke, were all submitted by me for planning approval, which was granted. Lastly, as the businesses developed, we obtained planning approval for more Bammant land at Newport, for about 200 chalets on 30 acres, to be developed in stages, and then on to California Sands nearby and other land at Scratby.

On the Bob Ludkin front, we bought an old RAF base at Hopton, near Lowestoft, from Ken Temple's company at Winterton, and developed it into a proper holiday 'camp' letting business which we named 'Mariners Park'. Bob and I also bought land at Rollesby, more land adjoining Willows End, and odd sites at Winterton and Somerton, all for residential housing.

The 1960s were also times of jumping land values and lots of speculation by 'amateurs'. We by now had an office in Great Yarmouth and employed an accountant, Derek Roll – of whom more later. We owned a certain, attractive piece of land near Burgh Castle and along came a 'wide boy' (name forgotten), likely from Essex, with a beautiful Rolls-Royce and a driver he called Maxwell. He wanted to buy our land, but we found out he was signing a number of contracts all over the place and was not always being able to complete on time.

We made sure he signed to buy our land with a big enough deposit he would not want to lose and then, as completion approached, he asked for an extension, which we gave him. He then wanted another extension, which we would not give him, and so he offered us some part-built properties on another estate in lieu of cash. That was fine by us if it would help him and, on the day on which completion was to take place, we got an agent in the area of the houses to check them out and see that we had value for money. Answer – no houses existed, just bare plots!

We finally got the correct plots, houses and value, but my memory is of the man being very angry indeed that we had found him out.

Let's just stop and reflect here for a moment. We were in the mid/late 1960s, me at 26 or so, still on my own, no other directors or managers, and with Bob Ludkin in the background. I was alone carrying out a phenomenal amount of work both building and selling holiday chalets plus proper housing, and all from a little, two-room office in Winterton before we moved to Great Yarmouth – and me loving it.

Geoff Balls reminds me of the sky-high interest rates at one time, and our having a dozen or so houses standing part-built and unsold. That was one of the earlier housing slumps that we see in Britain with increasing frequency, and your bank certainly needed to have great faith in you.

Bob and I had now formed a proper land company, *Larters Estates Ltd*, separate from my own building company, and Bob had by then also become Company Secretary of a listed public company in London, *City and Country Properties*, controlled by the Freshwater family. They in turn had bought out *WA Hills*, an old, established building company in Colchester, and then floated it, again with Bob as Company Secretary, and so it was really inevitable that they made a bid to buy *Larters Estates* and *O Larter Ltd*.

This was a very big move for me, and the total price paid by them in 1969 was £410,000, split between Bob and me, mainly an exchange of shares with me now, for the first time, no longer strictly my own boss. I remember Hills' 'due diligence' people not believing we could build holiday homes for the price we did, because they had no experience of prefabrication. If you look on the historical 'cash value' sites, that 1969 £410k would today be the equivalent of £5m, but did not seem remotely like that, which I think again illustrates inflation for you – an increase of 13 times the original value.

Hills was a real, old-fashioned construction company built up by Stanley Hills and his brother and, when I joined, consisted of Alan Hills, the nephew of Stanley, and Christopher Stowe as joint Managing Directors. Alan was the 'dealer' and Christopher was the engineer, together with George Woodgate, a very efficient accountant – all of whom got on very well with Bob Ludkin, who became Chairman of the company. I also met there a man I was to end up looking after in his very old age.

He was Jim Balls, who owned an accounting business, *Fruin Warner and Co*, and was auditor to the Hills. I think for Bob this was the best of times, because he was Company Secretary to some of the *Freshwater Group*, who controlled the Hills company, and they relied on him a bit to keep an eye on us. Also, he now had his 'family' of four 'boys' working in a company he understood, and we all liked and appreciated him.

I made a lifelong friend in Alan Hills, and one good change for me was that, under *Hills'* ownership, I no longer had to see to or plan the day-to-day actual building operation. *Hills* sent up a very tough and skilled building contract manager, John James, who did a superb job on a much larger scale than I had the experience to do. Whilst he was with us, John sadly lost his lovely wife in a car accident, but later married his secretary Lynne and they now live very happily in Cyprus.

Meantime, back at home, Susan and I had started travelling. The prefabrication of chalets really did earn a lot of money, and I know I was very proud to have one of the first E-Type Jaguars, followed by another – and wish I had them today. We parked the children with the Baker in-laws at our then Somerton Hall home, and took lovely holidays, including the West Indies one year.

In the late 1960s the West Indies were very simple and undeveloped, and I am not even sure there were jet planes then, so a long trip. Our first stop was Antigua and, going to the hotel from the airport, our taxi came across another which had broken down. We gave the passengers a lift and became friends with Joyce and Basil Bloodworth, giving me a serious serendipitous occasion which affected our future perhaps more than any other event in our lives and which also, in the second week, took us on our first trip to Barbados.

Before that West Indies trip, Mr Serendipity had turned up when Susan and I attended a charity dinner in Great Yarmouth. There was a raffle, with just one main prize – a weekend for two in Paris, all-found. Who else but us deserved that? I went to the agents who donated it and extended the trip to a week, and that really was our first 'breakout' from England – a very memorable trip, with all the 'Under the bridges of Paris with me' tourist sites visited.

Politics! Arising from being a Young Conservative (where are they these days?) and being persuaded by Dick Fairbairns at Martham, the Chairman of the Conservative party locally, I stood for the Conservatives as a County Councillor for the West Flegg area and, on 8 April1964, Councillor Joseph Larter was elected. I don't think there was much competition for candidates in those days.

This was no presidential 'fight to the death' with Labour, or whoever. I suppose I had an opponent but I do not remember who, and certainly saw no sign of him/her. No political meetings, thumping at the hustings, or anything, really. I recall my builders' truck being fitted with a public address system, but mainly just me driving around asking people nicely to vote for me. Mary and other YCs would deliver leaflets with my appeal to the electorate, and that was about it.

Here I was following a slight family tradition, as Father had spent many years on the much more local (and laid-back) Blofield and Flegg Rural District Council at Acle, where he was much loved and respected. George Hellier, the old-style Town Clerk there, and Donald Chilvers, the Chief Engineer and Planner, were both enormously concerned when Father was ill. The whole Council voted to send him a 'get well soon' letter, which was much appreciated by Mother. Mary was to later follow him as a District Councillor for many years.

I very quickly realized that politics and committees were just not my style. In those days (it may be the same now), if you actually *knew* anything about a subject you were not allowed on a particular committee.

Thus, as a builder, planning, construction projects and so on were all banned to me (and anyway, at 25, what did I really know?), so I got health and mental health – about which of course I knew absolutely nothing at all, but I did get to meet Andrew Scott, who was the Chief Medical Officer. The Chairman of the Council was Sir Bartle Edwards, who really was the most charming gent, but one had the feeling it was all a bit of a gentlemen's club.

The genteel ladies who formed most of the Health Committee were far more interested in the hourly price being paid to home helps than they were in the overall budget of several million pounds. Andrew and I would have a little meeting ahead of Committee so his pathway was slightly smoothed, because he was a very sensible Officer and we understood each other. A gentle Scotsman, he left the County Council in one of the shake-ups, and I met him again many years later when he had been Chief in Wellington, New Zealand and had retired to Rangiputa in the tropical North Island.

One side story here is that all planning appeals by builders in the Acle area (that included me) were held at the Council offices. Nothing like the ponderous system today, and all very civilized. The Planning Inspector was allowed to have lunch with all parties, so long as both sides were present and, of course, the case in hand was not discussed.

On the occasion I recall, at an appeal of mine, one of the County Council lawyers was relating a tale at lunch, mostly for his own great amusement, with loud guffaws as he reached what he thought were amusing points. It concerned an Inspector being taken to see a site on the Norfolk Broads. Standing in the back of the open inspection boat, he had made his viewing and when it came on to rain, the boat owner told his man to speed up and get them home.

So violent was the increase in speed that the Inspector was unbalanced and fell overboard. There was a very uneasy silence at the lunch until the Inspector said: 'Yes – I remember it very well, as it was me.' A lesson on opening your mouth, I think!

Not quite another serendipitous moment, but next, the Jim and Barbara Crampton I had met when helping Mother get suitable holidays for Father, now asked me to do something for them. Jim also later developed the start of Norwich Airport and *Air Anglia* with a colleague, 'Wilbur' Wright. Sometime, I would like to see a memorial plaque to them there because, without their pioneering, I doubt there would be much today. Norwich 'airport' was not much more than a few fields and an old wartime hangar in the early days.

Jim and Barbara had become taken with Malta and wanted to buy a property there, on the waterfront at Ghadira, just below Mellieha and on the bay. Would I look with them and advise if I thought it sensible? Another occasion where I am attributed with skills and knowledge I could not possibly have, but of course I said yes. Susan and I went out there with them, thought the property looked very good value, and they bought it. Whilst we were there, I spoke to the builder, a wonderful, gruff old man called Angelo Mifsud, and asked if he had anything else for sale along the waterfront.

He did not have anything, but said his brother had a roof space on the top of a concrete fishing-hut in the same row, and could possibly sell me that. It was agreed. Angelo then quoted for a simple, two-storey holiday apartment with a staircase through the ground-floor fishing part and, for about £3800 all-in, we had our first foreign holiday home – right on the edge of the water. Later the brother, who had another fishing store there, did the same thing again, and Jim and I bought that one between us. Thus, we had three holiday letting units which the travel agency in Norwich handled.

We had wonderful holidays there with the children, and I became very fond of the Maltese people, particularly Luis Fenech, a retired teacher who looked after the Malta side of the properties for us, and the wonderful Beatrix Bartolo (Beche) who cleaned and looked after us when we were there ourselves. We were all very close, and Jim, Barbara, Susan and I were honoured later to be invited to the wedding of a Fenech daughter.

Mr Mintoff – a communist – took over the government and hated the British and everything they stood for. He immediately banned the letting of properties by non-residents, so we could only use them ourselves. After a year of just costs and no income, we sold all three, and it did make us weep a little when we passed by a year or so ago and were told they were now each changing hands for £250k and more.

The Keith Sparks company I talk about later on, developed a tourist attraction there in Mdina and, long after Mintoff, I later returned to Malta in the 1990s. One of our contacts there, James Rizzo, the civil servant in charge of tourist development, asked if Bruce Cantor of Rex Studies at Great Yarmouth and I would look at providing a Sealife Centre.

It would have been perfect at a location in Buggiba, right on the rocky shore, in the same style as one I had seen in Monterey, California but, just as we were ready with plans, the government changed again and we lost it. Furthermore, the government were, in any case, convinced that it should not be in the main tourist area, but completely on the other side of the island, where there was no one staying. Their theory was that it would make tourists go to a different area. Such was their knowledge of tourism!

A real character I met in the early days of our waterfront properties was Lino Spiteri. Lino, an architect, had a home on the same waterfront and was a very extrovert character, later becoming an MP of some standing and, later still, a correspondent for *The Times of Malta* and a writer. One day he told me he was going over to Gozo, where he was supervising construction of a small block of apartments. Knowing I was a builder, he invited me to accompany him, which I did. I could immediately see that the visit was 'cosmetic' more than anything – just a site visit that had to be made every so often.

However, I was interested in the construction and drew Lino's attention to how some reinforcing was being laid, ready for concrete to be poured to form the base of the block. At that point he knelt down on the ground and peered closely, agreeing that the overlap was wrong or non-existent – but until then I had no idea he was short-sighted and could not actually see the detail!

Several years after the Malta Sealife idea I was back again, having been asked by James to look at Fort Ricasoli with Bruce Carter (opposite side of the harbour to Valletta), as a possible theme-park-type development. Again, government bureaucracy stopped any real progress, in the same way I was to see later in Barbados. However, Malta was another great experience I would not have missed, and it was just so different from what it is today, and less developed. When I asked a taxi driver on a first visit: 'Which side of the road do you drive on?' he really did reply: 'We drive in the shade.'

In 1965 Bob Ludkin moved into Norwich, and I bought Somerton Hall from him – a bit of a grand move from holiday bungalow via a little estate bungalow, to Hall in 5 years! It cost the princely sum of £10,000 in those days. On 25 July there was another big event, when daughter Rebecca was born there! Again great excitement, with the Bakers in particular coming to stay and babysit. It was a great property for two children, and the nearby beaches at Somerton, or driving up the road to Horsey or Mundesley, were just made for the family. We also had a small motor-boat, so we could use the river access at Somerton as well.

Somerton Hall stands on a hill and is next door to West Somerton church, which holds a curiosity you discover by going into the church graveyard actually by a side entrance, just a few yards from the Hall itself. There lies Robert Hales, famous as the Norfolk Giant. Born in a small cottage in West Somerton in 1820, Robert grew to be 7ft 8inches and weighed 450 lbs. He was a curiosity and performed in circuses, but retired to run a London pub; he died in 1863. The rather morbid story goes that, at his height, they could not get him into the coffin, so he had to be folded. Ughh.

In buying up various sites for development, I did buy a completely derelict clay-lump cottage behind what was the Post Office at Somerton, and only after we had cleared the site and built a new cottage there was I told it was the place where Robert Hales was born! I don't think it could have been preserved, but it would have been nice to have known before we pulled it down.

There are two Somertons – East and West. We lived in West Somerton but in the East, just across the road and on the Burnley Hall estate, there is the ruined church of St Mary. Inside the ruined tower grows a large tree, and the East Somerton morbid story says that it has grown from the wooden leg of an ancient lady buried there.

Another story of Somerton Hall was that of it being requisitioned by the Army for training during the war. Lessons on how to handle hand grenades were being given in what is now the main lounge or drawing room, and an accident occurred, blowing out all the beautiful, curved-glass windows there. I think there was a fatality but, if you look at the matching bay windows of the drawing room and dining room, only the dining room has the curved glass.

I was also told stories that a previous owner used to ride his horse into the hall and up the main staircase – possible, but I never tried it myself. Another was of there being a tunnel from the cellars of the Hall to the church (handy on a rainy day, I suppose) but, although there was evidence of previous owners digging to look, I never found anything myself.

Better news was that Bob Ludkin and friends had imported a barrel of French red wine to bottle for themselves, and had not liked the result. They left the 3 or 4 dozen bottles behind and, in later years, I found it had matured very well indeed.

Let's have a look at values and events for 1965 as we did for 1955, to keep our feet on the ground. Inflation was 5%, Hurricane *Betsy* hit the USA, it was the year of race riots challenging segregation there, and the Vietnam War was in full swing. Ronnie Biggs, the Great Train Robber, escaped, the 70mph speed limit on motorways was brought in, the Russian, Leonov, was the first man to walk in space, mini-skirts appeared, the Beatles were established and JK Rowling (*Harry Potter*) was born. Not quite as exciting as when I looked at 1955.

Four years after buying Somerton, Susan and I had found a lovely old barn at Blofield, near Norwich; we named it 'Two Barns' and, with the help of architect George Barnes, we turned it into the best home I ever built, with an indoor swimming-pool. But all was not well, and our marriage was not to last.

I was travelling a huge amount, always starting some new scheme, including one in Wales and, in 8 years, we had simply grown away from each other. Late nights, early mornings and, as now, my work was my hobby. The effect on the two children was a great concern, as it always is, but I hope they would say there were plusses as well as minuses.

We left Two Barns the year after we moved in. I bought Susan a house in Norwich and agreed that, as we had developed Blofield together, I would sell and not eventually live there with someone else. Thus I moved on alone to my next base, Barn Cottage at Carlton Colville, which was at least near all the coastal developments.

Running alongside all this was my developing the leisure side of *W A Hills*, as they were now, the owners of the Larter companies. In 1970 Derek Moorhouse, a freelance agent in Wilmslow, Cheshire, persuaded me to meet him at Caernarvon, in North Wales (250 miles each way, so how far away from Norfolk could I get?).

He wanted me to look at a leisure caravan and chalet development which was about to go under, as the owner had run out of money. He was Jack Enston, of a local quarrying family, and he really had bitten off more development cost than he could chew, led on by a Mr Easy, his manager. It was vast, but beautiful – 200 acres, two miles of salmon fishing, two lakes, and Jack himself living in a grand, mock-Tudor mansion – the Glan Gwna Estate at Caeathrow. How on earth could I handle that?

Hills were willing to fund the purchase and let me have men up there, so long as I would manage it; having the personal situation at home, I was more than delighted to do so – getting away, I suppose. By then I had an Aston Martin, so that was a joy for long distances as well. Bob Ludkin came up from time to time and we all got on with Enston and his charming wife, Rosemary. I never did even attempt to learn Welsh, but had some great local musical evenings in pubs, and met unusual, different people. A truly foreign country as far as the English are concerned.

Introduced to me by John James, the man who was most valuable for us there was Tom O'Hanlon. An Irishman who had worked for Hills ran the development for me, aided very ably by his office manager, Kate, who looked after all the sales and lettings and had come to Wales from Lincolnshire for me. Tom moved to Wales with his wife and daughter, and saw me through any number of troubles. Tom was just a very capable man, if sometimes very impatient. He had to build the place, furnish the bungalows and then liaise with *Hoseasons* – ours being the first estate *Hoseasons* had ever let outside Norfolk.

Much as I liked the Welsh, in short doses, the local lads occasionally clearing out our furnishings the night after they had been set out in the chalets for letting the next day did not help to endear me further to them. I think they saw the English as easy pickings. Tom was later to come down to Norfolk and only in 2012, aged 80, did he retire from being involved with me in one development or another, latterly managing some lettings which was his 'pension'.

In those days in Wales, if a development needed a liquor licence for a club, you had to form a committee of members, set out rules, and go through a ridiculous legal process to be able to sell alcohol to visitors staying with you. So off we set to form a club for our holidaymakers, and I consulted the local court and police doing everything by the book to make sure we had no problems.

We went to court two weeks before opening our club, and were thrown out within minutes. I went to the police sergeant who had advised me all through, and asked what on earth I had done wrong. 'Used a solicitor from Prestatyn and not from Caernarvon,' he said. He called their own solicitor (one ap Hughes) and asked that, if he arranged another court for the Tuesday would he, Hughes, act for Glan Gwna. Some discussion followed; his partner would act for the police and we got our licence on the Tuesday within minutes. What's that called? You scratch my back and I'll scratch yours!

On the application day, Hughes decided to ask the ancient Lady Chairman of the bench if she would also grant us a licence for fruit machines (gambling machines). In all seriousness, the lady said: 'Mr Hughes; fruit machines? Surely that is a matter for the public health department.' You could not make it up, but we got our licences and, from that day, any problem was sorted by a call to Hughes. To explain for the non-Welsh – 'ap' means 'son of', and normally it would be

Robert ap Hughes or suchlike. Although his first name was Gwylim, everyone just called him 'ap'.

Meantime, back at my new Barn Cottage bachelor base, things were also changing on a personal level. When Susan and I had our first child, Andrew, as I have already mentioned, a girl she had worked with as a secretary in the local Great Yarmouth Hospital, Betty Hayward, came with her husband to see the new baby – as girls do. In the years following, we made visits between the two families and, by the time I was divorced, so was Betty, and off working in Baghdad. She had made a big impression on me, so I was determined to find out where this lovely girl had disappeared to, and we managed to meet up on one or two occasions when she was home.

By 1971 Betty had at last returned to the UK, as her mother had become very ill, and it gave me a chance to make some very nice trips with her. She came with me to Wales, usually via somewhere like Portmeirion, the replica Italianate village by the water in North Wales, and location for the famed TV series *The Prisoner*. Quite different from the extreme north, where Glan Gwna was situated, and where we also had the opportunity to visit the Menai Straits and Anglesey. There were times when development was intense and time was short, and Bob Ludkin and I would fly in a private plane from Norfolk into RAF Valley, feeling very important and privileged.

On one occasion with Betty, we stayed in one of the estate bungalows for the weekend with her father, after her mother had died. In the bar on the Saturday evening, I remarked to the barman that, as the owner of supposedly one of the best 2-mile stretches of salmon fishing in Wales (every stretch in Wales has the best 2 miles, of course), I had never had one of my own salmon. He expressed his disappointment for me, and we left it at that.

The following morning, Betty and I went walking on the estate and, on our return, Betty's father held up a grand salmon which had been delivered, and for which he had been relieved of ten pounds. On asking the barman who had delivered it, he quoted a name like Taffy – the local poacher. Taffy had presumably stolen the salmon from my river and taken great delight in selling it to me, and probably been getting free drinks on the story ever since.

Bob Ludkin deserves a very special mention, as he really was my mentor – maybe after Father died I was the son he never had, and he was the father I had lost. He did not quite teach me how to eat, but he never hesitated to invite me to meetings, or lunch, or dinner in London, where I met some extraordinary people and where I benefited from his experience – or just listening to the conversations, during many of which I was completely out of my depth.

There were some 'shady' characters around (as I got to know them) and the meeting place was usually *Martinez*, the famous original Spanish Restaurant in Swallow Street. We met wheeler- dealers there and I heard amazing stories, one being of a restaurant (maybe *Martinez*) being won and lost in a bet, with the new owners then finding fine wine, worth many thousands of pounds, in the cellars. I remember one exceptional character being Freddie Smythson, a man with a huge personality, and it was through him I first heard of Robert Francis, with whom I was to become involved years later.

Freddie lived in a lovely house on the south coast and can best be described, in the nicest possible way, as a gentleman rogue. He was always arguing with the taxman, never had any money when he needed it, but you always felt that, if you were in trouble, Freddie would be the man to get you out of it. His son, Peter, was a highly-respected London solicitor Who was able to give us very sound advice when we needed it.

I think my favourite Ludkin/London story is of the building of the *Londonderry House Hotel* next door to the *Hilton* in Park Lane, where Bob was company secretary and I think Smythson and another serious stockbroker-type were both involved. It had been built by putting various bombed sites together, including that of the original *Londonderry House*, and had been very difficult. On opening, there was Bob and all the gang at the opening reception, very proud of what they had achieved.

A gentleman sidled up to Bob and said something like:

'Mr Ludkin, how will your staff and guests be able to get from Room 12 to Room 13 on each floor?' Bob made the obvious reply and then the man said: 'Well, actually, that will be very difficult, because if you examine such-and-such deed properly, you will find that my company still owns a 1ft strip between those two rooms.' I do not know the outcome, but I believe it was very expensive.

Being somewhat interested in history, I did read up on the original Londonderry House, when it was used as one of their family homes by the Marquis and Marchioness of Londonderry. If the history of a property ends up in the foundations of the next build, then *Londonderry House Hotel* will stand for all time! An incredible way of life there and so much power, almost more than the King and Queen and Prime Minister of the time put together. Everyone of importance of the day passed through, and many important Government decisions were made there. Lady L was a formidable lady.

The next that came up for Hills, and another eventual life-changing moment for me, was the availability in 1971 of the Gunton Hall Estate at Lowestoft, a holiday camp with a hundred acres or so of land adjoining. Maurice Whalley, the Lowestoft-based architect we had started to use, was instrumental in bringing the property to us, and Hills bought it for £380,000 which, you will see later, developed into something rather more valuable.

My old friend Alfred Hedges from Winterton, being a bit of a writer, researched the history of Gunton Hall for me and, so that Alfred's efforts are not all lost in the mists of time, here is a short summary of what he discovered. His book *The Gunton Story* was published by the Weathercock Press in 1977.

In the days when Great Yarmouth was not even a sandbank, and Vikings made their yearly forays into East Anglia, the Norfolk and Suffolk estuary coastline was forming and first mention is that, in 1190, the Manor of Gunton belonged to the church of St Michael in Norwich, with Richard de Gunton in possession.

An interesting historical note Alfred picked up on was that, in those very early years, it would be Saxons trying to protect themselves from the Vikings, and the style of very simple parish church with the round towers we know in Norfolk would be their base of defence. That's why the towers have no windows and most have one doorway several feet off ground level, so the entry ladder could be pulled up after the locals had scrambled inside for protection.

There are only 174 churches with round towers in the whole country and, of those, 160 are to be found in Norfolk and Suffolk. Just reminds us of how isolated East Anglia was in those far-off days.

In 1361 Gunton passed to Roger de Loudham and then, in 1451, to Sir Henry Inglose. The main value of coastal land at that time seems to have been the right to claim wreckage washed up on its shore. Wrecks by the dozen, and the same applied to the Scroby and Winterton Ness sands and wrecks mentioned previously.

1724 found the estate in the hands of the very rich William Luson. Two years later it was owned by his son, Hewling, who then went bankrupt! The whole of the estate, plus the manor of Fishley, near Acle in Norfolk, was sold at auction for £16,050 (£2m today). Now Gunton obtained a more interesting owner in the form of Sir Charles Saunders, Knight of the Bath and Admiral of the White Squadron.

Later he was to be Admiral of the Blue, leading a great fleet to provide a blockade of the St Lawrence River in Canada, whilst Wolfe made his famous assault on the Heights of Abraham and took Quebec for the British.

Feted as a hero on his return, 1761 made a Knight, 1770 a full Admiral and appointed Commander in Chief of all forces in the Mediterranean – a post he refused to take up as he was enjoying himself too much between Gunton and London. He was enthusiastic in developing his property, and took the opportunity to enclose for himself an additional large acreage of common land as well – no doubt for safety!

Sir Charles had no children and, on his death, Gunton went to a niece, Jane, who married a famous surgeon, and her second daughter, also Jane, married the 10th Earl of Westmorland – a bit of a lad who had, 18 years previously, eloped with the daughter of a wealthy London banker and married her at Gretna Green before the father arrived with his shotgun. Interestingly, Bob Ludkin sat on a company board with David, the 15th Earl of Westmoreland, and for a time, the Earl was also a Director with us on *Larters Estates*.

Those two families did not spend a lot of time there and, in 1802, now with a population of 36, Gunton was sold to Thomas Fowler who, in 1810, built the existing Gunton Hall as his own residence. A bookseller, John Downes, moved into the old hall (pulled down in the Second World War), followed by the Reverend Cooke Fowler in 1936. In the 1850s there were now 70 people living in the manor of Gunton and, even at the turn of the century, the number had only risen to 90.

One final matter of interest on Gunton. Hewling Luson, the 1726 owner, discovered by accident a very fine clay on the estate and which likely was excavated from what today is the lake. One Philip Walker rented the land, and that clay would not be important but for the speculation that the now much sought-after Lowestoft porcelain was made from it. Come 1764, Sir Charles Saunders also rented out the land, and it is thought the porcelain was made in a factory at Bell Lane in Lowestoft.

Between the two worlds wars the area around Gunton expanded enormously and, in the mid 1930s, the estate was bought by Charles Lambert, who was the first to provide a quality holiday accommodation business. During World War 2 Gunton Hall was a training centre for young soldiers, then taken over by the Admiralty in 1945 as a rehabilitation centre for sailors, and finally returned to Lambert in 1950.

Lambert had his plans so disrupted that he decided to sell, and a consortium headed by Commander Hammersley, who had been in charge of the centre for the Navy, bought it, and it was from them that we bought in 1969. I hope that's all interesting!

The purchase was on my East Anglian patch, so for me this was an exciting time because Gunton was planned to be a very large and exclusive housing development, as we had no interest in running a holiday camp – little did we know! All these things were mostly under my control, with me travelling between Norfolk, Wales, Lowestoft and, of course, the head office at Colchester – and going down for meetings with Bob Ludkin in London, usually on a Saturday with lunch somewhere – so that divorce was not perhaps so surprising.

Susan and I had seven years together and I was sad we drifted apart but, as she has said to me several times later, out of our time together came two great children, Andrew and Rebecca, and neither of us would wish to be without them or Rebecca's children. Then, as I was getting things really motoring with developing the East Anglian business, a little bombshell arrived in the form of *Galliford Estates*, who made an offer to buy *WA Hills*.

Sydney Grapes – The Boy John of letters to the EDP

Vote for Joe Norfolk County Council 1964,
youngest councillor elected at that time.

First day at Henstead School Suffolk backed by Joe. Alice 3rd left front row

Four Weddings and a Graduation

Rebecca and Mark 1985

Joe and Betty 1973

Andrew and Jan 1993

Rose and
James 2011

Alice at Reading University 2011

Joe's a winner.
Raising funds for the
Norwich Playhouse
on first day of the
National Lottery

Two 'old folks' at
home in July 2013

Chapter Five
1972-1978 – A Sale, a Buyback,
Some Lovely Travel and a Marriage!

During the early seventies, the price of building land went from something like £4,000 per acre to £40,000 almost overnight. My job had been negotiating whatever purchase I could find for Hills in East Anglia and, just before the boom, I had signed contracts to buy a large acreage in Stalham and more in Martham.

Developments were flowing thick and fast and, just before the Hills takeover, I had also put in hand a bid for a very big development being promoted by Great Yarmouth Borough Council, at Shrublands in Gorleston. As it was so large, I did this on a 50/50 basis with Robert Chase and using a design company run by Paul Robinson. I don't think our scheme was particularly magical but, out of ten applicants, we won.

Now Hills were on the scene and they did not want a joint venture so, in agreement with Robert, they paid him £5000 to move out and, as he said to me recently, that was perhaps the easiest money he ever earned.

Robert was a very efficient builder and was later to be a controversial Chairman of *Norwich City Football Club.*

I think he was a good Chairman and took the Club into Europe, but it seems he did not have the knack of keeping his supporters on-side (has any Chairman?) and there was eventually a very acrimonious departure for Robert. Over the years I have observed that seems to be par for the course in football everywhere, so maybe he was not so surprised, but I know he was very hurt by it all. I think mainly they did not like him selling players to balance the books, but in later years had to grudgingly accept Robert had made some very astute property purchases for them around the grounds and helped save their financial bacon.

Robert was a very strong supporter of the Conservative Party and well respected in London. I remember meeting Lord Avon, the son of Sir Anthony Eden, and other people from the Cabinet at his house for dinner, where Robert was in his controversial element and always a superb host.

As a young man, in the same way as me, Robert had taken over the Chase building operation from his father at Caister, but not because of illness, as his own father lived to be over 100. We helped each other in the very early days, experimenting with both equipment and prefabrication. In a different way, Robert had his own 'mentor' in the form of highly-respected Tommy Watson, who really WAS an entrepreneur. Tommy built up the Caister Group from a Great Yarmouth garage and went on to owning a lot of land at Caister with the holiday camp accommodation there, and then being taken over by Ladbrokes. We both learned fast.

Put all this new land together with what I already had at Larter's, plus Hills' own substantial developments in the Colchester area and rocketing land values, and I suppose we were just asking for a larger company to get interested. Major shareholders in Hills were *The Freshwater Group* – the VERY substantial Jewish family whose son-in-law was William Stern, later to become Britain's biggest-ever personal bankrupt (at that time)! Stern sat on the Board of Hills for a time, but we were glad he was not there when we had a takeover offer.

Who came to approach us? First we had *Galliford Estates* run by John and Cecil Galliford, who had approached Alan and Christopher and decided to offer around 50p per share. At the same time we were also approached by Robert Francis, who ran *Francis Parker*, also based in our area. I had met him previously with Ludkin and Smythson in London, and we all preferred him as a buyer.

After discussions, Francis said his group would offer 60p per share which was, in our opinion, well over the odds in value. With the offer in hand we went to Mr Osias Freshwater, the family Patriach, and a more charming, polite, absolute gentleman you would never meet. Bob Ludkin knew him well and was Company Secretary to several of the *Freshwater* group companies.

However, Mr Freshwater knew the market far better than we amateurs did, and said he was sorry, but his view was that because of the way land prices were rocketing, the price of the shares should be £1.00. No way would Francis pay almost double and, in the same way, *Gallifords* also laughed at it, and so we thought we were 'safe'. We hoped we could now go on and exploit all the land holdings we had built up.

Not even three months later, *Gallifords* came back (the market for land roaring away) and told us they would pay the £1.00, so back to Osias. Freshwater said: 'Thank you, gentlemen, but that was my price when we talked 3 months ago. Today, the price is £1.05' – and that, in 1972, is what we got. How can you not have the greatest respect for a businessman like that?

Obviously all the Directors would be receiving substantial sums for our shares, and it was a terrific deal, but this was my whole business life to date – gone! A completely new situation for me, and not unpleasant of course, but I love having assets, particularly land and property, developing them and taking entrepreneurial risks – now I had cash.

However, now along comes that old friend Serendipity again, to sit beside 'Cash Joe' at the lunch following the *Hills* takeover. This time he took the form of John Galliford, one of the takeover brothers, and I asked him what he would be doing with the non-residential developments I had been building up in Wales and East Anglia. 'Oh, we will dump those next week,' he said. So I asked: 'How about dumping them back with me?'

He said he had no problem with that, but it would need to be cash. On the back of a table napkin I listed for him what there was and what we had paid – including the all-important price of £380k only just paid for Gunton Hall, which he had never seen. The total I think came to something like £850k. 'Get a deal where you can offer me the cash with certainty in the next few weeks, and they are yours.' See how long the cash lasted for me that time – not even 24 hrs! But now I would have assets again.

I rushed out of that lunch, asked Bob Ludkin if he would come back in with me, and together we went to a private bank we had dealt with only once before, but liked – *Wallace Brothers Sassoon*. The Managing Director went by the delightful name of Jinks Gravety Smith, and we asked him if he would lend us half the money. He approved and put us on to a Peter Watts, who in turn introduced us to the aptly-named Peter Deal, whose very able assistant Peter Taylor made all the financial arrangements. I don't remember the terms, but it was fast and heady stuff for me at the time.

Again – just like that, we had the cash needed and, until we reached the awful 2000 years, that was what banking was like – and, in my opinion, should be today. Trust, and forming an opinion of a person, his honesty and ability based on his record and the security put up, is how it should be. Today it is only how a computer sees you, with no knowledge or even common sense applied at all. You are over 70 – no cash available. Property investment – no cash.

What a coup! I did not even have to move out of my office and, together, Bob and I now owned all the holiday developments in Winterton, Hemsby, Scratby and Wales and, of course, the all-important Gunton Hall estate – but we were back on our own and now had to make this really work. I think there was a collective sigh of relief amongst all our staff as, had the properties all been sold in the market place, there would have been no certainty for them. We were at the starting gate of a very interesting future period.

Now on the look-out for whatever property scheme we could find to get rolling fast, the first new purchase was *The Cliff Hotel* at Gorleston, a site we were told was for demolition and had planning approval for a number of flats. The property was owned by the Scott family, but we were advised by Jack Brown, a freelance agent who brought it to us, that we must not visit as there was a family dispute. The deal was that we were to complete on 1 January 1973, close the hotel and pull it down. It was just to be a future building site, and that is how we valued it and signed a contract, content to view from a distance and wait for completion.

Another personal serendipitous moment came that year, when our doctor friend and, by then, MP for Norwich South, Tommy Stuttaford, and I had both read the same property article one weekend in the *Sunday Times*. Two architects had bought Oliver's Wharf, an old warehouse in Wapping, but had run out of money because grants they expected from the local council had not materialized.

They needed help and were selling the basic 2000 sq ft units for £12,500 river front, and for £8,500 overlooking a park at the back – so long as the buyers paid in full up-front immediately. For that money they fitted out two basic bedrooms, a bathroom, kitchen and the lounge area.

Tommy was interested but had no time to look, and asked if I would go and view early next day as few were left, and advise him whether to buy or not. Train to London, quick visit and I was offered the only remaining back apartment at £8,500, so long as I confirmed and paid a deposit by 5pm that day.

Taxi to see Tommy at the House of Commons and I said: 'Buy'! He, however, said he had also been thinking and that, as he needed some private patients in London (and later became the *Times* medical correspondent), he felt his patients would not like to go down into deepest Wapping, particularly maybe leaving at night.

Wapping then was undeveloped, but had absolutely charming potential which has since been nurtured, but I could see his point at that time. No such worries for a highwayman like me, so back at the developers I wrote my own cheque for £500.00 deposit and, later, Betty and I had our first and, perhaps, the very best-ever base in London. I certainly wish I had never had to sell it.

As Betty and I got closer together, I discovered a talent for creating surprises which I still absolutely enjoy today. Maybe **the** best I have ever created for Betty was at *Maxim's* in Paris when she had a birthday coming up. I chose four friends and said: 'If you will get yourselves to *Maxim's*, please come to dinner with Betty and me on her birthday – but it is a secret.' I had not realized there was at that time a new restaurant in Norwich just opened and called – *Maxim's*!

Only later did our guests tumble to the fact that Norwich was NOT where we were going. No faxes or emails in those days, so everything confirmed by mail and, later in the month, I asked an extra couple to join us. Another letter, and the arrangement was that the guests would arrive 30 minutes or so ahead of us, bottle of champagne already open, and with Betty thinking we were just on a romantic evening for the two of us.

On the actual evening and me appearing more than a little nervous, so Betty tells me, we duly arrived after our guests. *Maxim's* had not received my second letter so, as in the tale of the Ark, the table filled up two by two and, at one time, my guests thought I had pulled a joke on them and we would not turn up.

The evening was fabulous, as you can see from the picture; none of us had been there before and *Maxim's* was (and, I think, still is) every bit as romantic as anything which has been written about it, and for we two the start of a long association with Paris. As we often joke, with such little events I tried to show I was no Norfolk yokel, and somehow I managed to fend Betty off until, in April 1973, we got married; but a lot happened before then.

Another trip we had made together in early 1972 was to Thailand – first to Bangkok, the city and the temples, which were stunning, and then out to Penang on the beach. Penang was then unspoiled and the locals made a great fuss of us. The security guard at the hotel insisted that on his day off we should meet up with him and his wife, and they provided a picnic for us on the beach.

Later, he also insisted we took his own small motorbike for the day and we toured the island, where we found fabulous scenery and a funicular railway to the old Colonial camp at the top of a highland area. There appeared to be no reason for their kindness other than they liked the British! In the evenings we would go into town where, at any number of 'hole-in-the-wall' vendors, you could find the most delicious and safe food.

Winter that same year found us on our way to Australia to see Betty's sister, as part of a six-week trip. I felt I had earned a break following the Hill's sale and then buy-back, and it was an incredible tour, six weeks round the world first-class, and about the only time we have afforded it that way.

First stop outbound was Fiji, recovering from a massive hurricane which had rather spoiled the landscape. We stayed in a lovely beach resort and I was determined to take Betty deep-sea fishing which neither of us had experienced before. The hotel tried to put us off because the hurricane had destroyed local fishing, and nothing had been caught in weeks.

The system there was that as you caught each fish, a flag was raised on your boat. Within a very short time Betty had caught an 80 lb wahoo and we continued in that vein, arriving back at the resort with 13 flags and a hero's welcome for having broken – as they say in cricket – the 'duck'. Needless to say, fish was on the menu at the hotel that night. Fiji in 1972 was very undeveloped, and we used a small, bus-stop, single-engine plane to get around. I recall a large percentage of the population being Indian, and believe that became a problem in later years.

On then to Perth in Australia, where I had a 'social' introduction to one of the big property agents through business friends in London; and they looked after us well. We also had the interesting experience of meeting the famous/notorious Alan Bond and seeing one of his very early developments. I recall finding a lone purchaser and one bungalow only, but covered in Union Flags. The buyer was from Britain and he was not going to let it be forgotten!

One year older than me, Alan was also from the UK, but was a 'larger than life' Australian property developer who, some years later, went to jail following a $1.8 billion bankruptcy. His big claim to fame in Australia was sponsoring the America's Cup challenge to the *New York Sailing Club* where, for the first time in 142 years, the USA lost the cup to Australia. I would have forgiven him a lot for that alone.

He was the most extraordinary wheeler-dealer, and Kerry Packer, the Australian media magnate who sold Bond his TV and radio stations in a $1billion deal, and then in the bankruptcy bought them back for $700m, once famously said: ' You only meet one Alan Bond in a lifetime, and thank God I have already met mine.' Alan and I had a mutual friend, Stuart McAlpine, in London and through him we met Alan's equally larger-than-life wife, Eileen, known as 'Red' because of the colour of her hair.

From Perth it was to Melbourne, where we were to spend Christmas and New Year with Betty's sister, Marjorie, and husband, Bill – plus Betty's father, Stan who, following the death of his wife, was having an extended stay with his daughter. Bill and Marjorie were a great case-study, being original £10 immigrants – a system to bring UK population to Australia, where their trip by boat was just £10 and included simple accommodation found on arrival whilst they sorted a job. Within the 8 years they had been there, we found them with a lovely house in Fern Tree Gulley, two children, Neil and Nicholas, and Bill very well-employed. We had a great Christmas.

Whilst with Marjorie and Bill, I had promised Neil and Nicholas that we would go on a trip before we returned to the UK, but the idea coincided with a national transport strike. Nothing was moving.

At the local airport I was directed to the Flying Club, and any number of pilots said: 'You hire a plane and we will fly you anywhere.' A single-engine Piper with John as pilot, Betty, the two children, Betty's father and I, took off for a very memorable trip to Alice Springs and back. We stopped at Coober Peedy, the opal-mining town, on the way out and then Alice itself. At Coober Peedy the residents mostly live in 'caves', or underground houses, because of the intense heat. Enterprising failed opal miners take tourists down an actual mine and show you how it is done.

We were fascinated and I duly bought Betty a real opal (that means solid stone rather than a sliver of real stone on a false background) and which, sadly, was stolen a few years later from our home. Alice in those days really did feel like the end of the world. Dust roads in the main and very little development – the true outback.

John, the pilot, told me I must book a hotel somewhere between Alice and Melbourne on the way back, as the distance was too long with no overnight stop. On the map was Oodnadata, a train junction and cattle outpost, with the *Transcontinental Hotel*. The international hotel group, I thought, so sounded good and was booked, with no one at the travel agents mentioning what we were getting into.

Between Alice and Oodnadata is Ayers Rock, which we dropped down to see, then just one motel, where we had lunch; the owner enquired where we were staying that night. He also made no comment at all when we told him, other than to say: 'You can stay here if you wish,' and off we flew, to one of life's more unusual experiences. Oodnadata then was one 'bunk-house', *The Transcontinental*, a landing strip and some shacks around the railway stop.

The 'Manager' of the *Transcontinental* was also the airstrip controller, and rolled out to see us land, tie the plane down for a coming dust storm and take us into 'town'. Our rooms were tin-roofed with iron beds, but clean – with the aborigines sleeping immediately outside our rooms under a veranda.

An above-ground pool was banned to the boys because the 'Manager' said he owned it personally - 'I pay for it and I use it!' and no amount of cash I offered would change his mind. We had arrived early evening so, to cheer everyone up, I took orders for dinner, only to find that the dining room was laid up for breakfast.

A lady, who I am sure was the model used in Blackpool in the 1950s to demonstrate just how bad a British seaside landlady could be, told me: ' You haven't booked dinner, so you don't get dinner,' and that hers was the only 'dining room' in town. A lot of fuss from me in the kitchen and she eventually produced for Betty a loaf of bread, a knife, some spread and a tin of camp loaf (corned beef) – from which Betty produced our 'dinner'!

Going to the bar, which was quite full of odd people, was a bit like the film *High Noon*. All talk and sound stopped as I walked in, bought my warm beers and Cokes, and started up again immediately I left.

Two telephone construction workers then told me later that evening I had not seen the worst of it – the 'Manager' was a nutcase – he always brought the people the mile or so *from* the airfield, but never took them back – you walked, luggage and all.

'No worries mate,' they would drive us out there in the morning – except they went to a party and lost their car keys and so we did – walk. The 'Manager', having watched us carry our luggage for the mile or so, then drove up in his car, opened the airstrip and we were able to take off. The first town in line was Broken Hill, where for breakfast two very small boys ate two very large T-bone steaks. That whole visit I would not have missed for a very large pension.

Back in Melbourne a call from Bob Ludkin, who had completed the purchase of *The Cliff Hotel* for us on 1 January, told me no way could we demolish it. We had bought a lovely hotel without seeing it! He had persuaded the Scott son, Rodney, to continue running it for us until I got back and we decided what to do. In later years we decided that, really, both holiday camps and hotels were not us, and for *The Cliff* we eventually made a deal with Rodney that he could afford and he bought it from us – to go on and become, locally, an exceptional hotelier and friend to this day.

Rodney is a natural hotelier and host, and gave some memorable parties – teaching me a lot about entertainment and giving me some good ideas. At one, he told me about his membership of the *Worshipful Company of Glovers* – a City Livery Company. For some reason *The Glovers* had stayed at the Cliff, where he befriended them, and they asked him to join the Livery – a great honour.

He asked me if I would also like to join and I did so, although to be frank we both realized the general Livery members were rather ancient and an injection of new younger blood would not go amiss, which was why we had been invited in. The trouble was that *The Glovers* is a cash-poor Livery, without its own Halls or any good financial backing – just living from year to year from the members' dues.

Most of the Liveries arose from mediaeval times when, to ensure quality and standards of work and traditions, Guilds were formed bringing like-minded workers together. *The Drapers, Vinters, Fishmongers* and *Goldsmiths* are but a few of the 108 Liveries mentioned today. *The Glovers* started before 1394, but there is now so little interest in glove-making or use, that I fear they will eventually lose all their strength and maybe have to combine with another Livery.

I did enjoy it for a few years, but could see I would never have the patience or time to get anywhere up the *Glover's* hierarchy at all, so my membership lapsed. I could not really contribute. One superb event each year was when we gave The Lord Mayor of London a dinner – in the *Mansion House*. Very formal, white tie and tails, and somehow that ancient historical tradition appealed to me a lot. Being at such a formal dinner in the *Mansion House* did make me feel part of British history.

Somehow you reflect on what went into producing the world as it is today, for good or bad, but our England did not just 'happen'. Real people, serious people, fought and struggled to make the future safe for us, and we should do our bit. History lesson over! But, if you watched the 2012 Jubilee celebrations for the Queen, you will understand what I mean.

When you join a Livery Company, you first have to be made a Freeman of the City of London; not the Dick Whittington or President Obama type of Freedom of the City, and actually anyone can buy the certificate for £25.00, but you do have to be formally sworn-in. You make an appointment, and the undersheriff will administer the Oath of Allegiance. Daughter Alice came with me as I was the only candidate that morning, and both the premises and the ceremony are interesting to see. Because I love the ceremony and pageantry of old-fashioned England, here is the Oath a candidate swears:

The Declaration of a Freeman

I Joseph Larter do solemnly declare that I will be good and true to our Sovereign Lady Queen Elizabeth the Second; that I will be obedient to the Mayor of this City; that I will maintain the Franchises and Customs thereof, and will keep this City harmless, in that which in me is; that I will know no Gatherings or Conspiracies made against the Queen's Peace, but I will warn the Mayor thereof, or hinder it to my power; and that all these points and articles I will well and truly keep, according to the Laws and Customs of this City, to my Power.

What lovely old romantic language we have at times.

The undersheriff was – how shall I put it? – a LOVELY man and very fussy. I swore my oath to the Queen and the Lord Mayor and, at the end, he said: 'I think that deserves a kiss!' Which rather startled me, until he added: 'No, no – not me, I mean your daughter,' and Alice duly obliged. He told us an American lady the previous week had reacted to the same statement by throwing her arms around him and giving him a real smacker.

Back in Australia, following the Oodnadata experience, Betty and I left her sister and family to go on travel for ourselves and headed for Sydney, where she had friends met on a previous trip there and wanted me to meet them. The next highlight was for us to have a week on Dunk Island on the Barrier Reef, only just discovered for development. It was a paradise.

We swam with an 800lb Grouper nicknamed 'Ulysses' (he was always to be found at the spot where the local fishermen cleaned their fish offshore – the lazy b*******) and, by making use of a large yacht the hotel sports manager had available, we went to visit an artists' colony on a small, nearby island.

In the evening it was all very casual, with few guests, and we were surprised to find Harry Secombe, the famous UK comedian and *Goon Show* actor there with his wife, who told us they more or less discovered the place. Trying to arouse any latent sporty side I might have hiding away, Betty also taught me to water-ski there.

This was a proper trip, so home was via the other side of the world and we had a week in Honolulu in the Hawaiian Islands. There we walked up the live volcano and could have cooked an egg on the recent, and still very hot, lava, and, with a pilot, took a private glider giving us stunning views of the whole island. I am sure we must have seen Pearl Harbor, but I do not recall it.

1973 brought our wedding and, being the second time around for us both, we made it a small event, not announced in advance except to my mother and Betty's father, to both of whom we supplied champagne to celebrate with the family. Mother was at home in Winterton and Betty's father *en route* to or from Australia on a boat. For us, we had our Wapping base already, and used the Marylebone Registry Office in London, six friends with us, for the marriage itself, and then a lovely lunch at *Claridges*, after which we went to Paris – finding Orson Welles waiting for us in the hotel Reception at the *George Cinq*.

During the time Bob Ludkin was involved with me, he was a member of *Lloyds of London*, the insurance agency, and in those days, if you were sponsored, you could become a member without having to put up any cash. He put me up as a member, and I was accepted.

As a *Lloyds* underwriter in those days you put at risk everything you owned, which one would never do today. At the time I joined, *Lloyds* had not had the scandals, frauds and 'Ponzi' schemes, all those disasters that came later, so I joined with no hesitation. We were very lucky indeed to be with our agents, *Fenchurch*, and they put us into syndicates which were very sound indeed. When, after two years, I received my first 'dividend' of well over £10,000, I could not believe this was my share after all fees and their charges. I actually wrote to ask how much commission I needed to send the agents. It happened for a number of years, and then came the scandals.

There was now fraud everywhere, but luckily in our case it was the reverse to normal. What happened in the 1970s was caused by the UK Labour administration raising Income Tax to 98% (Denis Healey, the Chancellor, saying he would squeeze high earners until 'their pips squeaked') whilst Capital Gains Tax was 'down' at 40%. That absolutely asked for manipulation by high earners to reduce their earned income.

The best syndicate we were in was *Brooks and Dooley* – motor insurance - but they were making *too much* money! At the end of each trading year, every syndicate has to look at its assets and liabilities and go to another syndicate to assess their net liabilities and take them on for a payment – called 'reinsurance', so a line can be drawn on profits. When the official report on the scandals came out, B&D featured not because the two men had been fiddling the books by hiding claims (for asbestosis, for example), as had a lot of other syndicates, but for the exact opposite.

Mr Brooks and Mr Dooley simply did not like us 'lay' underwriters having such high returns and they established a neat system for keeping more of the profits for themselves. First, they set up a company in Bermuda belonging to the two of them, reinsuring our real business themselves at a huge price, secretly to cream-off massive sums. Later, they would get proper reinsurance of their Bermuda company, which were the figures shown to us as their members.

All very lovely for them but the problem was, the report told us, how could they then get at the cash they had creamed off? Answer - they gave all their family members credit cards on the Bermuda account, for holidays and luxuries. Those were the days, but I was not a member of the family.

At our wedding, a spin-off from this *Lloyds* connection was that my own 'manager agent' there was also an adviser, or in some way involved with financial management, for the Queen or Queen Mother. On our wedding day he contrived to have a telegram sent from him congratulating us – but officially from Buckingham Palace to *Claridges*. A very nice man; and *Claridges* were duly impressed.

In 1974 Betty and I also took a huge step personally, moving from our little Barn Cottage to buying the beautiful Tudor Holverston Hall with 35 acres, near Norwich. The Harris family had lived there for many decades, but now the Harris father had died and mother moved elsewhere. The whole estate came up for auction and was bought by Timothy Coleman and his family – mustard, East Anglian newspapers and so on, and who owned the adjoining estate.

I went to the auction and afterwards asked their agent if they would consider selling me the house. I had to go for an appointment with Sir Timothy, and he agreed a price with me personally in a handshake, my agreeing not to develop all the wonderful barns that were included. A great shame since, when I sold because we needed the cash for development and consolidating our business and life generally, the next owners, a Dutch family, developed the lot!

We had to completely modernize the property, but we loved it there and inherited the very formal Leonard as a gardener. I think Leonard saw himself as a rather superior Steward of the estate – our 35 acres - and in later christening photographs he is seen drinking the champagne, more as part of the family than serving it or supervising the car parking! In November Alice was born, and Holverston was ready for her. Perhaps one of the loveliest family events we held there was her christening party on the lawns.

In 1975 I faced a blow, when Bob Ludkin's heavy smoking came home to roost and he died of lung cancer in December. We had a mutual agreement for either one to buy the other out on death so somehow I found the money, and was now truly on my own. I missed him.

Following Bob's death, the next cash call on me, in 1976, was that Jack Enston wanted to sell the Glan Gwna Hall in Wales and really I had no option but to buy, because to split the estate would be bad news for the future. However, THE big event in 1976 was daughter Rose being born, with more great excitement all round.

My involvements having to include Wales were too much, financially and location-wise, now that I was married again and with a growing, new family. We would have to be based either in Wales or Norfolk but we could not do both, and we chose Norfolk, which was absolutely correct.

Another piece of serendipity came as we were debating how to reduce our Wales/Norfolk financial responsibilities. Tom O'Hanlon had been left in Wales to carry on running the show, but it was not the same. Out of the blue, a telephone call to our Great Yarmouth solicitors informed us that a team from Wales was coming down to make us an offer to buy the Glan Gwna estate.

The potential buyers belonged to a local consortium that we knew had been disappointed when we bailed out Jack Enston in the first place. They had gone on to buy other properties, had now sold one to an electricity company, and wanted Glan Gwna in their fold.

We actually agreed a good price, but then the buyers decided to be less than pleasant. We had very carefully listed what we were selling, and left Tom O'H with the precise details of building materials and equipment he should keep personally, as he decided to stay up there and finish his own house – working for the new gang owning Glan Gwna for a time as well. With us gone and dusted the new owners, for whatever reason, decided to accuse Tom of stealing the very items we had given him and were listed in their contract as not belonging to them.

To this day we do not know what was behind it, but it went to full court, with me going up there and, after my evidence and showing him the contract, the Judge asking why on earth his time was being wasted and awarding Tom full costs. So ended the Larter Welsh period, and we moved on.

For us as one couple, having also taken on Holverston Hall, we had a huge amount going on, so 1977 saw us deciding we should sell *Olivers Wharf*, and then we were lucky to rent on the 23rd floor of one of the Barbican towers, so we still had a London base. Much more central, very cheap at that time and we enjoyed being there for 4 years. We needed to take some strain off, and that is what happened.

Chapter Six
Snow, Safaris, Desert Islands, The High Court and a Lot More Travel.

Alongside Gunton, John James, who had come up from the *W A Hills* days, developed a house-building company in which I was a partner, and he was very ably assisted by the Geoff Balls from *Larters Estates*. *Asta Properties*, as the company was named, developed various housing estates, including some wonderful old barns at Weybourne in North Norfolk. Nothing like the scale of *WA Hills*, but John also started his own private holiday development at California, near Great Yarmouth, and sorted any construction I needed at Gunton Hall and on other schemes. He was a very capable and successful man to have around, and much appreciated.

Somewhere during this time old Tom Bammant, the man I had started the chalet developments with at Newport, died, and his son – also Tom - from whom he had been estranged because of some family difficulty, inherited his estate. Tom Jr did not like me having been involved with his father AT ALL.

On the Monday after the funeral, he ordered me to remove everything from the new, 30-acre chalets development (where we had a proper lease to take up the land in stages) and, if not, he would start bulldozing, which he actually did by demolishing part-built chalets. We had to get an injunction overnight, and then we carried on in relative peace – but this was just a sleeping dog.

Tom Jr would make no contact with us or even speak to me if we met, and we all had no doubt that trouble lay ahead. When we needed to take up the next stage of the lease and gave notice to his lawyer, he instructed them to refuse permission, saying that I had exercised undue influence on his father to get the lease in the first place. Nonsense of course, but then it was ME who had to prove I had not done so!

What an expensive, drawn-out affair! Over a period of four or five years, ending in 1978 I think, Robert Killin and Sue Kent, my solicitors, saw me through the action in the High Court in London and, after a five-day hearing the Judge threw the case out, awarding us costs and damages for delay. Later in the year, as we were gathered with our expensive barrister to calculate the claim for delay, we discovered that, at the eleventh hour, Tom Jr had decided to appeal. So we were now off to the Appeal Court – you have to give me credit for clocking up as many experiences as possible during my business life!

At the Court of Appeal, the Lords Justice Oliver, Ackner and Buckner heard the appeal and, without calling the other side, it was dismissed. Oliver (the owner of a cottage at Southwold, on the 'bracing East Anglian coast', as he pointed out), delivered the judgment with some humour (so we knew then we had won), commenting on what he saw as the strange fact of old Tom Sr and myself naming our first development on that bracing East Anglian coast –*Hawaii Beach*.

In an effort to while away the days in both courts, when legal arguments were being discussed, I used to wander down and listen to the Master of the Rolls, at that time the famous Lord Denning. His judgments were like being read a delicious, adult, bedtime story, and he had the most wonderful way with words and a marvellous Hampshire accent.

When my time in the courts was at last over, I got a lawyer friend to write to Lord Denning, who had by then retired, and ask that I be allowed to arrange for him to record some of his most famous judgments, with him reading them out again in the same way Winston Churchill had done with his famous speeches after the war. He replied that he loved the idea, but had already signed-up to an agent so could not agree to what I wanted. A great, great shame because, actually, no one ever got him to do it. His entertaining, sonorous delivery was lost.

The final outcome of the case was that we had to calculate costs and damages and that, in the end, was settled part in cash and part by transferring to us the freehold of the site. Poor old Tom Sr must have turned in his grave, and what a sad outcome for the lovely relationship he and I had. There is a time when enough is enough, and we settled on selling the development as, after all the years of delay, my heart was no longer in it.

Let's slip into some travel and a personal, truly serendipitous moment or two.

As part of my sports 'education', Betty had organized a trip to St Moritz in Switzerland for us both to learn to ski. Thanks to her foresight (going a week ahead of me) and understanding that I was not perfectly formed for standing in line at ski school or any other lines, an old ski instructor she had met agreed to teach the two of us privately, and we never looked back. I loved it.

Robbie (as he was called) told Betty he would only teach me if, when we met, he 'liked' me. Over several years of going back to see him, we both understood that what he really meant was – does he like a drink? Always start the ski day with a grappa, make sure there is something during the day, and certainly always end the day with one! In many skiing visits to the Alps we had some great experiences.

Those friends Susan and I had made when we picked them up from a broken-down taxi in Antigua, Joyce and Basil Bloodworth, had decided that, having sold some land, they would retire from Basingstoke to live in Chateau D'Oex, a small village near Gstaad in Switzerland and also a ski resort. Betty and I had some very happy times staying in their chalet, honing our skiing and Alpine refreshment skills but, when we needed to take our very young children with us, we knew it would not work. The Bloodworths were not exactly children-orientated.

However, not wanting us to stop visiting, Basil found an old, wooden chalet in his village that had been rebuilt after a tragic fire and which was for hire. Locally, no one would take it because of a death there, but for us there was no problem, and it was one of those seemingly simple decisions that had far-reaching effects on the rest of our lives.

The hire cost was agreed at £1000 all-in for the whole winter season, incredible value even in the early 1970s. The price reflected the difficulty the owner had with its history – but it was also just round the corner from the home of David Niven. The plan was for Betty and the girl we had helping her, plus children, to live there all winter, and I could easily commute from UK each weekend, or more often. To paraphrase the Scottish poet: 'The plans of mice and men go oft awry' – and so they did.

I drove the family there, car overloaded to the gills with gear and the kitchen sink, but we quickly found that there was no way Alice and Rose could play outside. Temperatures of 10 or 15 below zero °C were quite common and, of course, they then got bored by the limited space indoors with none of their usual freedom, or having to be carefully wrapped up to go outside.

So we made Plan B. For that year: go back home, keep the chalet as it was so cheap, and we could have some nice ski trips with friends, and the children would be fine there in a year or two. In fact, going for a few weeks at a time before or after January and February was perfect, and the children in particular later became fine skiers alongside Betty, with Andrew and Rebecca also joining us.

The girl helping us at the time did manage to completely lose Rose on the nursery slopes on one occasion, but apart from her parents being in deep water with the local police, Rose having been put in the pound for 'lost dogs and children', she was personally unconcerned; nothing that a pizza at *Arc en Ciel* restaurant across the road could not put right.

Obviously I must have told business friends about the chalet, because Serendipity called on me again in the form of a phone call from Julian Snowden, an accountant in Freeport in the Bahamas. 'Peter (Deal from the *Wallace Sassoon* loan) tells me you have a chalet in Switzerland – can we rent it for January?' No way could I do that with the deal I had from the owner, who would have been mortified to see me apparently trying to cash in on his chalet. I told Julian that if he was a friend of Peter's then, if we were not using it, he could holiday there for a month.

That did not suit them as they did not know us, but the outcome was that, if they took the chalet for a month, we could live in their house on a golf course in Freeport for a month. Fabulous! The following night, a similar call: 'My name is Roger Aylen; I am a friend of Julian's and I have a house on the beach; can we follow Julian in February?'

Thus were born three lovely winters of sharing our chalet for two months each year with various people from Freeport and, in the last year, the second month was in a house at Deerfield in southern Florida – and we could still have our own ski holidays in Chateau D'Oex as well. One bonus with Julian's house was that Count Basie, the famous jazz musician, lived next door.

One anecdote from Chateau D'Oex is that each New Year's Eve, Betty and I would celebrate at *Chloisterli*, a lovely old farmhouse turned into a restaurant in Diableret, a ski resort up the road from Gstaad. It was always a fantastic evening and at midnight all the local farmers would enter the restaurant, each holding a large cowbell at his neck.

They would parade through the restaurant ringing the bells, and the New Year, in. One particular New Year's Eve, both Roger Moore and David Frost (James Bond and David of TV fame) were there, and I met them – in the gent's toilet. Not many can claim such an historic meeting in such an exotic place.

The sad end to the chalet in Chateau D'Oex story was that, in the third year of exchange in 1980, one of the borrowers put a cigarette on the wooden bathroom window-sill and burned a hole in it. With the history of the place being previously burned down, the owner quite rightly was beside himself with fury and, although we had one more year to run on the lease, I agreed to give it up.

In the late 70s air travel, particularly between the Bahamas islands and to Miami, was notoriously unreliable, and we spent many hours waiting for delayed (or sometimes non-existent) planes to turn up. Doing that, one developed a certain 'camaraderie' with other passengers, and we would make up acronyms and nicknames for the various airlines.

'If you've time to spare – fly Bahamasair'; 'Hughes Air Worst' (West); 'Take a chance with *Air France*'; '*BOAC* – Better On A Camel'; and an old chestnut, then my favourite: '*Alitalia* –All luggage in Turkey, aircraft landed in Athens'. I don't know what we would have made of *Ryanair* or *Easyjet* had they been there, something very rude, no doubt.

Serendipity comes as a pair in the Bahamas. In our third year there and us getting to know the place well, my mother came to stay and I took the opportunity to take Betty for a long weekend on a small island called Green Turtle Key. We flew to Marsh Harbour and then a small boat took us on to Green Turtle. Just the one small club was being developed at that time and the owner, Alan Charlesworth, who owned Birdham Pool in Hampshire, was there when we arrived.

We had a great time taking our own small boat to adjacent sandy atolls and swimming with huge rays that came basking inshore. We would meet with Alan and his wife and the few other guests each evening for dinner and drinks, and he wanted to know where we were from and what I did. On the last night he asked me if, before leaving the following day, I would please call at his bungalow, as he wanted to discuss something with me.

Next day I went to see him and he explained that, over the last few days, he had got to know and like both Betty and me, and he felt I was a genuine guy. 'I want to develop this little island into a first-rate tourist resort. If I give you a 50% share of the development, will you come out and develop the resort for me?'

For Betty and me it will be forever a 'what if', but I had to explain to him that I was just into the second year of the Dip Farm/Pleasurewood scheme, where I had sunk all the cash I had and could borrow, and there was no way I could drop all that for the Bahamas – exciting as the idea was.

Like the decision on Wales after Bob Ludkin died, I think it was absolutely correct, as I had no experience whatever of working in a non-European culture and, as Barbados was to prove later for me, that is not a good idea. Great offer though!

During our final year of exchanges in the Bahamas, and starting to get to know the USA, Mother had died at Winterton whilst we were visiting friends in Texas, and it made us reflect a bit because that was my side of the old family gone, apart from my elderly Aunt Eileen. They say 'end of an era', but it really was.

Mother was 71, so had 20 years or so on her own after Father died, and I hope she felt we all tried to look after her well. For Betty and me, we were delighted to have taken her to Los Angeles and Aunt Nora, to Las Vegas, and also out to the Bahamas. Whenever I see a Pina Colada, I think of Mother sitting with us on a Sunday in the appropriately named *Stoned Crab* restaurant in Freeport, having her favourite pre-lunch drink.

That last Bahamas exchange in 1980 brought us our first visit to Florida, exchanging with a lovely home in Deerfield on the Atlantic coast. By the time we left we had bought ourselves a small canal-side home in Hillsborough, which was the start of a safari of properties up and down the Florida Atlantic coast over the next 30-odd years. Alice and Rose were with us on that exchange, and Alice went to the Montessori school in Deerfield for a short time.

After our Bahamas period, Freddie Laker had set up his pioneering *Skytrain* airline offering £50 fares from the UK to Miami, and I had previously met John Seear, his son-in-law. John had bought investment boats from my *Priorycraft* company (mentioned later) introduced by Eric Humphries of *Hoseasons*, and had asked me to give him some property 'expertise' in Florida as they were looking at motels and so on. I, of course, knew nothing about property in Florida other than my small purchase but, as ever, was always willing to help if it was something different.

Freddie Laker is also worth a mention because, at the time, he was way ahead of today's *RyanAir* and *EasyJet*. He really DID pioneer cheap, transatlantic travel. Freddie conceived the idea of the 'Skytrain', a walk-on, walk-off, no-frills service. There was huge opposition and skulduggery from the big boys in the airline industry but, amongst others, he had Mrs Thatcher as a big fan.

He finally got going in 1977 after enormous and costly delays but overtrading, plus constant undercutting by *BA* and others to destroy him, caused bankruptcy in 1982. He started again based in Freeport in the Bahamas in 1990, but the scale was small and his time had passed. He did eventually get some major financial compensation for what *BA* and others did to him, but I like to think it was Richard Branson and *Virgin Atlantic* who finally gave the others their come-uppance on his behalf.

Another John, the *Laker* Manager at Miami, got to know me as a result of my several visits with John Seear, thinking I was a Director of *Laker* or, at least, someone important in the company. *Laker* was overrun with business at the start and sometimes people were sleeping on the Miami airport floor for a day or two in order to get a £50 seat home. No such problem for 'Skytrain' Larter, who would ring John the day before, or even the same day, and always be found a seat - on an occasion or two, the 'jump' seat next to the pilots. Those were the days......

Another trip Betty and I made was to South Africa, in part to see a customer on behalf of the Keith Spark's business (see *Pleasurewood*). He had supplied various models and promotional material to the *South African Sugar Corporation* in Pietermaritzburg and they needed a visit. The eager volunteer group of two set off for another memorable journey.

We based ourselves in the famous *Mount Nelson Hotel* in Cape Town, and had all the tourist experiences there – the cable car to the top of Table Mountain, and then the magic in the evening of watching the clouds fall over the 'table' as if from a waterfall. The SASC looked after us like a king and queen, and we then booked a safari to Schlu

Schlui, which was a small game park, but I think later expanded into one of the major State Parks – it was Betty's first-ever game park visit, and she was fascinated.

To get home to the UK, we arranged to drive ourselves the 'garden' route to Port Elizabeth via Wilderness – a very aptly-named small resort. Absolutely safe, Wilderness was so much like Winterton - sand dunes and uninterrupted views of the ocean - it was amazing. The Ken Temple I have previously mentioned in Chapter Four was immensely fond of South Africa, and I could now see how he came to develop his *Hermanus Hotel* at Winterton, with its 'rondaaval' round bedroom units, right next to our family home. A 'home from home' it certainly was.

When we stopped for the night in Port Elizabeth before flying out, we found a rather nice group playing music in the nightclub on the roof. We were last to leave and, as they were packing up, we discovered they were English. We asked them which area they came from, and were astonished to discover they were from Blundeston, next to Gunton Hall! They were homesick and we left carrying various messages and notes to pass on to their families, and promising to call mothers when we returned home.

We were hooked on the safari life and made several other trips to Africa, including one with our friends the Whartons, where we hired a driver in Nairobi. A beautiful drive through the Rift Valley to Mombasa, staying at the famous 'Tree Tops' resort on the way down. Being called up at 3am to watch a rare animal come to the water hole to drink is, I can assure you, worth every moment and any inconvenience. We were also impressed to be reminded it was Tree Tops that Princess Elizabeth and Prince Philip were visiting when her father died and Elizabeth became our Queen.

We did not quite become safari junkies but, in the seven years I was with first wife, Susan, we had made some pretty interesting trips, including a first visit to Kenya, and that had fired my imagination, staying in the Tsavo National Park on the slopes of Kilimanjaro. In those days there was still a 'colonial' atmosphere and, of course, apartheid, although not obvious to tourists, and all we noticed was very good attention and service. I remember one couple who lived there inviting Susan and me to dinner, and explaining how the staff they had were not always as experienced as they might wish.

They told the story of a friend who had a really good cook, but when they had a dinner party she simply would not use the serving hatch between the kitchen and dining area. In their rambling house, it meant a long walk from kitchen through other rooms and then to serve them. They got so exasperated they told the cook if she did not use the serving hatch at the next party, she would be fired. On the night, they waited with bated breath to see what would happen and, sure enough, the hatch was flung open – and the cook climbed through.

It was with Susan that I first went on occasional trips with Charles and Pauline Wharton – first going down to the *Imperial Hotel* in Torquay with another couple, John and Shelagh Mowson, and using the Rolls Royce owned by Charles' father. What luxury in the early 1960s, and then later, with Betty, we had some terrific sailing holidays in the Caribbean – but I am rushing forward too much.

On one Africa visit with Betty and the Whartons, we had taken a drive out of Mombasa to an absolutely remote and stunning beach for swimming, and with one small, thatched 'shack' as a restaurant, where we had a memorable fish lunch. It being my turn to pay, I thought we would have a joke with the waiter by offering him an *American Express* card, whereupon he stunned us all by saying, and meaning: 'That will do nicely, Sir,' the advertising catchphrase they were using at the time – and accepted the card!

Other safari trips included the Masai Mara and also staying at Governor's Camp where, one night, a herd of elephants decide to walk through our tented camp. One member of our party was so terrified she says she spent the night on her knees praying!

Having the pleasure of recalling all these visits (and many more yet to come), I am quite sure these ever-widening experiences gave me the open mind, and contributed to the knowledge I needed, for some of the future developments and the 'international' aspects of the eventual theme park business. A long way from Joe who had trouble selecting the wine at the Winterton tennis club dinner.

Chapter Seven
Tales of Gunton, The Old School Henstead, and Charities.

Hills sale and our buyback were done and dusted, and Bob and I now had to run the businesses we had bought, and we were literally on our own.

The first two years of Gunton Hall were of settling down, trying to understand how to run the place. That was not the intention when it was bought for *WA Hills* as it was to be a luxury housing estate, but suddenly the housing market collapsed (again) and we were lucky not to be caught out with huge debt and no income, as so many pure property developers were. Running it as a holiday camp, we could at least earn money to pay our loan interest which, in the 1970s, rose to 15%- 18% levels and more, and we had the Welsh Glan Gwna estate to finance as well.

Glan Gwna taught us a lot, as we were developing chalets and selling to the public, which brought cash back, profits from building, and then an annual income from lettings, the club and shop, and so on. We were sure we could do the same with all the land at Gunton eventually.

Actually running Gunton to start with was not the happy experience it should have been, because we inherited a certain dishonesty which continued after we had taken over. The dishonesty concerned hiding cash takings from certain amusement machines, so well-concealed that it took the courage and honesty of a long-term employee to walk me by the lake one day and indicate what was being done and where I should be looking.

With hindsight (marvellous stuff) I think we should have stood back and brought in really professional people as partners to manage Gunton, because this was a massive business to be responsible for, with our having no experience in that arena. Gunton took over 500 guests a week, served countless thousands of meals, and had to organize really good entertainment for both adults and children, week-long. In addition, of course, in winter Gunton was the centre of local events, and some very large dinners and celebrations took place there. Had we brought in proper help, we could then have concentrated on the development and property side of our business, which we had become good at.

Betty's father, Stanley, came to stay at Gunton from time to time and, to keep him occupied, in 1974 we bought Light Vessel No 82, which we placed at Great Yarmouth as a tourist attraction, and moored on a quay at Haven Bridge beside one of the *Asta* building company properties. Stan enjoyed it for a year or two, but was a bit lonely and he returned to Portsmouth, where he eventually married for the second time.

Owning Gunton was a great experience. I did not really relate to the holiday camp side (yesterday's business, I have been accused of calling it) but I did like adding a bit of style and quality to the décor and operation, taking it up-market a bit. We made a themed night club, *The Moulin Rouge* (Paris again), out of one of the bars, and were attracting more function and outside winter business.

A slightly eccentric and very energetic Irishman I had known for 20 years, Kevin Baldwin, was in between jobs and we engaged him successfully to be the night-club/events manager. For weddings we had a beautiful Brougham carriage bought from old friend Norman Chalk, and we upgraded the general furnishings and decorations in the hall itself.

The local silver band lost its venue in Lowestoft, so we gave its members sponsorship (I even bought them a real Alpine horn from Switzerland) and had them renamed 'The Gunton Hall Silver Band'. Jim Crampton, of the Malta involvement, was also a great cinema organ enthusiast and owned two or three, which he installed in the old water mill where he lived at Buxton. Yet another became available, and he persuaded me it was just what we needed for the ballroom – a great relief to his wife.

A large organ-loft was added to the roof and we could include summer entertainment 'Blackpool' style, and also have one-off Sunday concerts in winter. Terry Hepworth was the local wedding/organ man and he became a fixture at Gunton Hall, and later very much involved with us in The Bygone Village at Fleggburgh.

Our ballroom and the dining rooms at that time really were **the** places where you had your Lowestoft-and-area function. The Conservative Party locally, and Jim Prior as the MP for Lowestoft (later Waveney), all held several big events there and, on one occasion, I found my own office commandeered for a small cocktail party for Margaret Thatcher, who was Education Minister at the time.

Mentioned with a picture in another book by Hugh Sturzaker, one of the senior surgeons at the *James Paget University Hospital*, is that we put on a charity event. In 1980 we raised £13,000 or so towards the hospital scanner appeal he was running, a huge sum at that time.

To do that we sold 200 or so tickets, asked all our suppliers to give everything for free, and all our staff to work the evening for nothing. In addition we got superb auction items donated and, on the night, David Temple auctioned everything off for us. Kevin and Eve Finn, part of the *New Seekers* group and friends of Keith Sparks, came and sang for us and, in monetary terms today, we raised the equivalent of £52,000, so quite a figure for one night in Lowestoft.

I really liked using Gunton to raise money for charity, and I think I got that trait from my very young days at Winterton and Martham and being involved in fetes, fishing competitions and fund-raising for people like the Young Conservatives and various village halls. I did that from about 11 years old, approaching local business for help, getting handbills printed, donations, helping on the day and organizing the all-important insurance against loss because of the weather. Big business in those days. Stalls would be really quaint (for today): pick-a-stick, bowling for a pig (a real one), treasure hunt, and all the usual cakes, bring-and-buy, flowers, and anything anyone could think up to raise a few shillings.

Latterly I had a portable sound system and, at a fete for the Conservative Association in Martham, it nearly brought a very early end for me. Setting it up outside, someone inadvertently plugged it into the electric circuit, with me putting wires together. Some burnt hands and a damaged back from being thrown in the air, but I recovered enough to go to their social in the evening.

In those early days, on occasion we would have one of the local stars appearing in the pier summer shows at Great Yarmouth to open the events, as was the habit at that time. I recall being very chuffed at going to collect Ruby Murray, a popular singer in the 50s and 60s.

Any local organization which wanted a luxury event would choose Gunton, and that included the Round Table who, once a year, organized a 'men only' boxing event. Lovely dinner and then some set-piece rounds of boxing. Not really my scene, but I had to be the host and, at one of them, I invited Mr Clark of the *Fox and Goose* at Fressingfield, one of those early-days restaurants I have mentioned.

Clark was a notoriously difficult man to get to come out, and it took a lot of persuasion by his son, Adrian, and me to get him to agree. On the night, we were at our table and there was no Mr Clark. Twenty minutes or so later, the head waiter came over to me and whispered: 'I have got Lord Vestey at Reception, and he says he is in your party.' Absolutely no idea what was going on, I told him to show him in – and in came Mr Clark! When I questioned him later, he said: 'Well, we are both in the meat business (Clark having previously been a butcher), so I thought I would use his name.'

In 2013 Betty and I went back to Fressingfield to have a meal with the new owners, which was really excellent, and I joked that I had really come to see Mr Clark. Whereupon the new owner took me to a window overlooking the graveyard of the church which adjoined the restaurant building, and said: 'Count three gravestones to the left and he is there!'

He also told us that he has kept the chair in which Mr Clark used to sit in the bar and, on occasion, people swear they have seen him sitting there. Furthermore, one lady who had been a regular customer in the time of Clark came in and sat in the seat, ordering her usual drink. When it was placed on the table, for some unexplained reason it fell off, and she said: 'That's Mr Clark still here – he never did like me ordering that.'

After a few changes, Tim Jones and his wife, Janet, were the couple who settled down as our General Managers at Gunton. Janet was superb at organization in a no-nonsense way, and Tim was excellent with the customers and setting up the various events. Another big local night at Gunton Hall was always the New Year's Eve party, and some years Tim would arrange for bagpipes to see in the New Year. On those occasions, we had our 'New Year' next door at 12.15 to give the piper time to play for Gunton at midnight, and then race round to the converted stables, to where we had by then moved, and where we would be holding our own party, to play for us in the courtyard.

Gunton also gave Betty the chance to have great tennis parties - who else had four courts to play on? I developed my wood-fired barbecue system which, together with the tennis parties, made for some great evenings and Sunday lunchtimes. We always had so much support and so many friends around which, on occasion, were needed. Not quite Dr Cameron of TV fame, but our own Doctor John Dawson was a useful guy to have in nearby Gorleston.

Betty would get the tennis going and I worked on the final food and drinks, and got ready to cook on the barbeque. On one evening, in doing so, I managed to severely cut my hand with a 'freezer' serrated knife, and quickly realized I was in trouble. This was not a cut for a plaster, so I called John, who rapidly appeared and, as time was of the essence – i.e. there was none available! – I have this recollection of him in his best veterinarian pose with sewing needle I thought more suitable for a horse and, of course, no anesthetic as there was not time. Very much appreciated.

Other anecdotes at Gunton are of our Burmese cat, Holly, getting friendly with the children each week as they arrived for their holidays. Holly would sit with them, watching their entertainment, including the magician with the dove which appeared from the sleeve of his jacket. Holly thought this great and, one day, stayed hidden when the entertainment room was closed for the night with the dove left in its cage.

Betty had to make a considerable effort next day quickly to find the magician a new dove, and Holly was banned from the entertainment – as he was from weddings. At one wedding in the Moulin Rouge, one of the hosts enquired as to why we had a beautiful and innocent-looking cat sitting in the centre of the buffet.

Holly got his come-uppance later, when we went on a trip for a week. We arranged for him to be looked after and, on our return, the person doing the job told us that Holly had not been seen all week. Greatly concerned, we assumed the worst, until I happened to be walking past an 'above ground' wine store I had built myself in the courtyard. I heard a plaintive 'meow' and called Betty, for it must be we were going to find together a very emaciated, sick cat. Not a bit! I opened the door and Holly bounced out as bright as ever.

However, on entering the store I found out why! On the floor were several broken bottles of wine on which, of course, Holly had been living all week. I don't know how you measure if a cat has a hangover, but the Burmese as a strain are extraordinary and very intelligent.

What was also lovely there was that, on my 40th birthday, we held a 'Wartime' party. Everyone came to the *Moulin Rouge* in wartime gear - including Bill Barclay, from the *Golden Sands Holiday Camp*, as Al Capone complete with violin case. I had no more than a simple Army jacket, 1930's NHS wire-frame spectacles and a tin 'Warden' helmet but, standing beside Betty as we greeted our guests, she was constantly asked: 'Where is Joe?' The helmet and spectacles just completely changed my appearance.

Before we seriously get on to *Pleasurewood*, there are several other business and personal involvements I should mention, because of our being based at Lowestoft. Not least is the story of *Priorycraft* at St Olaves. From age 17, my personal bankers had always been *Barclays*, and we had been through some tough and interesting times together, especially surviving when interest rates got close to 20% or so in the 1970s.

A call from a local manager one day: 'Joe, don't question this, but we need your help in clearing up a bankruptcy we have had. You need to buy a plot of land at St Olaves, about 7 miles from Gunton, which is a disused boatyard and moorings. You will pay £25,000 and we will add that to your overdraft facility.' No problem, and nice for a bank to have that attitude and trust.

During the legal formalities I passed by to have a look at this 'plot', only to find a load of buildings and quite a few people working there. 'What the **** is going on here?' I asked. The men, led by Vic Martin and Dick Darkins, were building a fibreglass boat known as the 'Master Mariner' on their own account, and said the receiver had agreed they could do so, if they met all their own costs.

On hearing my story, they asked if they could continue, to which, after laying down some rules, I agreed. Later they asked me to make it a bit more formal, and they needed help. They sure did! I got involved with them and the first thing was to find out how profitable the boats were. They did not quite ask: 'How do you spell that?' but I discovered that their idea of pricing was to look around at what other people were charging for similar boats, and then charge a bit less.

Their main sales were to Denmark through a retired Danish Naval Commander, Willy Stenhild, in a small fishing town called Hundested. I got them listing the materials and labour involved, pricing the boats properly, and decided to go to Denmark to see Willy. Thereby hang many tales, not least the evening when he and his friends decided to introduce me to the ceremony of the eel – which involves drinking a lot of schnapps!

Although we cleaned out the mooring basin, got involved in building, selling and then managing Broads hire boats, it was too time-consuming and too cash-intensive, and I had to dispose of it. However, it was during that time I was to meet John Seear of the Freddie Laker connection in Florida, and other interesting people, as they bought hire boats from us for investment.

Because we obviously had large alcohol sales at Gunton, in another bankruptcy situation I was made aware of an investment wine merchant in Norwich who had run into difficulties. Again, either a bank or receiver wanted matters cleared up, and they had a barrel of *Louis Royer* cognac in a bond in Cambridge which no one would buy. To help, I agreed to pay £500.00 for it, subject to inspection, and duly went to view, taking with me Tim Jones from Gunton. The barrel was there and was full, so all was in order and we managed to sneak an 'in bond' tasting – delicious, we thought.

We discovered that a group of Beccles doctors had previously bought a barrel from the same shipment, but they had panicked in case they lost their barrel in the bankruptcy, and brought it out of bond to Beccles. Luckily for me, as they had bottled it, I was able to buy two or three bottles to see what we might have. It was more than superb, and I decided to give half the barrel to my daughter, Rebecca, and to organize for it to be bottled for us.

We planned an unusual bottle shape, a fabulous label and to aim it at the USA market – say Abraham Lincoln's birthday, or some such event. The Beccles group had their cognac certified as Grand Fine Champagne Extra by M Royer himself, and that was all I needed – certification.

M Royer duly tasted it and certified – it was more or less cooking brandy! What had gone wrong? We do not really know, but suspect it had not been well stored and was being opened later than that at Beccles. We were no brandy experts, but it was a great disappointment to me and Rebecca, and a great loss to the cognac drinkers in the USA! But we sold it 'as is' at auction, and at least made a profit. Two other involvements, and then on to *Pleasurewood*.

A local group of theatre-goers and players was trying to get a 'playhouse' established in South Lowestoft – very much for schools and amateur groups. They had great help from the education people, but were short of not a particularly large sum of money, which the local council was hesitating to give them. At Gunton we would always get stuck-in to raising this or that money for good causes locally, and I proposed to the Council members that, if I raised half the cash needed, they should give the other half. They duly agreed, and in 1977 the *Seagull Theatre* was opened by Alfred Marks who, to great amusement, said: 'I now declare the Seagull open – and may it sh★★ on you all.'

The other involvement was one of my better ones, and continues to this day with great success. Both our girls, Alice and Rose, in their early years went to a small, private school in Beccles run by a Miss Pagan. The trouble was, in 1977 Miss Pagan was retiring and the school closing. What to do? The school had been run by Ray Gillings as the Headmaster, and he now offered that he had found an unused, old, village school at Henstead, a village off the A12 near Kessingland. If parents would support him with a little cash, he would open a school there.

I gathered four or five other parents around me. We all worked like the proverbial slaves during the summer of 1979, and had to find a lot more money than the £500.00 or so Ray said he needed. In September, The Old School at Henstead opened with 22 children enrolled, a number which rapidly grew to near 100. I was appointed Chairman of the Governors (having never been involved in an educational establishment of any sort, so qualified in my usual way) and another quick learning curve was experienced!

Not least, within two years I was having to understand how to find a new Headmaster. I will be forever grateful to Laurie Rimmer of Framlingham School fame, for allowing me to drag him in and to advise me and then also to become a governor. After that hiccup, and an interim Headmaster, we acquired the outstanding Michael Hewett and his wife, who took the school forward in an amazing way.

I was very proud to be invited back by them in 2003 for the 25th anniversary, to present the prizes at the annual speech day, accompanied by Alice and Betty. Many buildings and new governors later, it is a thriving establishment, and I believe many feel we created an opportunity from which their children have truly benefited.

And so to my five minutes claim to fame – *Pleasurewood Hills American Theme Park* but, as we go in there, let's have a look at what the world was doing in 1980.

Snapshot of the year. We were all struggling out of the 1970's recession – petrol was now 28p a litre, beer 35p a pint, a loaf 33p and milk 17p. Unemployment was 1.56m, average wage £6,000, inflation 13%, the Iranian Embassy was stormed and Margaret Thatcher famously said 'This lady's not for turning.' In the USA, former film actor Ronald Reagan was President, inflation there 14%, interest rates 21%, and the USA population at an all-time record of 226m. Mount St Helens erupted, the first fax machine was produced in Japan, and *Post-It* notes and *PACman* were both invented. Quite a busy time for the world.

Joe's partner Robert Ludkin at the wedding of his daughter Ruth

Joe with model of Great Yarmouth Sealife centre

Ian Foster
(Manager) with
Jan and Andrew at
Hunstanton Sealife
Centre

Opening of Ripleys
Believe it or Not!
at Great Yarmouth

Sealife Centre at Hunstanton

Glan Gwna Hall at Caeathro outside Caernarfon

*Early Seaforths travel Christmas party – Jenny Mills,
Gary Hance, Alan Schoenherr and Joe Larter*

Bygone Village Fleggburgh first brochure

Ocean Park Barbados at night

*Tom O'Hanlon by the plane in Ripley's
Believe it or Not! at Great Yarmouth*

Aleks Szymanski and family inUSA

Chapter Eight

Pleasurewood Hills, Woody Bear, the Dutch Visitors,
We Go Public, and a Great Wedding.

If I ever had to justify the slightly awful title of 'entrepreneur', creating *Pleasurewood Hills* is the one outstanding event that maybe justifies it. Many would call it an act of madness but, as I said in my introduction, we all have the opportunity to make decisions, but then it is up to us. I completely believed in myself and, really, those wild horses again could not have dragged me from my objective with *Pleasurewood* once I had discovered what 'theme park' meant, no matter how much common sense might have dictated otherwise.

An interesting angle is that when I made the first tentative plans for the development of Dip Farm, which became *Pleasurewood Hills*, I had really never heard of a theme park as such, and planned a children's entertainment park, with holiday bungalows alongside. At one time I was considering an 'international holiday village', with blocks of apartments in various continental styles, Swiss, German, French, and so on, and of course the original Hills idea for development was housing.

Apart from the land being used for the Gunton Hall business itself, we had about 70 acres just as accommodation land - a nice area to walk by the lake or down to the beach. Between our own land and the sea was another area of 100 acres or so, belonging to Waveney District Council and on which, for ever, they had been discussing constructing a pitch-and-putt golf course and other leisure facilities.

After lengthy negotiations with them, I finally got agreement that they would give me a long lease on about 20 acres of their land between Gunton and the coast road, and preserve the woodland adjoining. Thereby they would give us a new access from the beach road and preserve our shelter from the sea, and we would build them the golf course and other leisure facilities they wanted for free. From press cuttings at the time, I see that in September 1977 I was described as 'a fairy godfather' for Lowestoft and, on 30 March 1979, Nick Brighouse, as Chairman of the Waveney Council, drove a JCB to start the scheme.

In the first place we just had a general approval for a family park, and I was not really sure what to do with it, but knew it would be entertainment and, I hoped, would improve the attraction of holidays at Gunton Hall. Just as we were thinking about it all, I read in the *Eastern Daily Press* that two men, John Edwards and Robert 'Happy' Hudson, garage proprietors, were going to build the longest private miniature steam railway in the UK, at Great Yarmouth, more or less on an open field. Serendipity again.

I arranged a meeting and showed them what would be an almost idyllic site through woods and beside a lake I knew I would eventually construct, and they agreed to bring their attraction to me. A great start, and we planned to have something to offer the public the following Whitsun holiday.

The arrangement was that they would build and run a 15-inch narrow-gauge steam railway, I would provide the land, and we would share the income. I loved the idea of steam, and maybe that was a throwback to seeing those large engines at the bottom of the garden in Repps Road, Martham, in the early 1940s, and then travelling to school by steam train all those childhood years ago.

The next call to me from them a month or so later, in October 1981, was: 'We are standing in the middle of your two grassed fields – where would you like us to put the railway station?" It was a wake-up call, because I had given no thought to design but, as we walked the fields, I told them I had just made a second visit to Disney (now open in Florida), so why not steal one of his ideas?

Disney developments always have a Main Street and a Station Square, so we started upside down with Station Square first and, later in the year, laid down Main Street - and that is how what eventually became *Pleasurewood Hills* was designed and started. A long and expensive design process and very professional!

We had very limited cash (would it ever be different?) for that first summer, so we excavated a street and square and, as cheaply as possible, filled up some of the space around the square. Using rough-split logs attached to concrete posts and wooden rails, we created a huge, wooden fort area on one side of the square and filled it with children's climbing equipment. We built a simple but hair-raising 'Death' slide based on a design from the USA.

To start to make the 'square' look like one, on one side we installed something entirely new, called Bumper Boats. They were round, rubber boats with real, petrol engines, all running around in a large wooden pond, but enormous fun as kids could 'drive' a real engine quite safely. We also bought a secondhand, plastic ice-skating rink from Newmarket Road in Norwich. John Edwards' brother ran a market at weekends, and we brought in odd animals like highland cattle from Billy Chapman at Martham. Refreshments were just kiosks, or you brought your own; with a shop in the station, that was about it for the first year.

Visitors paid to use each 'attraction' and, at 2.10pm on Saturday 22 May 1982, the steam railway was opened by local radio star John Mountford (great steam enthusiast) - and again the rest is, as they say, history.

For actual construction from then on, I was lucky that Tom O'Hanlon of the Glan Gwna experience had decided to move his family back down to the East Anglian area, and I asked if he would come and build *Pleasurewood* for me. Tom was always a bit of a loner and independent, but we suited each other – so much so that, right into spring 2012 some 30 years later, at age 80, he was winding-up another property investment we had in Gorleston.

Enter now, stage left, Keith Sparks – Sparky to everyone! Without Keith I would never have produced the leisure attractions I did, and certainly not *Pleasurewood Hills*. Keith died in 2012 so, in a way, this is a tribute to him - one amazing man.

Keith was a friend of Trevor Dodwell, the *WA Hills* lawyer I had met during the Glan Gwna purchase in Wales – Trevor being impressed that a Director of the staid *WA Hills* plc would buy a bottle of champagne to celebrate completion of the purchase. Keith had had an unsuccessful association with some previous partners and got left holding the baby on various costs and tax due, and could I help?

When we met he had a contract with Harry Corbett, a well-known TV presenter in those days, with his 'family' of Sooty, Sweep and Sue, hand puppets for a BBC children's show. Working now, literally, on his kitchen table at home with his wife, Mary, Keith was to make reproductions of the puppets for slot machines – insert a coin and the puppets appeared to play music. I provided the cash he needed, then more cash for production, and we eventually became partners in a proper business, *Sparks Creative Services*.

Very quickly Keith progressed to the Christmas window display business, with *Fenwick* in London and Newcastle, and *Alders* in Croydon as big clients. We rented premises at Hythe Quay in Colchester, and our Sparks partnership of the future was born. From there Keith tied up with the Golding brothers, also from Colchester, and they provided the growing audio side of his business. Keith was enormous fun, extremely talented, had a wickedly infectious sense of humour, and was truly loved in the theme park industry as it developed. 'A founding father of the industry' is not too grand a title to give him.

John Broome, of *Alton Towers*, thought the world of him and he developed major rides there and also for Geoffrey Thompson at *Blackpool Pleasure Beach*. In the early days, Keith had certain rights to the *Rupert Bear* stories and together we developed a very simple animated show, which we installed in the old Marina building on Great Yarmouth seafront.

The two Keith photographs show him with Rupert, and then with Geoffrey Thompson of *Blackpool Pleasure Beach* on his right and Kale Justander of *Linnemaki Park*, Helsinki, in Finland, on his left. Eventually, I became too busy to be involved directly in the Sparks business and one of the Golding brothers took over as his partner, but we kept in touch.

Pleasurewood Hills would be our joint claim to fame in the future, with my also introducing him to Bruce Carter of *Rex Studios* at Great Yarmouth. Keith was particularly impressed with the spectacular UV (ultra-violet) artwork *Rex Studios* produced, which was almost unique in those days, Bruce eventually winning 'Best stand in show' award at the 2003 International Association of Pleasure Parks and Attractions (IAPPA) show in Orlando for that work.

John Wardley was the man who really brought the idea of themed rides and audio-animatronic figures to the UK and, coincidentally, in his youth had learned so much of the basics of the entertainment industry at the feet of Jack Jay at Great Yarmouth. John knew Keith so well and, in 2013, published his own book *Creating my own Nemesis* (Amazon). He summed up the admiration the whole amusement industry had for Keith. I can do no better than quote one story from his book, and you will get the idea of the man.

'Keith was a larger-than-life personality. He came from a family of undertakers... but it was Sparky's sense of humour that we all remember, delightfully juvenile and matched closely to that of an eight year old school boy. It wasn't the joke that was funny but the **way** *he told it. Most of his jokes were filthy, but he did have one clean one and this is it:*

'"When I was a lad, we were so poor, we had to buy my uniform from the Army and Navy Stores. And, believe me, it was no joke going to Station Street Infants School dressed as a Japanese Admiral"

'Now, it's not the funniest joke in the world by any means, but when Sparky told it ,it became hilarious; by the time he had got to "we were so poor" he'd started to giggle. By "and believe me" he was in fits of laughter. After "Station Street Infants School" his face had become bright red with tears streaming down his cheeks. On the word "Japanese" his eyes were bulging, incontinence was a serious issue and paramedic attention was imminently needed. As far as I can remember he never did get the word "Admiral" out and it was many years later that someone else told me the punchline.'

As John also said: 'It was a joy working with Sparky.' And, for those of us who knew him so well, that says it all.

When I was first involved with him, Keith would talk at our business meetings about this or that theme park he was working for, and I asked: 'What is a theme park?'

'Come with me to *Europa Park* in Germany next week, and I will show you,' he said. I went over and was completely knocked out. The Mack family not only owned their park, but were big manufacturers of rides, and had created a quality as good as Disney, but on a smaller scale - and it was raining all the time but yet packed with people!

I came home and told my family and the team at Gunton, that we would be building a theme park next door; I had found my focus – my future. No market research or other consultations, just, in my heart, I knew it was right.

One early summer evening before I pressed the 'Go' button, I walked the seafront at Great Yarmouth and reminded myself of what was there – or rather what was not there. In the numerous amusement arcades I counted the crane 'grab' machines in the street-front row of the arcades and it came to something like 57 (and actually not many less today), and I said to myself: 'I am positive tourists must want something better than this.'

The *Pleasurewood* construction was difficult but fun; because there was little cash, everything was a one-off. Keith and I together literally designed it 'on the hoof', driving Tom O'Hanlon mad, but he did appreciate the challenge most of the time. I wish we had kept the dozens of restaurant and café table-napkins and menu cards on which, as we were discussing what we wanted over coffee or a meal in various countries, he or I would draw the design out. Because of our previous association and the constant travel we had made together, we could always say: 'Do you remember this or that?' referring to places we had been all over, and we knew instantly what the other was talking about.

It is easy for us all to forget that, even in the late 1970s, the communications world was nothing remotely like it is today. Bruce Carter reminds me that one day he and Keith called at Gunton Hall to discuss with me some matter about *Pleasurewood*, and I told them to come to my office as I had something new to show them. Keith and Bruce were by now working very closely together, but if either one designed something the other needed to see urgently, it would have to be sent to Colchester by rail or vice versa to Great Yarmouth, and then collected personally - infuriating for them, and so slow.

What I had to show them was one of the first commercial fax machines just invented in Japan. I had it on trial and told them that, if we bought three, they were only £2000.00 each! An unbelievable price, but we all bought, and our lives were changed for ever. Similarly, the very first computer we had at Gunton had to be lifted into place by a crane!

With faxes, mobile phones, emails and the internet, of course, the world is a different place today. Better, we all say, but it is a bit like when a motorway is first opened – you can just get to the next traffic jam sooner. Now you can receive and answer emails as you walk along the street with your smartphone. Interestingly, as you will see later, by 2013 my main work interest is an electronic fax business based in Austin, Texas, and run by my nephew.

I joined IAPPA (International Association of Pleasure parks and Attractions), based in the USA, run then by the indomitable John Graff, who always seemed to have time for everyone, even to visit little Joe Larter at *Pleasurewood*.

I started to visit attractions in the UK – plus I had immense help from Keith who, by now, knew everyone in the business in the UK, in Europe and in the USA. If Keith said: 'Joe Larter is coming to see you,' I got the royal welcome everywhere. As well as Geoffrey Thompson and John Broome, I met Colin Dawson of *Thorpe Park*, Ray Barrett and Michael Herbert of *Tussauds*, and the people at Chessington including John Wardley, *Windsor Safari Park*, John Collins - all the giants of the industry and they were unstinting in their help to me.

I went to all the various attractions in the Midlands – Drayton Manor, Lightwater Valley, *Gullivers Kingdom*, and others. I also joined the British Association of Leisure Parks, Piers and Attractions (BALPPA), of which I became a committee member which, as a 'new boy' amongst all the old, established attraction owners, I thought was quite a compliment. Our visitors liked our small, quirky, family venture – but I could see we needed a LOT more content, as tourists were getting elsewhere.

The sale of my ill-fated Newport development provided a chunk of cash and, combined with a very friendly Lowestoft bank manager granting me a substantial overdraft, we used that second winter, 1982/3, to start the building of a proper theme park. We built two large warehouse-type buildings with facades to form Main Street, and inside we housed food, drink and a shopping 'centre', plus themed attractions which Keith Sparks and *Rex Studios* in Great Yarmouth built for me. There was even a quality amusement arcade, but no crane-grab machines!

We also found a delightful old gentleman (Keith again), Fred Loades from Felixstowe, who had a wonderful and unique collection of miniature working fairground models, and we hired them to fill a space. Fred laid the whole collection out indoors as an actual fairground, and was on site all the time in summer living in a caravan. He continued making the models and, of course, was able to discuss and describe the collection to our visitors. He was absolutely in his element, and it was a lovely retirement occupation for him.

We needed something dramatic to anchor our 1983 launch as a proper theme park but could not, of course, afford the steel themed rides of Disney and *Europa Park*. What we did find was *Cine 180* – a vast, canvas dome inside which were projected dramatic, larger-than-life films of being on a roller-coaster, flying through the Grand

Canyon, and so on. In some ways it was even better than being on a ride itself, and the public loved it -standing only, large capacity, affordable, and perfect for us.

It was meeting the USA owners of *Cine 180* that gave me the idea that my 'theme' would be American – so much more dramatic in the quiet backwoods of Lowestoft. But what to **call** the park? In those days we used a Norwich advertising agency, *Foster, Seligman and Wright*, and really no one could come up with an original or appropriate name. We had a naming afternoon with the doors locked and we STILL could not come up with a name.

The following morning Ian Foster of the agency called and said: 'Have you noticed the name of the main road outside Gunton Hall? It's on your notepaper as part of your Gunton Hall address – Pleasurewood Hill! We added the word 'American' and thus a legend was born!

The other legend born at *Pleasurewood* was our theme park mascot – Woody Bear. Created by Keith, *FSW* came up with the name; he was truly one of the few original characters that have really worked in parks.

Woody was a small stroke of genius and, in 2013, four *Pleasurewood* owners later, Woody is still heading the park publicity and being very carefully nurtured. It is not an exaggeration to say that in East Anglia he has a standing equivalent to that of Mickey Mouse, and I was delighted to be twice reunited with Woody when I officially reopened the park, first in 2008 for its 25th anniversary, and then for the current owners on the occasion of its 30th anniversary on 2 June 2013.

In those development days, Woody led the publicity of the park and, in the end, had such a diary of events to attend at schools, hospitals, parties and opening summer fetes, that we bought a taxi and cut the roof out so he could travel in style with his driver – not unlike the Queen of England, and often with crowds about the same size! Jane Samkin was the first Woody, and then Sue McElroy (known always as Woody Sue) was Woody for the remainder of the time I owned the park, and she did really bring him to life in an exceptional way. In fact, on the Queen's official visit to Lowestoft, Woody did (I did not!) get to meet her.

What we also had to do was maximize the 'on park' spend by our visitors and, in-house at Gunton Hall, we had Martin Wilson. Martin started by just running the Gunton Hall gift shop, but took over the retail side of not only *Pleasurewood*, but all the other attractions as we developed. In the first full season we had a shopping centre with eleven different shops, but they were combined and reduced as the numbers grew and we learned that shopping needed space for layout.

Martin and his brothers were involved with the *Lowestoft Players*, and got on well with Keith, finding actors or puppeteers as we developed shows. When visitor numbers reached over 11,000 a day we had to have more than one Woody, as he was often at events 'off park' and, of course, all the visitors expected to see him at the park as well.

Even so, that was more than we could handle with just Woody, so between Martin and the staff they dreamed up a 'family' of Clarence the Cat and Ronnie the Raccoon to take some of the pressure – in the same way as Disney has to do with Mickey. He also developed soft-toy replicas with a firm in South Wales, and there is a picture of Woody presenting two to the Queen for Harry and William, on her visit to Lowestoft in 1985.

Woody, Clarence and Ronnie led a parade around the park each afternoon with clowns and amusement characters we hauled in to take the pressure of entertaining, but Ronnie and Clarence disappeared with the next two owners of the park, when visitor numbers dropped sharply. The current owners are bringing back the quality needed and, with numbers growing again, have recreated both of them for the 30th anniversary in June 2013.

The best attraction Keith ever built for me was the 'Woody Bear's Magic Music Hall', where he created his own voice-over and, to this day, I can hear his deep voice and see the action of the puppets which ought now to be in a museum of the Park industry. Superbly scripted, with a very skilled sound-track and actions, the show required three puppeteers and ran three or four times a day. In the end it was discontinued, as the cost was out of proportion to its use and, when we had 11,000 a day on the park, the capacity was totally inadequate. However, it was just about the best that Keith ever created.

Even today Woody is an important part of Lowestoft life. At the conclusion of this book you will see me involved with the *Marina Theatre* and, in Winter 2012/13, Woody appeared as a guest in the annual pantomime there and other street events. The latest owners of *Pleasurewood* treasure him and I hope that, in the same but lesser way of Mickey Mouse in the USA, Woody is a fixture in East Anglia forever.

And so ... after many birthing pains and advice from not a few potential midwives, on 2 June1983 *Pleasurewood Hills American Theme Park*, Lowestoft finally opened. We did not have the *Red Arrows* fly past but, at the precise moment of opening, a sky-diver landed in the park, bringing a baton inscribed with the opening time and date. That baton has long since been lost so, if a reader knows anything about it....

The challenge we had now was that a theme park was to be 'pay once and everything included', so we needed to offer great value for money. Our slogan was '£2.50 a day and no more to pay', and we scoured the land for anything we could beg, borrow or steal to try to fill our space.

An aerial picture of 1982 shows how thin we were on the ground that first proper year, and confined just to the first field. A visit with Keith to see the Florizone brothers in Belgium, Robert in *Meli Park* and Luc in *Bellewarde* - was an eye-opener for me and I found *Bellewarde* more or less the exact flavour I had in mind for *Pleasurewood*. Luc, in particular, spent endless hours talking to me and explaining why he did this and that – a real hands-on builder, like me.

From *Bellewarde* I stole the unique idea of running wood-fired barbecues all day long. When I meet them today, many a visitor from that era of *Pleasurewood* says: 'We used to come to your park on a Sunday so I could cook lunch on the BBQ whilst the family went on all the rides – do they still have them?'

For all the investment we made, it's strange how often a small and inexpensive idea sticks. No other park had them and I have suggested to the current owners, in a discussion on the future, that they might consider bringing one large, wood-fire BBQ back for special events, which I believe they are going to do for 2014.

That '£2.50 a day and no more to pay' slogan got us into trouble – but good publicity as silly actions can sometimes produce. A customer complained to the Trading Standards Office that 'no more to pay' was not true. He had paid his £2.50 but, when he went for his free food and ice cream, he could not get it! And there were slot machines which were not free. A pretty daft contention really, supported by an equally daft (in my view) Trading Standards lot, and we were prosecuted – but great PR! Robert Killin, Solicitor, to the rescue again and, although we were fined, Robert in court said that he thought what Mr Larter really **meant** to say was: 'almost no more to pay'!

We were also terribly keen to find out what our customers thought of us. We then knew no better way than to give out opinion forms, with tick-boxes and a space for comments. Our main advertising at that time was: 'Come to *Pleasurewood Hills* – your biggest day out ever.' As I have said, in that first year we were thin on the ground and it was a rather extravagant claim to make. One gentleman left us a message on his opinion form, putting us in our place by saying that: 'If I have just had my biggest day out ever, then I have very little in life to look forward to' - very amusing, but he was so right at that time.

Those early days in that first year at *Pleasurewood Hills* really were traumatic and, at the start, absolutely frightening for me personally. You could not fault our PR, publicity, presentation or advertising material, but we opened on that June 1983 day and really no one came – just the odd hundred or two here and there, when we needed them in thousands.

All through June we did everything to get ourselves known, but still no big numbers which we now had expected, at least at weekends. I explained to the staff and my family that it must just be timing, and the schools breaking up around 20 July would be the turning-point. At the same time, I was desperately thinking to myself that maybe I simply had not created anything exciting enough, although I had borrowed all the cash I could. That depressing period gave us time to settle in staff, get our systems right and so on, but still no one came – even when the schools DID break up.

Right at the end of July, and with no one there, I had to say to Betty that maybe I had made a colossal mistake. Other 'helpful' people were then pointing out that half our catchment area was the North Sea and that might be the reason. Utterly depressed and really not knowing what to do, we now reached the first weekend in August when, on the Saturday, we got hit with 2500 visitors in the one day (knocking us for six as we were totally unprepared) and never looked back. Jubilado!

To this day we do not really know why it happened, but we ended the year with 246,000 visitors and made a profit. In fact, for reasons you will see later, our peak number eventually reached around 552,000 for the season in the 1990s, when we had by then over 50 rides, shows and attractions.

What I THINK happened in those opening months was that East Anglian people are notoriously cautious about anything new. A theme park? They wanted to hear what others thought before trying it for themselves. People actually loved the 'folksy' American style we had created with so much 'make do and mend' and, as I have said, the BBQs were important way beyond their appearance and cost. By then they were being carefully looked after by Chris Tooley, who had taken the catering concession next to them. He started to provide sausages, burgers and simple pieces of meat, so even those who had not thought about it in advance could cook for themselves. The attitude Chris had was just exactly what we needed to 'nurture' our visitors, and good for his business as well.

For me, financial times were tougher. Gunton needed constant updating and, as we moved into the *Pleasurewood Hills* phase, we had to consolidate – me always trying to do too much with my limited cash and ability to borrow. The Bammant case had ended; we sold the Newport development in two parts, and then sold our lovely Holverston Hall, thereafter converting the old stable block at Gunton Hall into a lovely home.

Another important event at that time was that I persuaded Andrew, my son, to take overall charge of the catering, which was his expertise, and it was a great relief for me to have him there. He also took charge of all the catering as the various other leisure schemes developed.

We started to add new attractions at *Pleasurewood* for the second season and, in February, went with my local bank manager to his head office to meet his Regional Director and (supposedly) to congratulate ourselves together on the first-year profitable success, and thank the bank for its support and discuss our plans and cash needs for the coming season. By now we had a loan on overdraft of just about £1m. What I did not know was that the Regional Director I knew, and who had actually been to the park, had left and moved to New Zealand to open a bank there.

The new man, a rugby-playing bully (my description) looked like thunder as we walked in (he had invited us to lunch) and his opening words, never to be forgotten, were: ' You two (the bank manager and me) have stolen £1m from our bank and you have 7 days to get it back to us.' That was so outrageous there really was no answer, but it appears the local manager had not kept head office totally informed on what he was doing. Huw Walters, who was with me, said: 'You did not look concerned,' which is true, because it was – so silly.

An interesting 'Don't be so daft'-type conversation followed. He eventually said we had better stay to lunch as he had invited us, and I insisted on showing him a video of the park we had brought with us so he could actually see what he was talking about. The outcome was that he gave us a month to repay, and I left saying we would discuss. In fact, during the meeting I realized the problem he had, but it was one he did not trouble to explain to us, as I think he had just made up his mind not to like us. His bank really had no security – what do you get back if a theme park fails?

All our main security was Gunton Hall, where another bank had a charge on the property, and a very successful holiday-based business. One call to the Regional Director of that bank, where I was well-known, to explain my problem and I was told to ask the other bank what figure was outstanding and they would clear it for me, so there would be one loan and one charge! Not something that would be happening today, but I mention all this to show that entrepreneurs don't have it easy all – if any – of the time, and that trust and reputation are everything.

It was in about June of the second full year that my friend Serendipity decided to join me at *Pleasurewood* and created for me another absolutely life-changing moment. A call to my office told me a small group of people from Holland had arrived on the park and would like me to go over for a cup of coffee – to be the first of hundreds in and out of Holland, but I did not know that then.

The Bembom family had arrived. Father Bembom did not speak much English but he had with him his sons, Willem and Henk. Mr Bembom Sr was a man extraordinaire! Already written about in many books, he is a legend in Holland and has been entered into the Hall of Fame at IAPPA – and here is what he did for me.

The sons explained that their father had heard about *Pleasurewood* and they had come to see for themselves, and immediately understood what I was trying to do. They told me they owned two or three theme and holiday parks in Holland and France, and Father wanted to know if I had plans for steel thrill rides. I told him I certainly had, but with no money to spare right then, we hoped to add one a year or so in the future. He said he had an idea for me, but first would Betty and I please come to their home base at *Slaghaaren* in Holland the next weekend as their guests, to see the operation there.

No problem, and Saturday found us in Holland with another cup of coffee and a great welcome. After a lovely hotel and dinner that night, we were told to be in the father's office at 10am on the Sunday. Meantime, Henk and Willem showed us around the amazing *Slaghaaren*. Self-built and including more steel rides than I could imagine, but as a builder I could immediately relate to the super DIY-style of development with amazing constructional ideas. Lots of bungalows for the tourists to stay in. If you stayed there, the park was free – rather like I had hoped for Gunton but could not progress.

Back in the office Sunday morning – another cup of coffee and: 'Mr Larter, do you still think you would like to have steel rides?' 'Yes, Mr Bembom but, like last Wednesday and yesterday, I still do not have any money for them.'

Whereupon he threw down on the table the pictures of five very large rides – a big carousel, a Round-up, a swing-boat and so on. 'We have surplus rides and would like to send these over to you, show you where to place them, install them and give you an engineer for the season to run and maintain them – and train your employees on their use.' Those rides were worth £3 million if new, so how on earth was I to pay for them?

He explained that I should go home, double the price of the park from £2.50 to £5 (the rides were worth far more than I had spent on the whole park at that time) and he would charge me £65,000 to be paid as the season progressed. If it did not work, he would take them all away again at the end of season, for free. Stunned is about the only word to use and, of course, I accepted. There was eventually a very simple season agreement in the form of a letter, and Betty and I went home asking each other: 'Where is the catch?'

As we discovered over the years with the Bembom family, there wasn't one. I actually think Betty had more influence than we realized (how could I be a bad guy if she had married me?!) because, as we left, Bembom Sr invited her to go with him alone to another warehouse, where he had a huge collection of Dutch mechanical organs. He picked one out and said he would send that over as well, for the coffee shop, so that when he visited he would be reminded of home!

From that meeting grew a lifelong and valuable friendship with the family but, for me particularly, with son Henk, who went on to buy Loudoun Park and Castle in Scotland. That meeting and agreement were THE making and success of *Pleasurewood* – no ifs, buts, or maybes: that is where our success eventually came from. Over the years more rides were added and exchanges made, and I think at the end of my ownership we were paying maybe £400k /500k rental for the season, but had a chairlift, log flume, Ladybird and other thrill rides, and achieved 552,000 visitors in our best year.

In 1985 we needed more cash if we were to develop fast, and were lucky to meet up with a venture capital fund, led by Gareth Pearce, in the form of *Electra Investment Trust*. Gareth reminded me of his first visit; London financiers being met off the train at Oulton Broad and taken to the park in spring, in pretty, remote Suffolk, where Gareth decided he wanted a ride on the giant swing-boat, which he never should have contemplated.

We watched in horror as he turned from a very pleasant, happy, rosy-looking city gent to an extremely pasty-faced, rather ill-looking…. We tried to make his visit as pleasant as possible as he recovered, and I think he went away with his compatriot, Josh Dick, reasonably well impressed with the park. The investment funds in those days had a deadline of 31 March to invest, and he wrote later saying that they had really allocated all their funds this year and would look at us again next year.

A little downhearted we started looking elsewhere, but thought our chances of expansion for the coming season were lost. Four days before the deadline, Gareth was on the phone: 'We have been let down and we have about £400k we could put into *Pleasurewood*, but it HAS to be completed by 31st.' A developer's dream, because there is no time for excessive checks and investigations. We lived in London for the four days and, beyond midnight

(lawyers stop the clock when they need to!), we had our first major investor.

However, not before, at about 2am, our own lawyer Bruce Westbrook, of *Cameron Markby*, decided that Betty, as an individual shareholder alongside me, ought to be separately advised before we signed for her to be part of the deal. I said: 'Great, Bruce – Betty will be delighted to hear from you, you deal with it!' He decided a phone call would suffice and, at about 2.30am, I am calling Betty in Suffolk to introduce her to her new lawyer.

The Electra cash meant we could install far better attractions, including a well-loved sea-lion show and pool, the Tikki Tikki tent with a parrot show and, for a time, a BMX facility. We could also plan expansion for the company, and Huw Walters, an accountant friend from the *Wallace Brothers* days, joined as non-executive Director. We were heading towards being a proper theme park.

In the second stages of *Pleasurewood*, Keith designed for me a haunted castle. I had seen them at *Alton Towers*, in Europe and Disney, of course, and every park has to have one. It was a part-animated, part-real person show, and Keith had a real sense of the macabre (I think from his days when, as a young man, he worked for the Co-op Funeral Services in Colchester). To shock people he devised an opening where, with a piercing scream, a model with a noose around his neck dropped right in front of the audience – made by Bruce at *Rex Studios* of course.

Very scary and dramatic, and all went well, but the model was not strong enough for such constant treatment. There came the day when it dropped and broke in two, with the head coming off and landing in the lap of some poor woman sitting in the front row. I think we all did find it very funny, but the woman was terrified and no doubt today we would have been sued to high heaven.

Keith had previously been burgled at Hythe Quay and had some rather valuable books stolen. On the principle of 'don't get mad, get even', Keith set up a trap for the next burglar, using the same hanging-man device. The Hythe was an old maltings and had a 3-storey atrium in the centre where grain had been hoisted.

He set the device to drop down in the dark with a piercing scream and a flashing light, triggered if anyone walked through the atrium on the ground floor. Never tested at night, I am glad to say, as I think there might have been another customer for the old Co-op business he used to work for.

In an expanding company the need is always for more cash and, if we were to grow, we needed a cash source, so inevitably we thought of becoming a public company. Our Electra investors lead us to *Guidehouse Securities*, who promoted a public issue of shares for us and, on 27 February 1986, the *Larter Group* became *Pleasureworld plc*, and we raised £1.8m, gaining 100 or so shareholders.

Just at the wrong moment, the Government changed the rules for fund-raising in the budget that year and we had to stop in mid-flow. I wrote to the then Chief Secretary of the Treasury, John MacGregor, who was an East Anglian MP and, tongue in cheek, told him that as a penalty he would be made to visit *Pleasurewood Hills*. To my enormous surprise he agreed to do so with his wife Jean, and we have always kept in touch from time to time – he now being Lord MacGregor and living in Pulham St Mary.

£1.8m was an enormous help and gave us a much more solid base for development. We acquired the energetic and always enthusiastic Peter Rowledge as a non-executive, and were delighted when Jonathan Peel, of *Norwich Union* insurance fame, agreed to be our plc Chairman. Respectable at last, with Jonathan being the direct descendant of Sir Robert Peel who, in 1829, formed the Metropolitan Police with his men known as 'bobbies', or 'peelers'. Our team was ready for take-off.

Things moved on rapidly from there and I knew I had to concentrate on the theme park business and tourists, which was what I loved. The *Warner Holidays* people came along and, in October 1987, we negotiated the sale of Gunton Hall, not exactly top price but it produced funds for the theme park and other developments and removed my responsibility for running something in which I did not have my heart.

My offices moved to downtown Lowestoft but, as a family, we still lived in the converted barn in the woodland next door to Gunton Hall and which we had not sold to *Warners*. Did I have mixed feelings? Not really, because I felt the chalet accommodation we had inherited at Gunton was dated no matter what we did to try to improve. That *Warners* in 2013 planned to demolish the lot and build a new apart–hotel (apartments in the barn of a hotel) really confirms my view. One look at *Potters Leisure Resort* at Hopton today tells you where we should have been in quality at Gunton.

1998 brought a planned visit to *Pleasurewood* by the Duke of Gloucester, who was to be in the area for various functions. In the event he was very ill, and we had the pleasure of a visit by his wife, the Duchess, instead.

At this time a lady who was to be involved with me for almost 40 years came on the scene. Pat Dowsing has been my secretary or PA on and off, firstly working for Tim Jones at Gunton Hall, but then with me at *Pleasureworld*, *Seaforths* and now *The Courtyard*, and still puts up with me. We have been through some good and then some pretty tough times together and she has been, and is, much appreciated.

We had the usual minor and major staff problems of course – one *Pleasurewood* manager deciding to steal quite a bit of money from us in a complicated fraud he set up using the entry system. Another sad event was the departure of our long-time accountant, Derek. I knew Derek and his wife had become seriously religious in the recent years, but I did not know just **how** much.

One morning, in the period when we were producing budgets for our financial advisers and the bank for the following year, Derek asked me into his office; I was told to sit down and not interrupt until he had finished speaking. Agog, I did so, and he read me a passage from the Bible. He then asked me if I understood what that meant and, having not listened because I was so stunned by what he was doing, I said: 'No' and he told me: 'But it means we do not have to go to the banks for finance – God will look after us!' He said that if I did not understand and agree, he would have to leave the company, and I was truly sad when he did just that. We had been through so much together. Arthur Marshall again: 'All part of life's rich pageant.'

Gavin Briggs was Derek's young, unqualified assistant, and he proved very capable indeed in taking over. From our waterfront offices in Lowestoft, we now tried to build ourselves into a proper leisure plc. It was Gavin who discovered the cash thefts going on at *Pleasurewood*, and also who helped me to assist another old friend, Ronald Toone.

Ronald was an architect who had bought another small holiday camp, known as *Golden Sands*, along the coast at Hopton. His son and others who ran it for him really had got into difficulties and, to save a bank taking over, Ronald asked me to move in like an unofficial Receiver – written authority and everything. With Gavin as my assistant (i.e. in charge!), we had an interesting time collecting keys to cash- and amusement machines from members of staff and others who wondered what had hit them. We got the cash flowing into, rather than out of, the right places and, in one season, did save it, only for Ron to take back control - it was lost the next year.

Another BIG event at this time was the marriage of my daughter, Rebecca, to Mark Tassie on 30 August 1986. More or less next-door boy- and girl-friend in Norwich, Rebecca wanted a little different wedding (taking after someone we know?), and we settled on the Mississippi River Boat based at the *Swan Hotel* at Horning.

Martin Wilson roped in friends to decorate and the kitchens at Gunton and our two stalwart waitresses, Betty and Barbara, from the restaurants, organized the on-board catering. With a jazz band on board, the happy couple and their guests sailed, not into the sunset, but into some very romantic Broadland settings and a very happy marriage; but I am reminded by them that the weather on the day was terrible. Great fun was had by all and even if her biased father says it, he was very proud to walk a beautiful bride down the aisle of the church at Old Catton. Mother was equally very proud of her, and Andrew was to follow his sister a few years later.

At the time we sold Gunton to *Warners*, we already had a planning application in (and had arranged a sale to *Tesco*) to construct a superstore on some of our land adjoining the A12. In 1988 that store was given planning approval and brought a further injection of £3.5 million for the company which was to change our financial life, but unfortunately not in the way you might think.

Before we get to that, let's explore the American connection and what I learned there.

Chapter Nine
Florida Properties, Hurricanes and USA Travel.

Because in both personal living terms (we have had a home n Florida for over 30 years) and the business connections, through the IAPPA international theme parks association and the two medical businesses, the USA has meant a huge amount to us. I have allocated the USA a section of the book of its own here but one business, *SecureCare*, has its further space later because of its importance. It is confusing to try to slot the various stories into their years, so my apologies that in this chapter we will run a bit ahead of the main, UK-based part of the story.

Our first trip to the USA was in 1976, to take Mother to the west coast to meet up with her Aunt Nora, of wartime food-parcel fame. Cable cars, Fisherman's Wharf, restaurants at the top of skyscrapers in San Francisco - and then on to Los Angeles with Disney and *Knott's Berry Farm* and to Las Vegas. As a first trip to the USA we were all stunned by the quality of everything, and Mother could not believe some of the illusions at Disney. She forever would not believe that the submarine ride did not take you right under the ocean.

Mother had not seen Nora since her trip to America with her own mother, Blanche, in 1936, and I believe Nora and family had emigrated in about 1932 following a brother who had gone a year or so earlier. So here was Mother, 40 years later, back again and having the time of her life and, for me looking back, was one of the most satisfying things I ever arranged for her.

We left her with Nora for a few days so they had some time to reminisce alone, and went ourselves to see the themed hotels and attractions in Las Vegas, arranging to meet her there a few days later. None of us was a gambler, but the shows were fantastic and it was a delight to take Mother to see the favourite entertainer for people of her age – Liberace. He was a very camp, over-the-top vocalist and pianist in the 1970s and appeared dripping in jewels and with a customized Rolls-Royce. He would bring it on to the stage and was the highest paid entertainer of the time – the Danny La Rue of his era. Walking to the front of the stage to show off his jewels, he would say: 'Have a look, ladies – you paid for them.'

This was all in 1976, years ahead of any theme park ideas I was to have, but must have sown the idea in my mind, alongside my becoming involved with Keith Sparks and his business in Colchester two years previously. I am sure he must have pointed me in that direction. It was not until 1978 that I got myself clear of, first, the Newport scheme, and then Glan Gwna, so I think I had a 'germination' period after that, where the knowledge I picked up from Keith and various visits in the USA helped put the *Pleasurewood* idea in my mind.

The Bahamas interlude in 1978/80 brought the purchase of our first holiday home in Florida and, of course, Disney had by then opened in Orlando. We took all the children at various times, and grandchildren later – plus seeing all the other parks in Florida as well - Seaworld, MGM, Universal Studios, Busch Gardens. Maybe I had become a little 'Americanized', and the creation of *Pleasurewood* just four years later all fits in.

Our '*Pleasurewood* Years' - 1982 to 1990 - did give us an amazing time of visits. Every year, IAPPA had a huge meeting (3000 delegates and more) in locations which were very limited because of the meeting size – I recall Los Angeles, Atlanta, and New Orleans, and latterly they met only in Orlando because it was by then becoming the centre for theme parks and the IAPPA show is simply massive. There were also visits to State Fairs at Springfield in Massachusetts, to the *Six Flags* parks, which were some of the largest around, but also to 'folksy' places more akin to the UK. One just had to take the scale out of what was seen and imagine how it could be applied to an idea for one's own park.

Fitz Otis of *Cinema 180* introduced us around, and one friend of his in particular remains in my memory. I do not remember his name and am not quite sure where he fitted in but, if we were in a restaurant and not getting served with the speed he wanted, he would break into an operatic aria – full-blast baritone. We got service!

I think what made the deepest impression on Betty and me was the sincere hospitality provided everywhere - not only food, drink and often accommodation, but real time to explain how their parks worked and always a promise to come and see us – which many did. If you owned a park anywhere in the world you were simply part of the family, and they often just loved to hear Betty speak English, as still happens when we are in our USA home.

There was no problem you could raise that someone would not try to solve for you. What one always had to have in mind was the limited knowledge most Americans had then, and many still have today, of the rest of the world. The majority just does not travel, and even now 80% of 'the people on the street' do not have passports. Whilst writing this book I was astonished to read, in March 2012, in the *New York Times*, that only that week had *Macy's*, the famous departmental store, decided to cater for online sales outside America and had to set up a system to actually ship the goods. In 2012!!! – Where have they been hiding?

The people at Disney were notorious in the early IAPPA days for **not** joining in and providing any support – they felt they were too grand, I think. However, there came a year when they decided that the competition was so hot they should join us, and provided an evening where they closed down part of *Disney World*.

We were told to go to a certain car park in the evening and enter Disney by a certain gate – some three or four thousand of us. It appeared to be chaos, with a huge queue to get in and us saying Disney could not organize the proverbial party in a brewery if they tried, but we were wrong. Disney had hired a large number of teenagers to pretend to be our fan club, screaming for our autographs on the **other** side of entry. They then laid on a meal spread amongst the various major areas, as we experienced the various rides and shows - a truly memorable and spectacular evening.

One IAPPA trip was through Canada, after having been to a meeting to see the first hotel with themed bedrooms, at Edmonton. A bedroom, for example, would be called the 'Automobile Room' – which would mean the bed was in the body of a real car and the room themed with traffic lights actually flashing red and green if you wished. The mind boggles!

There was also the 'Carriage Room', where guests would sleep in the frame of a real horse-carriage and a couple of fibreglass horses in front of them. We then took the trip through the Rockies by train to Vancouver for another meeting, to see developments there. If you ever do that train trip, be sure to get your timing right, as we unfortunately found the best scenery had passed us by – at night.

In Vancouver we wanted to treat Geoffrey and Barbara Thompson, of *Blackpool Pleasure Beach*, to lunch in a lovely mountainside restaurant we had found with some great effort, to repay the enormous help and advice Geoffrey had given me. When we arrived for this memorable experience, the cloud had come down and we could hardly find the entrance door of the restaurant, let alone the magnificent view we had come to see. Vancouver, and Victoria on Vancouver Island, must be two of the most beautiful locations we were ever to visit.

Let's just say a bit about Geoffrey Thompson, another absolute legend in the theme park and entertainment industry in the UK. I first met him at Blackpool, when Keith was making one of the first major changes there. Geoffrey lost his father very young, as I did, and he had just taken over control from Mrs Thompson Sr who, even at aged 80 years or so, was a formidable lady and very much had her say.

Busy as he was, he was always the perfect host and, later, was always ready to discuss ideas of what I planned at *Pleasurewood*, visiting me there from time to time. One memorable evening, which Betty and I considered an honour, was being invited to the *Savoy Hotel* in London, where Geoffrey gave his mother an 80th birthday party. Many years later, and after *Pleasurewood* was sold, Geoffrey was giving the father's speech at the wedding of his daughter, Amanda, finished the speech, and simply dropped down dead from a heart attack. We shall miss him forever.

We had friends living in Seattle and, following the Canadian visit, we went south to visit them, then flying on to San Franciso again, before taking a car down Route 101 to Los Angeles. It is one of the most beautiful drives you can take, and includes Pebble Beach, the famous golf course, Carmel of Clint Eastwood fame, and Monteray. At Monteray they have one of the world's most outstanding aquariums and I am sure that, later in the *Pleasureworld* era, my visit there influenced our decision to build *Sealife Centres* in the UK, and certainly I was thinking of Monteray when I was designing what should have been built in Buggiba in Malta. It would have been stunning.

Continuing south, as we reached Santa Barbara and before Los Angeles, we found Hearst Castle. Most British have never heard of it and certainly would not be able to imagine it. William Randolph Hearst, a mega-rich newspaper magnate, inherited several thousand acres as a holiday estate from his mother, and got fed up with just 'camping out' on the coast there, although with his cash it would nevertheless have been camping in grand style. In 1919 he asked an architect, Julia Morgan, to build him 'a little something' so he would be more comfortable.

By 1947 she had built her 'little something' for him - the castle of 165 rooms with 125 acres of beautiful gardens. Hearst had, meanwhile, in the 20s and 30s, been around Europe and bought up the interiors of any historic building for sale. He now had warehouses in New York full of the contents of castles and stately homes – including many from England. In 1919, Morgan had a budget of something like $10,000 a month (that's about $370k in money today), and they would decide together what room to theme in what way as they went along. Walt Disney, way ahead of his time. The 1941 Orson Welles film, *Citizen Kane*, was said to be based on Hearst, and he was so furious he banned any mention of it in his newspapers.

Even today, those warehouses in New York are full of the materials Hearst did not use, and one occasionally reads of people in the UK buying a stately home which had been stripped, researching, and finding Hearst had taken their interior. In the odd, genuine case where people are not just trying to make money, if the carvings or fittings are still in store the *Hearst Foundation* will return the materials to them, which is a nice, patriotic gesture. We made a second trip to Los Angeles, when IAPPA had a meeting based on the old *Queen Mary* cruise ship, which is moored downtown, where we all had accommodation on board.

On that second trip to Los Angeles we also visited the 'Spruce Goose', the one and only example of the H-4 'Hercules' seaplane built by Howard Hughes when he had the *Hughes Aircraft Corporation* during and after WWII. Another mega-business magnate and philanthropist who, after inheriting the *Hughes Tool Company* from his father, became famous producing films and romancing the actresses, but became increasingly eccentric as he got older.

The USA Government financed the whole H-4 project, with Hughes to be paid only after the first flight. The plane was vast and totally impractical, with a wing span of 319 ft, but he HAD to fly it or lose a fortune. Hughes finally got it to take off on a one-mile run 70ft above the water, and got his money.

On the personal side Bob Tabor, the 'realtor' – estate agent – who sold us our first home in Hillsborough, became a good adviser. When we decided we would like to build a home on the coast to mirror one we had stayed in on our Bahamas interlude, Bob found us a plot about 100 miles north at Vero Beach.

The development was planned to be an exclusive, gated community of about 20 houses. We chose a plot on the beach, but first had to be interviewed by the estate owners, who were also local bankers. Puzzled as to why, we never really found out (we were 'approved') but suspect it was, in those days, something to do with the colour of our skin, or which part of New York we might have come from. British – no problem!

Although I had the house designed, at that time we were consolidating in the UK ready for *Pleasurewood*, and I got cold feet about the actual building and its cost. In other words, I did not have enough cash. We sold that plot for more or less what we paid, and found a lovely apartment a bit further north at Melbourne Beach, again actually on the beach, and we and the girls enjoyed Melbourne for several years. However, later developments in 1990 saw us pull all our resources together, and we sold the Melbourne Beach apartment and, for a few years, were without a property in the USA.

Once in recovery mode again we missed our winter base, so went over, hired a car in Miami, and drove north to see what had happened in the intervening years. We had no real intention to buy straight away, but when we reached Hutchinson Island near Fort Pierce (that's about level with Disney and on the Atlantic coast), we got bowled over. A developer had built what was called *The Atrium* – an unusual 12-storey block of 48 apartments, and we were hooked. We bought on the 10th floor and returned later to furnish.

After two years in *The Atrium I*, in 2002 we bought the penthouse on the 12th floor in the identical *Atrium II* block next door, and that is where we are based in the USA today. During the *Atrium I* days we got my daughter, Rebecca, and her family to take a Disney holiday in Orlando, where Bruce and Leslie Carter of *Rex Studios* are now based. Bruce and Leslie kindly took them round all the parks for a week, which was much more his cup of tea than mine.

Bruce I have mentioned in connection with Keith Sparks, and by now he had decided he wanted a holiday home near Disney. Unlike me, he would (and still does) happily spend a day at Disney, *Typhoon Lagoon*, or *Sea World* and, by the 2000s, he had obtained a Green Card (a resident's card) and now spends more than half the year there. Perfect for looking after my family!

Betty and I did one day with Rebecca and family in Orlando and then, after all the theme park visits, went back to collect them for a beach stay with us. It was lovely to have Rebecca et al to stay, and I think the highlight with us – at least for Ben, my grandson - was the visit to the *Kennedy Space Center* at Cape Canaveral.

In Orlando, before we brought them to the coast for a week, we arranged a stretch-limo evening party, with a 'bar' on board, collecting them as a surprise from their hotel. The three children thought it the most luxurious thing they had ever seen or done – real 'cool', I think the kids call it today.

The other experience we had in *Atrium II*, and one which we would like to have avoided, was in 2004, when two hurricanes visited in the same month – *Charley* and *Frances*. Our damage could be repaired, but the unit adjoining us was trashed. The main air-conditioning unit from the roof of the block next door was ripped off and thrown through their front window.

With the whole of their space open to the elements, the force of the wind was so strong that, after destroying their interior, it partially blew down the internal walls between their unit and ours.

We were lucky, but I visited Florida later that month and the devastation to the whole area after a hurricane has to be seen to be believed. The main problem they have in Florida is that most of the power lines are overhead cables, so imagine how long that took to put right. When I tried to visit, our area was still in 'lock down' and I had to be identified in order to visit our property – looting, I think, was the big problem.

Worse was trying to find anywhere to stay, because it was only when I was actually driving across from the west coast that it sank in - I would not be able to stay in the apartment. Eventually I did find a place some 50 miles away at Yeehaw Junction – which is as 'hick' as its name implies.

I got the last 'room' they had, sharing with a few wall animals, but it was clean and comfortable and I did have an amusing evening – just like being in The Blitz, I imagine. When I went to leave the following morning, handing in my key which had required a $5 deposit, the proprietor and his wife said they had had an argument after I had gone to bed, because a hysterical woman turned up and would not accept that they had no space. The husband apparently suggested that, as there were two beds in the room they had given me, they should wake me and ask if I would mind sharing. They did not tell me what the woman looked like!

We live on what is known as the 'Treasure Coast' – so called because of the Spanish treasure galleons that gathered to go in convoy across to Spain. So many were lost as they moored in those same summer hurricane seasons, and 85% have still to be discovered. There are literally billions of dollars of gold, silver and jewels lying not far off the Florida coastline, right in front of our home.

The most famous ship eventually discovered was the *Nuestra Senora de Atocha* (whoever she was, she must have been quite a lady!), which went down in 1622 and was finally found by the legendary Mel Fisher in 1985. The Mel Fisher story is well worth reading, and some of the $450 millions of what he found can be seen in two museums – one in the old Naval Station at Key West and the other at Sebastian, near us at Vero Beach.

Mel coined the phrase 'Today's the day!' but, in spite of finding the famous ship, the tale of Mel Fisher is nevertheless sad because, during his 20-year search for the treasure, he lost his oldest son and his daughter-in-law in a boating accident. At the time he was searching in 1960s and 1970s, the law of 'finders keepers' applied to treasure hunting offshore.

Mel raised millions of dollars from private investors to find the ship and its treasure but, when the immense value of what he had found was understood, the USA Department of the Interior stepped in and claimed it all. No compensation, nothing for all his years of work and the investment.

Mel was forced to spend more millions on a huge number of court cases, with the Supreme Court finally finding in his favour and awarding him more or less 99% of the value. A lesser man would never have survived. Mel also found $20m or so with the *Santa Margarita* (sister ship to the *Atocha*), which went down at the same time.

The most interesting piece of information on all this is that what Mel found was only half of the *Atocha*, and the sterncastle half of the ship, containing the greatest amount of treasure, has never been found and his team are still very much looking for it. When I suggested it must be nearby so what was the problem, I was told that it was more buoyant than the main section and, breaking up in a hurricane, could be literally anywhere - anyone for diving?

Our friend Phil Ratcliff, who lives in Vero Beach, is a great treasure-hunter and, in fact, introduced us to John Brandon, who had worked closely with Mel Fisher, and from whom I bought a silver coin from the *Attocha* for Betty to make a medallion. In the two hurricanes of 2004, Phil remained at his home – the most terrifying thing he has ever experienced, he told me later. Phil and his pal aimed to be first out on the beach as soon as the hurricane was dying away, and to get their metal-detectors finding anything the hurricane had exposed. He tells me the lost gold and jewels simply sink lower into the sand every year, and the hurricane is the best sand-blaster he knows – but a bit extreme.

It is an illustration of just what is out there, that Phil very quickly found two 1-escudo gold coins of the 1700s period worth about $8000, plus some silver and other bits of gold and jewellery. His friend, who stayed longer, found five coins and other items. Phil still says he would not do it again – but I wonder.

I think once the treasure bug gets you, you have it for life, and Phil now has a small 'treasure' boat with a 'blower' arranged around the outboard motors, and which he takes out every summer season. If you stay put through a hurricane, as the 'eye' approaches the wind just screams with an absolutely terrifying high pitch, followed by absolute silence as you sit in the 'eye' when it arrives. However, shortly afterwards the screaming starts again just as terrifyingly, as the hurricane moves away.

I am sure Betty was a mermaid in a previous life. She and the two girls have all been scuba diving off Florida and in Barbados, whereas I cannot stand being under water with a mask. If Betty goes down with a group (who are usually men), she will always be the last one up with the dive master, having used maybe 30% of one tank of air, whereas the others will have used their two tanks in full. That really reflects her very calm, patient nature which, as I have told her, reflects her time living with me, when she has been able to hone that skill!

As in the rest of the world, the USA, and maybe Florida in particular, has a problem with obesity – serious obesity in some cases. On occasion, the local newspapers there run competitions to get people on a healthier eating regime. The copy of an email below, which I sent to my children, shows how not everyone is working in the same direction.

'April 24th 2013 from your Dad to Andrew, Rebecca, Alice and Rose.

I know you will all have been concerned as to Betty (in particular!) and me having been able to eat properly and well and keep slim whilst we have been in Florida this year. Be assured there are plenty of opportunities. The local press in Fort Pierce have recently run a competition for their readers to vote on the 'best' of everything in the area. Food featured prominently including where to get the best breakfast – which I am keen on when I go out to get my *New York Times*.

'Today they published the winners and the best breakfast place is deemed to be the Berry Fresh Café in Port St Lucie, not too far from where we live. In the same magazine, Berry Fresh took out a full page advertisement, and one of their regular customers wrote a review for them, I quote:

"It is our 'to go' place when people come from out of town, because the food is simply amazing! We order the Berry Fresh Slam which is two eggs, a sausage patty and red potatoes.

"It comes with pancakes but we ask to switch out of pancakes for their… Chocolate, strawberry, Nutella stuffed French toast"… wait for it, *'This droolworthy French toast is challah bread stuffed with cream cheese, Nutella, bacon, bananas and strawberries'…*wait, there is still more. *'They then roll the French toast in cornflakes, which adds a great crunch to the outside. Pure yummies!'* – so, I thought, there you have it.

But no there was even more! *"To top it off it is served with caramel drizzle and topped off with whipped cream".* I kid you not. For breakfast!? Anyone for lunch there?'

Another thing the Americans are very good at is the use of words for publicity. I wish I had made a note as I travelled around, but sometimes their use in business names makes you laugh out loud. I have seen a ladies' hairdresser called 'Hair Today' which is nothing out of the way, except the next-door travel agents called themselves 'Gone Tomorrow'.

There are endless tourist shops that sell pithy, written 'notes' to put up at home. 'Housework never killed anyone but why take a chance' and 'I smile because you are my sister, but I laugh because there is nothing you can do about it,' are two of my favourites.

In my office I have long had a plaque hanging there which, if you think about it, helps us all to look at business problems in the right way.

'The objective of all dedicated employees should be to thoroughly analyse all situations, anticipate all problems prior to their occurrence, have answers for these problems and to move swiftly to solve these problems when called upon to do so. However.................... When you are up to your ass in alligators it is difficult to remind yourself your initial objective was to drain the swamp'

I have described my two USA business involvements in a later chapter, but one by-product of them was meeting Richard Corlin, the long-suffering President of *SecureCare*, who is the much respected ex-President of the *American Medical Association*. Richard has become a business friend, I think simply because he won't go away and I am still here. In the mid 2000s I was a Liveryman of the *Worshipful Company of Glovers* in the City of London, as I have mentioned in Chapter Five, and thinking on how Americans just love the British way of pageant and ceremony, I invited Richard and his wife to the annual banquet the *Glovers* give for the Lord Mayor of London in the *Mansion House*.

Because of work commitments, Richard simply could not come over, but as a result he invited Betty and me to the annual Black and White Ball in Los Angeles, held at the *Beverley Wilshire*, where we stayed. Oh boy! It is somewhat out of kilter with what we have in the UK, where I am used to raising money for charities. First, on entering the reception for about 500, there were enough bar staff on hand to be making individual cocktails for each guest.

Richard's wife, Katherine, was the Chairman for the evening, aimed at raising substantial money for the new wing of a cancer- or heart hospital nearby. During the meal, various guests would stand and make statements like: 'Richard, we got together as a family before we came over, and we have decided to give you another $1 million' – several of those. Then it came to speeches and the chief 'Honoree' as they are called in the USA. I am sure I exaggerate the figures, but he was a Bill Gates type, who gave them something like $5m, to be followed by $1m a year for 15 years. Incredible! I have been used to raising £10,000 on an evening and calling the event a huge success!

However, best of all, at the end of the dinner another of Richard's friends got up and said that, although he did not have any millions to add to the funds, he had prevailed on an old friend of his to break a world tour and appear for the dinner. Would we please welcome Burt Bacharach!!

For Betty and me the perfect end to a most wonderful evening, dancing to the original Burt. Even I could not arrange a surprise like that, so maybe I am excused for the next five years. In typical American style, as we have discovered, by about 9.30 or so the floor was almost deserted and everyone gone home to bed, so Burt was playing for the two of us and maybe three other couples!

Betty and I still talk about travelling Route 66 in a luxury campervan as, in spite of all our time and travels in the USA, we know so little of the interior. I perhaps doubt we will ever do it in that style now, but we did take one other trip not yet mentioned, to Alaska.

Because I am simply not the gregarious party animal that some can be, I have never been interested in cruise-ship holidays. However, we found ourselves arriving in Vancouver in order to go down to Seattle later to see our friends there, and thought a six-day cruise to Alaska to the origin of the goldfields would be fun and interesting. I had just read James Michener's *Alaska* and my imagination was fired up.

The first problem I imagined was: would we be designated to sit and eat for a week with people we did not like? No problem, we got the Chief of Police in San Diego and his family, who turned out to be great fun. At the end of the trip, and knowing a friend of mine was the Chief Constable in Norfolk, he gave me an 'honour' badge and appointment of him as Deputy in San Diego, which I made a great fuss of presenting to him the next time he came to lunch.

The trip was everything we expected, except there was no time to walk the actual Chilkoot Pass, which is what had fascinated me in the book. Great seeing Juneau and Skagway, and we really got the feeling of the old mining towns. We should have gone cruise ship one way and plane home, as the return trip was boring, with the ship-owners simply trying to sell you anything they could. There was a 'fine art auction' advertised, which we went to inspect before the actual auction. There was nothing on display except prints of various pictures which we thought must be photographs of the real thing, because estimated prices were between $1,000 and $10,000.

Imagine our astonishment when we were told by a bow-tie auctioneer that they were what you would be buying, and also: 'First we have had all these works of art 'appraised' by Bloggs, Bloggs and Bloggs of New York, and there will be a flat $100 fee for a certificate of value from them. Second, as they are all stored in our New York warehouse, they will be mailed to you and there will be a set $100 fee for that mailing. Finally, there will, of course, be the usual 10% auction fee added to the final sale price.' Only when we asked if the prices included frames did we discover you would just be mailed a rolled-up 'print'. How many would you like?

But they did sell for thousands, which just shows what the right setting and atmosphere can lull USA tourists into spending. I had cause to write to the cruise company later and, in passing, said that if they ever put the 'fine art' enterprise out for tender, to let me know.

Betty with 80lbs Wahoo caught in Fiji islands

The Transcontinental Hotel in Oodnadata Australia

Surprise party for Betty at Maxims Paris

The £1000 ski chalet in Chateau D'Oex

Grandchildren Ben, Imogen and
Abigail Tassie at Disney Florida

Vineyard party
invitation 2003

Joe and Betty Larter
request the pleasure of the company of

David and Margaret Barnsley

....

to **SUPPER** *and* **JAZZ**
on March 29th 2003 to celebrate
their first grape harvest at
the Northbank vineyard, Tuamarina Road
Blenheim,

6.30pm onwards at the vineyard.
RSVP joelarter@hotmail.com

Betty in Northbank vineyard, Blenheim South Island New Zealand

Twin sister Mary (Lovewell Blake) as Queen Victoria when Palmers Stores in Great Yarmouth celebrated 150 years of business

Mary with Prince of Wales when she retired from Great Yarmouth College EDP 2012

Chapter Ten
Sealife, Bure Valley Railway, Pleasurewood Hills Sold, a Disaster and a Great Wedding

Back in the UK, with £3.5 million from the *Tesco* sale banked and lots of plans to expand, we were on a roll. We were a public company with about 100 shareholders who loved us and were making money, and I was set for the tourist, and not the holiday camp, industry. We even had a happy bank manager!

Looking around for new ideas, we did not want to start charging all over the country to build things, and I hoped to quietly expand from our Norfolk base. Brian Soloman, the tourism officer for Waveney, whom I had got to know well during the *Pleasurewood* land negotiations, came to see me and asked if I would consider building one of the new *Sealife Centres* for the seafront at Lowestoft.

Knowing nothing about them, I contacted David Mace, who was leading the *Sealife* company, and visited Portsmouth to see what they were all about – brilliant, I thought. They had a 'wow' factor with the big fish and a glass, walk-through tunnel; it was all about education as well and, unlike *Pleasurewood Hills*, they were year-round, indoor attractions. With *Sealife*, we signed a 5-centre deal – that we could build three centres in the UK and two abroad, and the parent company would get a small percentage of turnover for the use of the name and logos.

Unfortunately for Brian, it seemed very obvious to me that Great Yarmouth seafront was the place to have one in our area, not Lowestoft, and I think he was disappointed, because it was his idea. Chris Mitchell, a local surveyor with *English Estates*, had now joined the company to look after the property side and help Tom O'Hanlon with construction, and he negotiated a Great Yarmouth seafront site.

However, before we could get down to detail, Chris had also found another intriguing site by the sea at Hunstanton, on the other side of Norfolk – an old boating lake. Hunstanton Council was equally keen to have a centre and we thought it not too close to Great Yarmouth to spoil the scheme there. We negotiated a long lease, and our first *Sealife Centre* was constructed at Hunstanton.

Actually it was quite good for us to put our toes in the water with a smaller scheme, before the much bigger attraction planned for Great Yarmouth. Hunstanton opened in 1989 at a cost of £1.25m was, and still is, a great success and addition to the town. Where we disagreed with David Mace over the centres was that he never quoted enough as the likely cost.

Yes, you could have a tin shed and no windows, or catering for the sort of £700/800k he always talked about but, for long-term quality and investment, which is what we as a public company were about, we spent twice what he suggested at Hunstanton and three times at Great Yarmouth.

At the time we built the Great Yarmouth unit, it was the largest *Sealife Centre* in Europe. There is no doubt that, for the area at that time, what we built at Great Yarmouth made a significant difference to the future of the seafront and tourism, and complemented our *Pleasurewood* park at Lowestoft. When they had a local authority tourism conference in the *Marina Centre* that year, I was asked to address them about what we had done. I remember one rather pompous lady at question-time asking me what I thought about keeping animals (i.e. fish) in captivity.

I rather flippantly replied (because she had irritated me so much!) that I understood why she had asked her question, but at *Sealife* we were very fair. We used the local fishermen to catch for us and, when they got a fish, they always asked it if it would like to go to the fishmongers or to the Great Yarmouth *Sealife Centre*. It drew not one titter! But there were no more questions.

However, my favourite story from that meeting was of its Chairman, the much-loved, absolutely larger-than-life Gerald Milsom, who owned the famous *Le Talboothe* restaurant in Dedham, near Colchester. He was Chairman of the East Anglian Tourist Authority at that time, and the sponsor of the event was the *Midland Bank*, and some high official was sitting beside him.

Gerald opened with hardly a welcome and then said: "Once upon a time an old couple in Colchester went to their local *Midland Bank* and asked to borrow £500 towards buying an old property on the river at Dedham, where they wanted to open a tea room (that of course is now *Le Talboothe*). The Manager would not lend, and told them not to be so silly, as it would never work, and Gerald said: 'That is why my family and I never have banked, and never will bank, with the *Midland Bank*." He did not get much of a laugh either, but we both appreciated each other!

Gerald was a gentleman in the true sense of the word, and he had style! There were times when Alan Hills, of the Colchester building firm, invited both Gerald and me to sail with him for the day on his fabulous Swan boat, the *Surveyor*. On occasion we would end up at Harwich, where Gerald had a great fish restaurant. On arriving at the dock, his 'man' would be waiting with a silver tray, a bottle of *Veuve Cliquot* champagne, and three glasses. I like it already.

At the same time as we developed our *Sealife* ideas, 'Happy' Hudson and his partner, John of *Pleasurewood Hills* miniature steam fame, came to see me again and said **they** had been negotiating with Mid-Norfolk Council at Aylsham, and we could have a 10-mile stretch of disused railway between Wroxham and Aylsham for a steam railway. We drove the old track in a Land Rover and agreed it would make a great route and attraction.

They planned a 15-inch narrow-gauge steamer, and would build the stock themselves at Great Yarmouth – with the main base, with station, shop and restaurant at Aylsham, and a station at the Wroxham end – very close to the mainline station. Betty and I visited a number of similar ventures, including again the *Romney, Hythe and Dymchurch* I had ridden all those years ago as a cadet at KES. We were all hooked on the idea and, although we did not see it making mega-bucks, it would make an important addition to the collection of attractions we hoped to develop.

All lives and businesses have peaks and troughs and, looking back, I think I can say that *Pleasurewood Hills*, and the constructions of the first *Sealife Centre* and then the *Bure Valley Railway*, coincided with the peak of my business life with me just 50 – maybe I should say the peak of my 'first' business life.

Around this time, *Pleasureworld* attracted the interest of a listed public company run by Robert K (Bob) Francis, the same Bob Francis I had met with Ludkin in the days when he was trying to take over *WA Hills* in Colchester. So that we would know each other better, he got me to events and to join a charity known as *The Guild of The Nineteen Lubricators*, I believe originally started by nineteen oil executives, and where Bob was very much the lead. I joined, but immediately realized that this hard-drinking, very much racehorse-orientated group was not really my style. I did, however, enjoy the two or three events a year with Betty, including a great group visit on the actual Derby Day.

The main fund-raising event for the *Lubricators* is a huge charity dinner on the eve of The Derby, where they raise many thousands for poorly-placed children – a lot in the East End of London. We had the Bishop of Salisbury and another Bishop, John, who was based in the East End, as our 'chaplains', Salisbury in particular being a very unusual and amusing man. I recall him introducing his wife to people when they met, saying: 'This is my first wife.'

During the charity dinner, the guests can buy tickets to 'draw' a horse, or at auction afterwards you can 'buy' a horse – the 'owners' then winning a large sum of money in the £000s according to where 'their' horse ends up in the race itself the following day.

During my membership I invited 6 or 8 business people from Norfolk to join my table for the dinner and, of course, they all bought tickets. We did not have the winner of the race but, for some obscure reason, the horse that comes LAST is also awarded a very substantial sum, and we were last! Some very amazed Norfolk people received a meaningful cheque from me a week later as their share of the winnings.

You could not help but like the energy and 'charisma' of Bob, and one day he said: 'Look, I would like *RKF Group* to take over your company. *RKF* already has a property side, two printing businesses and an engineering arm. If we add your leisure side, we would have a really interesting mix so that, should one business section be down, another will be up and we ought to have a safe and evenly balanced company.' That seemed sensible, and we invited him to make an offer.

When the offer came in it looked generous at about 1/4 more than we had expected, and we thought our shareholders would be pleased and well looked-after. For me personally, he said that within three years he would step down and he hoped I would be ready to take over control of *RKF* plc and develop it in my way, as no other members of the Board were interested.

Bob suggested that we *Pleasureworld* shareholders took reasonable cash (he was selling more *RKF* shares to the City to raise it), and I in particular was encouraged to keep a high share stake in what I thought would shortly be 'my' company. At just 50, this was a very flattering position to be in – but here I was handing over my life's work of over 30 years into the control of a group of strangers with 80% (£5m) of my value in their shares, albeit quoted.

In selling the takeover idea to the city, he got me to endless meetings, explaining what we did and how we hoped to expand – more *Sealife Centres* and including a second theme park in Cleethorpes, where Chris had identified another site. We were going to need a lot of cash, and I was delighted at the prospect of supposedly having that responsibility taken away from me by the *RKF* finance department.

One very good thing to come out of the takeover was our hiring Clive Preston as Managing Director of the whole company, so I could get on with acquisitions. Clive had a great history with *First Leisure* and other companies, and had a whole new approach to running the attractions. Sadly, he hardly had his feet under the table when *RKF* fell into trouble. Clive went on to help another troubled public company owning bars and pubs, with enormous success, and then to start his own pub group. I met up with him many years later and, of course, had the 'what if' thought together on what we might have achieved.

In the two years *Pleasureworld* was owned by RKF we managed to complete the second *Sealife Centre* at Great Yarmouth and also the *Bure Valley Railway*. I think what we did with *Sealife* was inject theming expertise and make realistic settings for the marine life - reefs, sunken treasure, wrecks, and so on.

One nice side-effect from the *Sealife Centres* for me was that Jan Jaworskyj, who was the lovely young lady assistant running the Hunstanton Centre, came over to run the Great Yarmouth Centre – and also to run my son Andrew's life as well – not before time, I hear her say. They married in 1993 and we were all very happy for them. We had a lot of fun, with a great wedding in Freethorpe near their home and a rather emotional Jan.

Jan has reminded me that our Manager at Hunstanton, Ian Foster, returned £400 to our first visitors from his personal money because they complained his 'walk under water' advertising led them to believe they would be walking under the sea itself, and not just a tunnel. About as realistic as the *Pleasurewood* man who wanted his food and ice cream for free because we said there was '£2.50 a day and no more to pay'. People!

I hadn't heard that story before, and certainly would not have agreed to him spending his own money, but he felt responsible. The Great Yarmouth *Sealife Centre* was opened on 3 July 1990, by Michael Fish of BBC TV weather fame.

The *Bure Valley Railway* was a lot more difficult to build and run than we thought, because of engineering technicalities and all the health and safety regulations to follow. We got to the opening day on 10 July 1990 and Miles Kington, the author and great steam enthusiast, came to open it for us. **Everyone** wanted to come to the opening, as it was such a dramatic project for the area – but we invited too many!

The plan for the day was for us all to ride from Wroxham to the main Aylsham base and have a tape-cutting ceremony and reception there. Bank managers, directors, press, TV and all the great and good were on board, with two engines to ensure there were no problems. Problem! Wroxham requires an uphill start, and that's something we didn't manage!! One of the more embarrassing moments in my business life was to see the staff, directors and anyone we could get, including me, leave the train to – push. All taken in great humour, as 15-inch narrow gauge is really quite small, but something we could have done without.

The theme park site which Chris Mitchell had found us in Cleethorpes, although not the centre of the world, would be more or less free and the local authority wanted it developed. I got out a design based on some infrastructure already there, and we planned a Lincolnshire *Pleasurewood Hills*. We thought we had a good basic plan now – nothing too over the top, but a good family attraction, barbecues of course, and a whole new catchment area. Tom O'Hanlon moved to a weekday base there, started planning and construction in a small way, and we would have had it open for not a lot of cost.

But RKF now rapidly ran into trouble and, within 2 years of buying us, could not fund any of the schemes on which we had embarked. The £3.5m we had when they came in had gone to 'central accounting' on day one, and I was now stunned to be asked to find a buyer for *Pleasureworld* itself as it was the best part of the company for RKF to sell, and within months we were in full receivership. How on earth had this happened? On our own we could have used our £3.5m plus, say, another £3.5m raised with it, and had all the developments we wanted.

With that wonderful stuff, hindsight, it is easy to say we should have investigated our buyer before selling out, but we were dealing with a fully-listed plc.

It seems that, before the *Pleasureworld* purchase, *RKF* had made some large, off balance sheet, joint investments in property to be developed with another company, but with *RKF* guaranteeing the investment funds and picking up the interest downside if it happened – which of course it did. Maybe all sensible at the time it was done, but not when it went wrong and annual interest was running finally at about £3m – more than the whole of *RKF* earned in a year. Those property investments with wrong timing are what took the company down, and no amount of pleading would get the banks to ring-fence that financing and leave us to continue the other profitable businesses.

As a person to be a future major investor in *RKF* through the shares I got for my sale, it would have been nice to have known of these 'investments' at the time.

Worst of all for Betty and the family, we still lived in the company-owned converted Old Stables near Gunton Hall which we had sold to *Warners*, and which we had not asked to buy because we wanted to live more centrally. We could have had that property included just for taking less shares, but now most of the cash element I had received had gone to a lovely, old, moated property we were restoring near Stowmarket. There we hoped to live and make it easier for me to commute when needed to Worthing, where *RKF* (my!) head office was based. That all had to be unscrambled at a great loss, with us never even moving in, and we were left camping for the time being in our home now owned by the (I have to say, soon a very sympathetic) Receiver of the *RKF Group*.

Property developers are always optimists, and you can perhaps blame this on timing, but I think the £3.5m sitting in the *Pleasureworld* bank was the reason for making a good offer to us and, overall, the situation was not far short of a fraud – at least on me personally. I can only add that Bob Francis died very shortly from a cancer he had also kept quiet about, and you could not imagine a sadder end for what ought to have been a very exciting time.

I now had to scramble to get together what other funds I had, and sell property or whatever so that we could survive with a viable future, including selling our little London flat where I had so carefully cleared the mortgage. The frightening realization that came to me in the middle of many sleepless nights was that I really had lost the bulk of all I had built up in 30 years.

This was not stock market investments, that go up and down but, like the parrot in the John Cleese sketch, this was dead, caput, L.O.S.T! It would never be coming back to life. I had to more or less start again, and my base from which to do it was gone as well, alongside a lot of my personal esteem.

Maybe I overreacted a little as, when I stand back, I did have other much smaller investments, and I was certainly not going to be penniless. It was just a huge, huge shock to the system, and very difficult for a while to see the wood from the trees. That is where Betty's calm, scuba-diving make-up came to help, and we worked out a plan forward again.

Within a few months (which seemed like several years to me) the Receiver decided, in 1991, that really the only buyers for the old *Pleasureworld* set-up would be the original vendors. When I had recovered some confidence, and with the considerable assistance of Huw Walters, who became our unofficial Finance Director, we persuaded *Legal and General Ventures* to back us, and a new company rose from the ashes of *RKF*.

We did leave the *Bure Valley Railway* behind, as we could not put forward a good case for it being hugely profitable – and that left Happy Hudson and John Edwards at a loose end. *BVR* was bought privately, and has since been very successful, building up a large body of skilled volunteers, which makes it more viable. For a new group like us, on mostly borrowed capital, it would have been a luxury.

So now, with the team of me, Huw Walters, Gavin Briggs, Tony Shorthose and Peter Hadden, plus an appointment *Legal and General* made as their Chairman (who was NOT a happy appointment and soon left, with Huw taking over), rather like *The Owl and the Pussycat*, we set off across the seas in a new boat called *Pleasureworld II*.

Our base was now in Oswald House at Southtown, Great Yarmouth, which I had bought with my small personal company a few years before to house *Seaforths Travel* for Jenny Mills, of which you will hear more later. We had *Pleasurewood Hills* (where Peter Hadden was the Operations Director) and the two *Sealife Centres*, with Jan and

Andrew much involved and Andrew looking after catering in all the attractions, and me looking around for new ideas.

First was something I had seen Geoffrey Thompson put in at *Blackpool Pleasure Beach* – a *Ripley's Believe It or Not!* I went to see various *Ripley's* attractions in the USA, where the idea originated, visiting four *Ripley's* in six days, and came back to look for a site. In the USA I had seen some amazing presentations, and one I particularly liked was in the vaults of a bank in Hollywood.

Bob Masterson and the *Jim Pattison Group* based in Canada had acquired all the rights and artifacts originating from Robert Ripley, who had spent the 20s and 30s collecting the weird and the wonderful – the biggest, the tallest, the fattest, the most awful and the most strange, from around the world. The *Pattison Group* had put them together as collections, like a *Guinness Book of Records* come to life, and Masterson and his gang had continued to collect all over the world. Buying parts of the Berlin Wall as it came down was a typical example of what they did, and I have a piece on my desk to this day.

I could not find a bank I could empty, but I persuaded *Pleasureworld II* that we should take a lease on the old *Windmill Theatre* in Great Yarmouth, opposite our *Sealife Centre*. I spent the winter altering the building and preparing the site with Tom O'Hanlon, and then alongside Sylvia Matiko and Norman Deska, the *Ripley's* VPs of Development and Marketing, installing the collection allotted to us. Absolutely brilliant and, in my view, the best quality attraction I ever built. We even had a replica of Mr Ripley himself, standing beside a real, single-engine plane inside the building, one that had crashed elsewhere and which we had bought.

I met various *Ripley's* franchise-holders at IAPPA meetings, two being the charming Mario Rabner and his English wife, who had the franchise and a museum in Mexico City. They invited Betty and me to stay at their home and showed us Mexico City itself, including the fabulous temple, Templo Mayor.

The temple had been built by the Aztecs in 1325, but partially destroyed and covered over, including the contents, by the Spanish in 1521, and then largely forgotten. Not until 27 February 1978 was it finally properly discovered, by some electrical contractors working in the city. A large number of buildings had to then be demolished to excavate the temple, and those excavations were affected by the 1985 earthquake. Some absolutely amazing artifacts had been discovered.

The other thing we experienced in Mexico City for the first time was the driving system whereby, if you owned a car, you could only use it on every **other** day. As Mario pointed out, often these government-made rules, so well-intentioned, have unintended consequences. People simply bought two cars and increased traffic, rather than reduced it.

After our visit, Mario sent us off to stay in their holiday home in Acapulco. We had a great time there; I caught 'Montezuma's Revenge' (a local tummy-bug) but recovered, and we invited Mario and his wife to stay with us in Norfolk, although I am not sure how the castle at Norwich and the Norfolk Broads measured up to a 1325 Aztec temple.

The trouble was that we really could not make *Ripley's* work in Great Yarmouth, no matter how hard we tried – somehow the UK public did not get the idea. I believe Geoffrey Thompson had the same problem in Blackpool but, being on the *Pleasure Beach* there, he had a captive audience. Those who did go inside loved it.

We had a great opening, having hired Christopher Greener, an accountant who is the tallest man in the UK at 7ft 6.25ins, and we had an amusing story to tell our guests. Since *Ripley's* is a walk-round attraction, we could not have a tape-cutting ceremony, especially in June when the Great Yarmouth season had started, so he and I greeted everyone at the entrance. Our guests then looked round and went across the road to the *Sealife Centre* restaurant for the reception, where we then introduced *Ripley's*.

Bystanders gathered to see what was going on and, at one point, a little girl dipped under the protective barrier and asked Chris if she could have his autograph 'because you are the tallest man in the world.' He gladly obliged, and then she handed me the book (standing at 5ft 3ins against 7ft 6ins) and said: 'And you must be the smallest man in the world, so can I have your autograph too?!' which I happily gave her.

Although we tried everything, we could not make the sort of return our venture capitalist investors (and we) expected and, very reluctantly, at the end of a five-year lease of the Windmill, we had to dismantle and return everything to the USA. But by then we were also ready to move on again.

I think the problem we had at *Pleasureworld II* was that a theme park-type group cannot be run by a committee. I had been the creator of *Pleasureworld*, and not always do I know exactly why I want to do something, or even get it right, but most times it turns out OK – or at least very interesting. Of course, also, we did not have that £3.5m in the bank and the asset base I had spent 30 years building up, and we were properly constrained by L&G to get returns for them and us on the borrowed money.

Not quite like getting a return for shareholders' investment, with interest to pay on borrowed money as well, you really have to earn it twice. Also the team with me, who were now equal directors and shareholders, and not just executives, had different desires and aims – although Huw did his best to keep us peaceful.

No one particular thing triggered it, but for me, with no freedom to be myself and, maybe, not being on the park day-to-day, I became very unhappy and we all agreed it would be best to find a buyer. This we did after a couple of years, in the form of Philip Mason and his *Queensborough Holdings*, who bought the business in April 1996, giving us a modest profit, and we each could get on with our lives.

Gavin Briggs went with *Queens*, with great future success, and Tony set up a joint marketing business with Ian Russell, of *Wroxham Barns* fame. Peter Hadden stayed to run *Pleasurewood* and, when *Queens* bought *Lightwater Valley* in Yorkshire as well, he ran both. When *Queens* sold out its leisure attractions to concentrate on the caravan business, Peter was able, with his wife, to buy *Pleasurewood* himself, and ran it very successfully until he in turn sold to a French-based group.

In 2008 the French group invited me back to cut the 25th anniversary tape on re-opening day. I remember a lovely girl, who did not know who I was, giving me a wrist-band and explaining carefully that I could go on all the rides as many times as I liked. In turn, that French group sold to another one and, in June 2013, I was again on the park with Woody to cut the 30th anniversary tape. Déjà vu!

The new French owners really do understand the park has to have quality and they are also bringing back the American theme for Woody, and my barbecues.

For me after *Pleasureworld II*? Well I had the base at Southtown Road and my *Seaforths* involvement, so it was time to move on, and for the next stage of my complicated business life.

Chapter Eleven

Seaforths, Dutch Again, Bygone Village, Recovery, Some Fun, and Woody sees off Mr Blobby

My *Pleasurewood Hills* era was at an end and, in a way, it was 'Been there, done that and got the T–shirt,' let's move on to a new life. During my momentary success at the time of the *RKF* sale, I made an investment to help out Jenny Mills, a friend of Betty's. The lesson learned here is that, in my opinion, it never hurts to be kind and helpful to people when you are in a position to do so.

Jenny Mills had a great travel business based in Great Yarmouth, Lowestoft and Aberdeen, at which she had worked hard with an aunt when she was younger, and had taken over when the aunt died. She and her partner, Conrad O'Riodan, had built up a business with a high reputation as the best agents in the area, with (luckily, as it turned out) a very loyal customer-base, and Jenny was a bit of a legend in the area and very popular.

She had phoned Betty one week, very worried; she had a business problem, which Betty encouraged her to come and discuss with me. 'Could I help?' she asked, as we sat over coffee one Saturday morning and she related her story. Conrad wanted to retire and, under the terms of the partnership agreement, she had to buy him out, which she did not at that time have the cash to do.

However, her real problem was that the people working in her offices in Great Yarmouth had other ideas as well. They saw Jenny as very vulnerable, particularly as one of the gang forming against her was the company accountant, who also looked after her personal affairs, tax returns and so on.

Thus armed with the inside information that she did not have £ thousands to buy out the partner, the two had turned up one day at her house before breakfast and told her not to bother going to the office much more. They were forming their own company and, as 'they' were the guys on the shop floor, of course the customers would move over to them. She had, they said, had her turn!

Jenny was beside herself with fury, as she had been a really generous employer; but what to do? After discussions with Jenny, I arranged to meet the ringleader in the Great Yarmouth office and offer him could the chance to a buy proportion of the business, paid for out of future profits, as it seemed ridiculous to be fighting with a man who had apparently been a good manager, although that was Jenny's view.

'Stop interfering' was the message I received so, on behalf of Jenny I didn't get mad, but encouraged her to get even.

I went to Jenny's office and told her that when I had gone, if she wished, she could tell the man that as of today *Seaforths* had a new partner – I would buy Conrad's share. I do not get outraged very often – but that was one time when I did.

Next, Jenny and I went to Aberdeen to see the operation there, meet the staff and reassure them, because we thought they would have heard about the rebellion in Great Yarmouth. Too right! The manager in Aberdeen had been very ill recently and Jenny, in her usual style, had looked after him; full pay whilst in hospital and recovery.

When we carefully explained the situation to him, his reply was that he knew all about it and he and his staff were all leaving as well. I asked him when they would be doing that, and he said that they had intended to leave, with the exception of one person, on the following Monday, and they had not intended to tell Jenny in advance. Nice people.

Jenny and I were both stunned, and went to another office to regroup! We could not fight fires on all fronts and did our best to persuade him and his wife to stay.

I made it clear to him in no uncertain terms that, after all the support Jenny had given him, no way was he leaving at what was now three days' notice, and we shamed him into agreeing they would all stay until the end of the month. Dear Eleanor, the one member of staff staying, was a brick and helped us enormously up there until she retired many years later. Large G & Ts on the plane on the way home, as we still wondered how we would cope. Whereupon, Jenny had her own serendipitous moment!

A travel agent called Gary Hance, running a branch of another large travel business in Aberdeen, was not exactly happy there. He called Jenny the following day and said he had heard on the grapevine of the problem she had, and could he help? We duly met and interviewed him that same week at Heathrow, and appointed him on the spot as the new partner in Aberdeen. He had to give a month's notice to his old company, and none of us was to mention his joining *Seaforths* until he had worked that out.

Contrary to what the manager in Great Yarmouth had expected, Jenny retained all her customers and, over the next two years, the business settled down and *Seaforths* rented and moved into a building on Southtown Road, which my own small company had bought. The rest became storage units as 'U–Store' in the American style and, later, our *Pleasureworld II* offices as well.

With later expansion as our oil-related customers set up bases in Bracknell, we opened an office there. Gary Hance was very much an IT man and, as *Seaforths*, we developed some of the first internet and online booking systems, which were to hold us in good stead.

Meanwhile, in the winter of 91/92, Joe Larter still had his *Pleasureworld II* hat on and, whilst I was constructing the *Ripley's Believe it or Not!* attraction at Great Yarmouth, another Dutchman turned up; Henry Holterman. From that first meeting we were to have an over-15-year involvement together.

Henry had been sent to me by Henk Bembom Sr of the *Pleasurewood Hills* days, and had a problem in that he urgently needed a *Sealife Centre* built in a tourist attraction his employer, Dick Wessels, had in Vlissingen on the coast of Holland. Henry had asked Bembom to provide it, but had been told the man to see was me, as I had just built two of them. For Mr Bembom – anything!

The problem was that we had no time and no building team, so we sent Henry to another group, who designed and quoted but then, at the last minute, said they too could not build it after all. Back to me and, because of the Bembom connection, we really could not say 'no'. With Chris Mitchell and Tom O'Hanlon, we somehow put together a European construction team and carried out the contract PDQ. A bit of a nightmare in an old building and some cracked glass at a late stage, but we got it open and a friendship developed between Henry and me, although a relationship entirely different from that with Bembom.

We followed the Vlissingen aquarium with Bruce Carter and I restoring *Miniature World* at Walcheren for Wessels, a lovely park for, small children, and we put in (of course) a miniature railway. I never got to 'know' Wessels, as he spoke no English and I no Dutch and, for later, I think that was a pity.

Before we move to the development of *Seaforths* and IT, I was still *Pleasureworld II* until 1996 and had people turning up on my doorstep with ideas and proposals, not all of which the new *Pleasureworld* team would look at.

First up was 'Happy' Hudson who, since the *Pleasureworld II* venture did not buy back the *Bure Valley Railway,* had been looking for his own next venture. After several false starts, he came to me with a receivership he had found – *The Bygone Heritage Village* at Fleggburgh, eight miles north from Great Yarmouth and which we eventually renamed *The Village.*

A strange mixture of a collection of antique steam engines and fairground items, it needed turning into a proper tourist attraction. Who better than the very guys who had started and then brought *Pleasurewood Hills* to the 552,000 visitor attraction that it became? A piece of cake, we thought.

Business plan made, Receiver negotiated down to £800,000 and investors assembled, including Ken Sims of the nearby *Thrigby Wildlife Park* (ex KES school with me) as our Chairman, and loan arranged. On 13 June 1993 we bought the collection, all the properties, and about 40 acres of land. To get a reasonable return we needed about 120,000 visitors for the year and, although we added some really nice, quirky items over time, including old-fashioned rides, an original Cake Walk and a Haunted Room, we never could get past the 100,000 level.

Pleasureworld II would not agree to invest in this, so my share was on a personal level. With the other feelings floating around, I think that also contributed towards us ending the new *Pleasurewood* business, as we were not on the same wavelength. Let's just talk 'illusions' for a moment, because they fascinate me.

What I learned from my original Disney visit in 1976 was that, in darkness, you can make believe anything you like. Simply by tilting the floor of a room against you and painting sight-lines in the wrong direction, you could be totally confused. You think you are going to walk 'up' but find you are actually walking 'down'.

The old 'haunted' room we bought for the Village was an original classic but, in reality, was simply a large swing-seat in the centre of a room. A 'real' room with windows, doorways, furniture against the walls, flowers on a table, and so on. The visitor sits in the swing-seat (six at a time) in the semi-darkness and *thinks* the chair is starting to swing, whereas it does not!

It is the **room** that starts to revolve around you and eventually goes completely over 360 degrees. Imagine how the 'rider' feels. You see them gripping the seat sides and each other for dear life, and people have come out totally disorientated, not believing what had happened, when actually they had not moved at all. At the same time the room has to be totally enclosed, hiding it from the public waiting for the next 'ride', so as not to give the game away.

It was for the same sort of reason that my mother would never believe that the submarine ride in Disney is not actually under water. It is all done by paintings on the wall of the channel as they move along, and bubbles, giving the impression of going down. One 'illusion' that terrified both Betty and me was in one of the downtown Orlando attractions, when they had them in the centre there. I have forgotten what it was called – 'House of Horrors' maybe, but you entered what you thought was a horror museum except that, as you went through, you found some of the particularly gruesome models were real people.

Frightening! And, right at the end, one ghoulish chap came alive and started a chainsaw, chasing you through rooms and corridors, and finally into a room with no exit except a large, mouse-type hole near the bottom of one wall, through which I can assure you we left as fast as any mouse.

At *The Village*, we tried everything we could think of. We inherited a large, steel barn, so added a section to it and installed really nice catering for big events, organized by Andrew and Jan. We then had Terry Hepworth, the organ buff from Gunton Hall, build up what was heading towards being the largest theatre-organ in Europe, for daily and special concerts.

All, in the end, to no avail. There was a bit of profit one year, a bit of loss the next, and the Board decided in September 2004 to close it and we auctioned the remaining collection the following month. No one could say that in 10 years we had not tried. To try to recover our investment and get a return for our investors, we applied for planning permission for houses on some of the land. We got a very reluctant approval for limited building and, in due course, sold the whole scheme to *Tredwell Developments* in 2006.

Why did it not work? I think we just had bad luck on timing. The previous owner had built the Bygone Village as a personal hobby, with no understanding of how to attract, or even look after, the public. He got his bank to finance a collection of steam engines and old rides expecting them to rise in value enormously, which they did not. As a result, the history for the visiting public was terrible and we had first to overcome that; but also, whereas *Pleasurewood* had coaches coming weekly from all the local holiday camps, the camps themselves were declining and had by then woken up to the fact that they could earn more money by keeping everyone in-house.

Another business approach I had was from Reece Hedges – the son of the Alfred Hedges who had been so good to me at Winterton in the days after my father was ill. He was Alfred's son, so I felt I had to help him if I could. Reece had been working for a company called *Caddymatic*, which manufactured electric golf-trolleys in the Midlands and, in fact, were No 2 in the market, which is what attracted us.

Again a personal investment, but could we find £14,000, I think it was, to take over from a Receiver (again)? He would run it. With Huw Walters, I went to see him and the company; we liked the idea and backed him, only to discover neither we nor he were made for the manufacturing business. We made an enormous effort with Reece, but the trolleys just had too much competition, and Reece would agree he is no manufacturer. In the end, after three years of trying, we were happy to hand it over to a German customer for nothing, and even they did not survive.

Also during this period, I got involved in an advisory way with Philip Mason of *Queensborough Holdings* after he had bought *Pleasureworld II*. Nothing very serious, but I think we liked each other and he was involved in building up his group as fast as he could. I had experience and maybe I could help.

Philip had a park on the Isle of Wight, which I visited several times, and was also involved in an attraction at Land's End that had been built up by Peter de Savary. It was very impressive and there was a lot to discuss with one of our ex-*Pleasurewood* managers then running it. Philip was also involved with Noel Edmonds of TV fame and the *Crinkly Bottom* attraction in Devon, and we did try to give some good advice there. I also remember looking at *The Cheddar Cheese Company* with him, which I really liked, but we could not agree suitable terms on which to buy it; I also spent some time with him at the old Liverpool Garden Festival site.

In *Pleasurewood Hills II* days, Tony Shorthose in particular wanted us to tie up with Mr Blobby of the Noel Edmonds TV show, which we did attempt, with me leading the negotiations. However, we already had our so-famous (locally) Woody Bear, that Blobby was not the attraction he might have been elsewhere. The idea was that he would be in the Castle show and we would get an occasional visit from Edmonds – in return for quite a high fee.

At the same time, it was decided to remove the word 'American' from the name '*Pleasurewood Hills*', and so I think, in a way, we started to lose our previous very focused direction – again a committee running it. The focus today is more and more on steel rides, and I see the latest owners now call it *Pleasurewood Thrills*, but Woody Bear still leads the publicity.

These things were all happening in the early 1990s and, in November 1994, the National Lottery was launched, with Noel Edmonds leading the way as presenter. I had nothing to do with the Lottery itself, but it was right at the time I was meeting Edmonds over Blobby, and maybe this was to be my second 5 minutes of fame.

Betty and I had friends, Jane and Henry Burke, who were very serious about amateur dramatics and who were building their own theatre - *The Playhouse* – in Norwich. They came to a small dinner-party at our house when they were still short of about £400,000 to finish the main construction, having already put a very large sum of their personal money into the project.

Betty's food, a lot of my wine, and I was asked the question: 'We have tried everything to raise funds, but you are the man with all the ideas and who created *Pleasurewood*, etc. – how would YOU raise the last £400k?' I had no idea but, after more wine, I suggested in fun that the only way would be to try to win the upcoming first National Lottery – some 6 or 8 weeks ahead, but we all really knew nothing about it.

More wine and later still, I suggested we should each write to 100 friends and ask that they send us a £5.00 note so that we could gamble on the lottery. The deal would be that the first £800k of winnings would be split 50/50 and, after that, the funders got the lot. What optimists we were! Amazingly we got sent £8,500 in fivers and they were handed to me with a note –'Your idea, so please organize it!'

I duly saw my friendly postmaster, David Thompson, at Filby and asked him to sort it for me, only to THEN discover what the Lottery was about. I would have to fill in 6 different numbers for each of the 8,500 x £1 bets. I persuaded an IT company in Great Yarmouth, *Corby and Fellas*, to write a short program to provide 20,000 x 6-number combinations between 1 and 36, and then the *Seaforths* staff to sit with me one evening filling in the entries. I think we got it wrong, as it was such a big task, because we opted for the same number three weeks in a row to cut down the work – whereas we should have thrown £8,500 at the first draw.

We needed publicity for *The Playhouse*, but Thompson was concerned about security and asked that nothing went out until I had turned up with my £8,500 cash and he had locked it away. Under Lottery rules, the money could only be cash and he was concerned at having so much delivered to his small, isolated village post office. We understood his problem and put out a press release embargoed until 10am that day – but one radio station ignored us and, at 7am that morning, made a great thing about Joe Larter turning up at Filby with all the cash!!.

Pandemonium. Thompson threatened to close unless the police were involved for security, and in the end my son, Andrew, took me in his less-than Porsche-looking car to Barclays Bank, who wrapped the cash in a brown paper bag, and then on to Filby Post Office, with the police alerted.

At Filby it was like a night at the Oscars – TV, press, radio, and interviews. You name it, we had six of everything, and I have a wonderful scrapbook of that day and the following weekend, as Betty and I were pursued each day because everyone wanted to know what we had won. We had the front pages of both the *Daily Mail* and the *Daily Express*, and something in every other paper. It really was not a big deal, but they all wanted a new Lottery story.

David McCall, who was a trustee of *The Playhouse*, was in Sydney, Australia, and tells me of passing a news-stand near the Opera House and seeing my picture on the front page of the *Express* and wondering if maybe I had murdered someone.

In the end we actually won £1800 and, later, the Lottery Fund itself gave *The Playhouse* what it needed. Did we help? – We know not. Except for two people, everyone gave up their 50% of winnings because the amounts divided into £1800 were so small. Interesting that two people insisted they should have their £1.05p winnings and, of course, there was the inevitable criticism that we should have just given the £8500 – but that would not have been fun, and *The Playhouse* did get huge publicity.

The Monday morning following the lottery launch, I actually had a meeting in London with Noel Edmonds over our Blobby contract and, as I walked in he said: 'I can't believe it – I was running the b★★★★★ thing and you got more column inches than I did!"

Henry Burke had an illness, not at that time life-threatening, but from time to time he would simply faint. Jane and he were on a London-to-Norwich train in the early days of mobile phones, when they were rare but also very cumbersome – you could not fail to know if someone had one.

On this particular occasion travelling to Norwich, Henry fainted. Fortunately, a man in the same carriage had one of the new phones on which he had been loudly, pompously and irritatingly calling his friends all the way from London. Jane quickly asked him if she could use the phone to call their family and be sure a car was at the station to collect them. To the astonishment of Jane and the other people in the carriage, the man absolutely refused, and put the phone away. They all pleaded with him to help, and finally he had to admit the phone was not a real one.

In the *Pleasurewood I* days, and whilst *Seaforths* and the other businesses were building up, Betty, the children and I were pursuing our skiing and other holidays. Visiting Zermatt one November for what they call their 'White Weeks' – that's the weeks right at the start of the season – we met a couple of Germans, the Weinsteigers, Bert (Berthold) and Bruni and, over a number of years of going back to the same place, got to know them well.

We had great ski holidays with them and, when their son, Arin, wanted a summer-holiday job, he came to Lowestoft, stayed with us at Gunton Hall, and worked at *Pleasurewood* for one season. A charming young man, as were the whole family, but all very German – precise, I think, is the way to put it.

The following year, inside a Christmas card from them, was a note written in German, which they knew we did not understand, and it was not until April, when *Pleasurewood* opened again, that we had a German-speaking member of staff to read it. What did the note say? It was an invitation to a fabulous party in June! We quickly called to apologize for the delay in replying and chide them for writing in German, and then went to the party, staying at their house.

The party was spread over two days, and each guest was supposed to 'perform'. I got away with something simple, but one man sat through the main party meal and then, in a speech afterwards, apologized for his wife not being there. Beside him he had a large, cardboard model 'computer', which was asked embarrassing things about Bert's life and spewed out paper replies. At the end of the performance the computer burst open and his wife stepped out, having missed the whole meal! As Betty said, that is way beyond the call of duty and could only happen in Germany.

Bert and Bruni lived in Felbach, near Stuttgart, and had a great collection of friends. They took us to see wine growers, butchers and florists, and I got the feeling that they, and Germans generally, devote far more time to enjoying themselves socially than we do in the UK.

One friend was also the Development Director of *Mercedes-Benz*. On an occasion when I was not with Betty, they went out to dinner with the Director, and he took her onto the test track at *Mercedes*. Having driven round the track, he told her she had just ridden in the first Mercedes powered by hydrogen (i.e. a water-powered car). I think electric has taken over now, but at the time we were most impressed.

Regularly over this period, we made use, on the various French canals, of a boat which our friend Keith Gregory, who owned *Crown Blue Line*, loaned us. He used to like a report from me on our return, but taking a six-berth 'Broads Holidays'-style boat on those canals, with just the two of us, was perfect.

Not at all organized with bases, as in the UK, we had two bicycles and each night would tie up to a tree, or whatever was going. There would be a towpath to the nearest village, where we would cycle to find restaurants of varying degrees of quality but, almost without exception, good.

The canal system demonstrated the French skill at engineering and innovation. Locks were moving from being manned by lock-keepers to customer-orientated control, and then to automatic. We experienced them all and, after a few years, were quite happy to give a teenager a   1 piece to wind the lock gates for us if they were not then automatic. The MOST impressive innovation was somewhere near Alsace, where an engineer who must have had ski experience tackled a location. To get up or down that hilly section, you needed to operate the gates of about 8 locks. That's a lot of locks and a lot of time.

The engineer's solution was to stop the lock at the top of the hill and also at the bottom and throw away the locks in between. He then made two new, portable, sections, each large enough to take either one barge or four tourist boats, and would slide them up and down the hill on rams, one counterbalancing the other. Brilliant! And it is also the best tourist attraction in the area, with thousands coming to watch each summer.

Each season we would come across some little village along our route for that year, where they still held a summer 'fete' or celebration – very simple village entertainment in the style of England 30 or 40 years before. Even the smallest canal village would have a massive firework display for 14 July (Bastille Day).

Unlike on the Norfolk Broads, mooring your boat on the canals is a rather more casual business. Find a tree or knock in a stake by the old towpath and it's yours for the night. My delight was always to walk down to the nearby village next morning to get bread and other naughty things full of calories which tempted me, whilst Betty got herself and the boat ready for breakfast.

On this particular occasion I came back to the boat, and stood on an old piece of tree or planking to jump back on board. Except that I didn't! The next is a bit like the Gerard Hoffnung *Bricklayer's Lament*.

The wood broke as I jumped and, spread-eagled to try to catch hold of something, I hit the edge of the boat full on to my ribs and then mouth, falling into the water between boat and canal edge. I was completely winded, unable to speak, and could only make a groaning noise, rather like Chewbacca in *Star Wars*. Betty was in the shower at the time and heard nothing for some minutes, after which she opened the cabin door to see what was going on.

She saw a drowning rat with a bloody face trying to climb on board the boat, but thought she recognized something familiar! After I had been helped on board in absolute agony, Betty cleaned me up; but then what to do? We were at the very start of a 'do-it-yourself' canal – no auto-locks or lock-keepers. No pain-killers until we could find a chemist, but we just had to move on.

We edged our way to the next lock, but no way could we handle getting in and out of a lock with Betty alone, about 1000 turns of the lock-gate handle we counted to get in and out of the lock. We put a rope round a tree to consider our options and waited – and along came some 'forceful' Germans, who rather rudely went straight into the lock first - canal boaters usually take their turn in line. We quickly followed, hooking a rope to a support and letting the Germans do all the work. I liked that! Three locks later we reached a small town, and painkillers enabled me to get through a day or two of recovery.

We are both very fond of France and, when Great Yarmouth twinned with Rambouillet near Paris, Betty was a member of the Gorleston Tennis Club, which had arranged a tournament, so we got to know a French couple, Bernard and Brigitte Tinur, who came to stay with us. I do not speak much French, and Bernard did not speak any English, but it is amazing how much Franglais you can speak after a bottle or two of wine. We have remained in touch and, when on the canals, at Cahors we would moor and they would come down to see us from their retirement base.

Although we never bought a property in France, we did have friends who had them, and we would visit. On one occasion we headed for Nice, where the Kurzners had a lovely home and had invited us to stay. We thought we would have an unplanned visit to the area for a few days ahead of seeing them and, using various guides, we ended up on a particular night at the *Chateau de la Ch è vre d'Or* at Eze, along the coast. A fabulous place for a romantic interlude, and the bathroom we had was actually carved out of rock and had cave paintings on the walls as from the Stone Age. I have a picture of Betty in the bathroom.... with clothes on! Preparing for a lovely supper, we went to have a drink on the beautiful 'terrace' from which you could see Nice in the distance.

The 'terrace' waiter came along with a small, hand-held board giving a description and asked if 'Madame would like to have the speciality of the terrace this evening?' The board announced a pot of caviar and a glass of *Dom Perignon* champagne. Now Betty likes caviar, which I do not and, of course, who could refuse a glass of Dom P? He then turned to me and dropped his hand a little so I could also see the price of what he was offering. I told him I did not wish for the caviar and also, could I please have a glass of ordinary champagne?

He duly returned, gave Betty the smallest pot of caviar I have ever seen, accompanied by a very small glass of champagne, and then turned to pour me a glass of the same. I put my hand up to remind him I had asked for a glass of 'ordinary champagne', whereupon he drew himself up to his full height and said: 'Sir, this IS our ordinary champagne!' and poured me an equally small glass. When he had gone, Betty asked: 'What on earth was that all about?'

I told her I did not ordinarily ever question the amount we spend when we are on a lovely weekend such as we were having, but when he had let me see the price of her tiny offering, the 3-figure cost had made me wonder if I would need to rob a bank before we departed. In fact, we had not known it was the Grand Prix weekend, when everything trebles and more in price. The dinner we had so carefully chosen from their menu was also 'off', with a 'set' Grand Prix meal instead, and I will not embarrass myself or you by saying what we in the end had to pay for a Grand Prix night of being there. Another part of Arthur Marshall's rich pageant of life!

Pleasureworld II buying back the old assets from the Receiver also meant an end to us, as a family, camping out at the Old Stables at Gunton Hall. The Receiver wanted to sell but I did not have the cash to buy, and Betty wanted to be nearer to Norwich and a fresh start.

Autumn 1991 found us renting The White House at Intwood, near Norwich, a lovely Georgian rectory-type property. We said we would be there for a couple of years, but in fact we stayed for six, and very happy years they were. I really got myself established again, as you will see, and in 1996 we had a lovely 60th birthday party for Betty in a marquee on our lawns. No surprises, just all our friends and, I suppose, saying we are back; it was the best party we ever gave. I think we got lazy as the house was so nice, but we needed to get our own property again. No matter where I looked I could not find what I wanted – an unspoiled wreck in the country to do up and enlarge.

Easter weekend 1997 I set off south of Intwood determined to really search the area and, at the first stop in Long Stratton, found an advertisement for the White Horse Cottage at Hapton, a Grade II-listed wreck. I went to that small village to search for it as the agent was closed for the weekend, and discovered later that, in the 1700s and right up to after World War II, the property had been a small 'farmers'' public house.

The cottage was empty and pretty derelict, sitting in 1/3rd acre of land, so I could get a good look round, including scouting to see if there would be enough land for Betty to have a tennis court and, if not, whether I could buy some.

I found the land adjoining, with a fantastic view invisible from the cottage because of overgrown hedges. Next was to take courage in both hands and see if the farmer would sell me a small piece of land – farmers being notoriously possessive of their holdings. Not a bit of it. Alfie Bartrum, as he turned out to be, could not have been more friendly, and more or less said I could have as much land as I wanted, but to be sure I bought enough. I did not 'buy enough', as I could not afford it, but over the years he was very kind and we bought more as we went along.

I rushed Betty there; she took me on trust that I could turn it into the lovely home it now is. It was *Believe It or Not!* again – bought in June and, in November that same year, we moved in to a place double the size of the one we had bought and now with one acre of land and the precious tennis court.

We have been there 15 years – for us a record, so champagne all round, please, and remind me always to have an interest in developing a property, as perhaps I am good at that. In planning this book, I first had to make a 'time capsule' record of what we have done and where we have been. Even I find it hard to believe that in the USA and UK, including rented properties as well as those we owned, Betty and I have lived in 16 different homes, and me alone in 20, and excluding those with Susan, my first wife.

Another bit of history. Great-great-great-… grandfather William Larter was the landlord of the *World's End* public house at Mulbarton in 1735, as I have related, and I am sure he would be much amused that his later relative was buying an old public house in a village 3 miles away. It would have been nice to compete with him.

During 2012, Barbara Lawn (nee Woods) called to see Betty and give her more of the history of our property. From 1924 to 1954 her parents were the landlords there, having taken over from Anna Gray, her great aunt, who was there from 1902 to 1924. Before we developed it, the property was just one long building about 18ft wide, and our study was, in fact, a cart shed. However, NINE people lived there – the Woods, their 5 children and their parents! There was a small cellar under what is now our kitchen, and our winter sitting-room was the bar – called The Clubroom.

The way they used spaces was amazing – what we have as a clothes cupboard was a bedroom where the babies slept until they got older! No running water, a 'privy' at the bottom of the garden and, no doubt, as one Highland gent told me on a visit to a Scottish pub in my youth when I enquired about male facilities, the patrons of the pub would have had 'acres and acres' to use outside!

Mrs Lawn said that during the war her father befriended a quiet gent of military bearing, and he started to frequent the pub. Later he stopped coming, and only after the police turned up to discuss him did they discover he had been arrested as a German spy, living at Tasburgh and signalling the German planes using equipment hidden in his chimney to guide them on to Norwich.

The Woods family moved to Hempnall and Dr and Mrs Wells bought the property, with our buying it after Mrs Wells' death. 15 years, and time to move again.

Chapter Twelve
Seaforths' sale, Dotcom Bubble, NZ Vineyard, Dutch Joint Venture and an Airline

The Dutchman, Henry Holterman, with whom I had now become involved, was an accountant who had been appointed by the Wessels family to help invest a fortune they had made in construction. Wessels had built up one of Holland's largest public construction companies, and Henry was looking at various ventures in the UK. Having got to know each other through Vlissingen and the *Miniature World* in Walcheren, increasingly he involved me in his thoughts, in order to understand the English ways rather than the Dutch, which are so different.

One of my earliest positive involvements with Henry for Wessels was in buying the engineering moulding businesses in Folkestone, and later in Maidstone, to complement what they had in Germany. He then discussed with me how in Holland they had made an investment in *ATP*, a travel company similar to *Seaforths*. He had also got involved with a UK company developing a system called *Telme*, supposedly already running. He made an investment there, only to find the system was not actually yet complete as he and others had thought, and needed development.

Henry met Jenny Mills, an idea was born and, in 1996 Wessels, through *Reggeborgh Beheer*, would take a 30% stake in *Seaforths*, eventually linking all three businesses together and seeing what Gary Hance could do with the internet side. This was a very new line for me, but I could see how technology was taking the world by its pants and was delighted to be on this roller-coaster, as it turned out to be. The years 1995 to 2000 were known as the 'Dot-com bubble' years, and so they were.

Various developments down the line, and *Reggeborgh* took an investment in a public company, *Phonelink*, where we met a huge city character – Sir Gordon Brunton, the Chairman. Graham Ramsey, who was head-hunted by Sir Gordon, was appointed CEO to turn the company round, which he achieved with remarkable skill. I think another life-changing moment for me was when I met Graham with Henry for the first time in the *SAS* hotel off Portman Square. All new stuff to Joe Larter, but let's go with it.

I cannot claim much credit here on the travel side, except in interpreting things occasionally for Henry in an 'enabling' way, writing the odd document, and so on, and we all owe Graham Ramsey an enormous 'thank you' for pulling it all together because, quite frankly, *Phonelink* was of little substance before he came along. The first real internet success for Wessels was when he made a 1996 investment in the Dutch internet service provider, *World on Line*, being developed by Nina Brink, and it is worth summarizing the history of that deal, which is on *Wikipedia*.

The company was started by Nina Brink in 1996 and, on 17 March 2000, she was planning an IPO (initial public offering) which valued the company at €12 billion and €43 per share, an enormous price and value for what she had created. I think maybe Wessels and Henry had a 10% interest in the company, so a very important investment. There was a lot of controversy and concern because of the price compared to other similar offerings but, in the grey market and then on the first day of trading, over 80% of the capital in the company was traded for up to as much as €50 for a short time.

The whole company then collapsed within a day or two, with great embarrassment and loss to the banks involved, when it was revealed that the previous December, Brink had actually **sold** her own total holding for $60m to *Bay Star Capital* in the USA – at $6 a share! And without telling anyone what she was doing. Her small investors and company shareholders were, understandably, furious. As I think I have said somewhere else, there is serendipity – and there is luck! What the *World on Line* profit provided Wessels was capital for various other ventures, including later property investment in the UK.

In the 1997–1999 period Ramsey led *Phonelink* to great success, and then it was decided to split all the travel side away from the telecoms part. Ramsey took control of travel and would develop it into a major company and eventually, with partners, buy out from *Reggeborgh*. Freed of control, he has grown it to USA$1.2 billion revenues in 2012. Our original *Seaforths* investment was now part of the *Telme/GB* Group, a public investment company, and took off with the dot-com bubble. Nina Brink had her fun in March that year and we had a rocketing price for *Telme* in May, when I was actually travelling with Betty in the far north of New Zealand, which places us nicely for the next part of my story.

In 1999 friends near our own home, in Framingham Pigot, received surprise callers at their 'cottage' (they actually own a complete village there). 'TJ' and Rex Brooke-Taylor, from New Zealand, had come to the UK to find their long-lost relatives. In due course they were introduced to the neighbours, including us, and we told Rex we would be visiting New Zealand the following year to see my old friend from the Norfolk County Council days. Andrew Scott, who had been Chief Medical Officer for Wellington after he left Norfolk, had retired to Rangiputa, in the extreme north of North Island.

Rex and 'TJ' had developed one of the first vineyards in Marlborough, at the top of South Island, and called it 'Framingham' because Rex knew of the UK family connection, although he had no contact at that time. We agreed to call and see them, and so May 2000 found us with the 'Kiwis', first staying with Andrew and his wife, Maggie – me on the phone at night frantically trying to keep pace with the rocketing price of, and demand for, *Telme/GB* group which coincided with our visit. We did well, but should have said: 'Sell the lot'! At last, something for me to set my *RKF Group* losses against, and maybe the Larter fortunes were turning up again.

We had the most fabulous trip and, when we reached Rex in Blenheim, he showed us round all the grape-growing areas where I noticed, as builders and property developers do, a small, 10-acre property with a nice house and growing cherries, and with a 'for sale by auction' board outside. Rex told me it would fetch about £40,000 equivalent (the price of a small, terraced house in the worst section of Great Yarmouth) and would be cleared and planted with grapes as a 'boutique' vineyard.

Seeing my looks, he said he would buy and develop it for me if I was interested; was this my wine gene, triggered at the dinner in Winterton all those years ago and my constant mention of liking an investment in France, coming to the surface? Combined with some of that *Tel.Me* cash coming in and, although it was not what Betty really wished me to do so far away from the UK, I asked him to bid in due course.

We then went south down to Queenstown, with great experiences all the way. At the *Wilderness* (not far from Mount Cook) we stayed in a camping-type cabin, where a famous NZ naturalist was in residence and took us walking at night to explain the night sky. Until that moment we had not thought about where we were in the universe but, of course, we were completely 'upside down' from England. We saw the Fox glacier and went by boat to see Milford Sound, the only time I have been with about 200 people as the tallest man there – the rest were Japanese!

I think, like all visitors to New Zealand, we were stunned by the extreme beauty of the two islands – but also by the sheer dramatic range of the country. Sub-tropical in the far north of North Island, and then ice, snow and glaciers in the far south of South Island. The sequel to all this, before we return to business life, was that, back in the UK, I received a call from Rex.

He had changed his mind and thought the auction price for the 10-acre plot would be silly in NZ terms, and he would be locally embarrassed bidding for me. Instead, he had located another plot – 20 acres with a house and barn adjoining a new planting of his own at Kaituna, on the river Wairau – and would I consider buying that 50/50 with a lady vintner who worked for him?

I had to trust his judgment without either seeing the property or meeting my proposed partner, but there came from that purchase a lovely association with Barrie and Shelley Mangos, who actually developed the whole property – mostly Sauvignon Blanc but with some Pinot. I went back alone the following year to see what we had bought, and to meet Barrie and Shelley. A tremendous meeting, first with Shelley, who will not mind me saying, could talk the hind legs off three donkeys without drawing a breath.

She met me at the airport (24 hrs and more non-stop flying already, Auckland and then down to Christchurch where they lived). 'How are you feeling?' she asked in the hotel foyer, as she had laid on a day of vineyard visiting for me! 'Let me have a shower and a clean-up and I will be with you,' I replied.

There followed a day of meetings with various owners and others, lunch and then, mid-afternoon, Shelley asked again: 'How do you feel?" Well pretty good, with my tiredness overtaken by the interest in what she was showing me. 'Oh good, because tonight there is a black-tie dinner of all the wine growers in the region, laid on by *Penfolds of Australia*, and we got you a ticket, if you feel up to it.'

I had no DJ of course, but I had a blue jacket, bought a bow tie during the afternoon, and I was in for one of the best evenings I have ever attended, with some great people. It was ME who, at midnight (now 48 hrs since I had seen a bed), when they said they were going to another party and would drop me off first at my hotel, said: 'No way! And I will be buying the champagne to thank you.' Those were the days…er, I think I mean I was younger.

Shelley and Barrie turned out to be wonderful vineyard partners, not least because they had to do all the work as I was in the UK, but never once have I had a complaint from them. It was to be in March 2003, three years after purchase and planting, that we were to pick the first grapes. Betty and I decided to be there and, for any friend who wanted to come, we would give a small party – so we thought!

To our astonishment, as the confirmations came in (guests made their own travel arrangements and booked accommodation, but the party was on us), we were to host 75 people from all over the world. Suddenly this was not going to be a 'barbie with a few steaks' in the barn! We had a major event on our hands, which Rex offered to sort.

On our own arrival a few days before the Saturday event, I found he had done little, because he wanted to wait for us. Bit of a panic but, in three days, we organized a marquee and all the kit, a restaurant to close and bring their kitchen to us, a great band and, of course, for us, we stayed for the first time in the lovely house we had acquired with the property.

So much fun was had that we extended the party to the next day and, during the evening, booked a large river-boat trip on Marlborough Sound itself, to take us all on the Sunday to a restaurant for lunch. John Leslie and his wife, Julia, from Norwich, were party guests, John being a great jazz musician and, on the night, he kindly played for us. Sadly, he's another who is no longer with us, as are John and Shelagh Mowson and Keith Harvey, who were also there.

We will never forget the party, and I doubt we can ever repeat such a success, except we had a good try for our daughter Rose's wedding. Of such things the great mosaic of an interesting life is constructed.

The grape-growing and wine business out there has not been plain sailing. The big boys moved in during the early 2000s and New Zealand planted far too many grapes. Although we managed to sell our grapes each year it is a very difficult business to be in, and I take my hat off to the skill of Shelley and Barrie in keeping us solvent and, mostly, profitable.

My original expectation was to have been the UK importer of the wine made from our grapes (we could produce about 8,000 twelve-bottle cases in full 'flow', I think) and it would have been a nice 'retirement' hobby, with us going out there every other year. Prices world-wide have fallen so much that there was no hope of ever doing that, and so our lovely grapes are sold in the market to the highest bidder; but New Zealand still makes the best Sauvignon and we have had the experience of a lifetime. Had it been nearer we might have tried a 'wine-share' arrangement, where individuals buy or rent two or three rows of vines.

Because of our age and 'been there – done that – got the T shirt' attitude, we made a proposal to Barrie and Shelley in 2012 and, in February 2013, we agreed to sell our shares to them. A great adventure, and one I am glad not to have missed.

On the way home from New Zealand that year, we went via Sydney in Australia, which has since become my favourite city. We saw *Mamma Mia!* at the Opera House, walked the upper archways of the Sydney Harbour bridge, ate a lot of fish, and even saw the news-stand where David McCall had seen my *National Lottery* pictures. So, back to the grind in the UK.

Henry Holterman now suggested that Wessels wanted to invest some of his cash into real estate in the UK. He asked if I would be prepared to do that for them, rather than setting out on my own again. I had to think hard about it, because I had always been independent before but, on the promise of 'autonomy' and Henry stressing the personal relationship we had now built up, I agreed. Looking back, it was a mistake to give up independence, but I'm not complaining.

We set up *Rivercastle Ltd* (English translation of the Dutch word Reggeborgh) on a joint venture basis, with Wessels providing the cash and me doing all the work and having a 10% stake and a salary, and arranged that the following year, when he retired as Crown Estates Commissioner, Sir Christopher Howes would join us.

In 1998 I started with a small, rented office in Prince of Wales Road, Norwich, because we made our first purchase there – Charles and Wensum House. A big learning curve for me again, administering large properties, but I did it on my own for the first two years without agents involved. With Christopher joining us, we needed a London base, and Henry wanted a London apartment, having now married Gerita, one of Wessel's daughters. A bit different from the carefree guy I had first met.

After selling out my own interests to *Queensborough* in 1996, I had bought a London base again and we now had an apartment at York Central, King's Cross, and so London working during the week suited us all. York Central was a bit like the Oliver's Wharf warehouse in Wapping, in that we bought it bare and did our own fitting out. Not £8,500 though, and this one overlooking King's Cross railway station.

For *Rivercastle* we found No 8 Upper Grosvenor Street as offices, almost next door to the American Embassy. This was an expensive, £3m purchase Henry and Gerita wanted but which, as property investors, we needed like a hole in the head. However, for Henry and Gerita it was a beautiful building and made a superb flat for them, in the right location on the top floor, with us having offices on the lower floors. Christopher was now there, as was Graham Ramsey, running the *ATP* company for Wessels, as well as *Phonelink*.

Quite by chance, Christopher and I were together with two American visitors at Upper Grosvenor Street on the afternoon of 11 September 2001, when the first plane hit the Twin Towers in New York.

The ATP company now became too large for our premises, and the flat was not used. I was now buying some quite nice investment properties – Leeds, Bradford and so on, and one of my scouts found us No 10 Leake Street, by Waterloo Station. A great buy at the time, we converted several floors and let others, and that was our base until I departed from *Rivercastle* in 2004.

Our Wessels association was nothing like the success it could have been, because neither Christopher nor I was allowed to be 'entrepreneurial'. I had to buy properties that gave an 8% return, which meant they would always be 2nd tier (8% was too high a return for the A1 areas in London or main cities), and I could not create developments as I had done all my life.

I was out of my operational zone, and it would have been better to give me a pot of, say, £10m on a 50/50 basis to use in East Anglia, and let me do what I had always done best in the past – speculate and develop. It was all very well to have £8-£10m available, but most likely we would have needed £50-£100m to make the sort of deals Christopher was skilled at with the Crown Estates. I know he was bitterly disappointed.

The other unfortunate matter was that, having married Gerita, Henry then fell out with the Wessels family and Dick in particular, and left the main family company to set up home on a Greek island and buy a large motor-yacht. We kept in touch, but from then on I was in business with people I did not know or relate to, although I did my best to teach them about England. After I departed and they came to sell all the properties, they made a very respectable profit.

In 2004, the eventual settlement of the value of my share of the business was not a happy one. However, I had made some money and had gained very valuable experience in the property world on a much larger scale than before. Henry returned to the Wessels' fold a few years later, but too late for me, and time was now moving on rather fast.

2004 finds me aged 65 but with no intention of ever retiring; that is for old people and, in any case, what would Betty do with me? On my leaving London Gary Hance, of the *Seaforths* and then *ATP* days, asked if I would meet a man from Iceland who was now living in Aberdeen; together they had been planning to start a small airline, *City Star Airlines*, which would fly oil executives from Aberdeen to the islands.

They had been let down on some funding at the last minute, and Gary knew I had a settlement from *Reggeborgh*. He asked if I would invest some of the cash with them, and I was sympathetic because of what Gary had done for *Seaforths* all those years before. I looked at an excellent business plan for travel, where the idea was to use only small, 38-seat turboprop planes.

With very strict rules laid down about minimum occupancy, ticket pricing and so on, I agreed to invest. They appeared to have good support in Iceland and Lee Sharpe, a quite well-known UK footballer, was already involved. I met with Lee because he had a very considerable sum involved, and we agreed we would try to keep together on it but, in the end, we just failed to exercise any influence, no matter how hard we tried.

The Icelandic team simply did not follow the rules, and I discovered by accident that, less than 6 months after I invested, Gary had left the company, although no one had told me. When I asked why, they were dismissive.

As always, a few other people followed me as investors and, to this day, none of the investors in UK can understand how that small airline, supposedly making £800k a year in October, was out of money and bankrupt the following January, which is what happened. Two of the other investors actually lived in Aberdeen, with one of them using the planes every week. Neither of them could get to the bottom of what happened and, of course, the language barrier was ridiculous; we could not read anything the 'Board' in Iceland wrote.

Eventually there was a police investigation in Iceland, because a lot of money had been lost there over buying and re-selling planes which we knew nothing about, but nothing came of it. Let's stick to English (or if not, then American!) but it is a business that had a great plan, was a great success, and should never have been lost. We innocents in the UK were even supporting the excellent purchase of the ground-handling facilities of Aberdeen airport, right up to the time of *City Star* ceasing to trade – we were that ignorant of the situation.

Chapter Thirteen
Bungay, Barbados and Cliff Richard

You remember that roller-coaster I mentioned? Well, in this period we are on a downhill section, but the rider is hoping for a sharp upturn at the end before coasting to a stop. 2005 brings the suggestion that, as he had parted from Wessels and I had left *Reggeborgh* in London, Henry and I should plan a 50/50 joint venture for developments and business together in the UK.

Henry had retained as his assistant the very able and likeable Raymond Hekkert from his *Reggeborgh* days, and was already investing in small hotels in Holland. He had an idea about financial services and saving VAT for rich people, purchasing large boats which would require a Channel Islands financial base and should be run from the UK.

As a base in East Anglia we bought a beautiful old house in Bungay, Suffolk, which I decorated and furnished for our joint venture, and we explored the VAT business, Henry being able to fly easily into Norwich and our expecting high-net-worth clients to be visiting us.

Whilst the idea would have worked legally, the advice I obtained said it was pretty certain the VAT people would not like it, and Henry was also by then not actually liking the sort of people who wanted the service! End of that story, but then Henry reversed his personal family position and returned to Wessels as the main Operational Director. The reason for us doing anything more together had disappeared.

However, we were both already involved in Barbados together, where I was trying to look after our interests.

Two years before Bungay, David Mace, of the *Sealife Centres* connection in the UK, came to see me. They had built up a group of 17 centres in Europe and had sold out, and David wanted to know if I would be interested in helping him start a chain of centres in the West Indies. I said no, but a year later he came back and said he had found a site in Barbados, and would I have a look with him?

I knew Barbados from the past as very 'English' and liked it, so it was very tempting, and I put the idea to Henry. He was interested in Barbados, having his luxury boat there on which to live, and I think he envisaged some very pleasant winter months travelling the Caribbean islands, as I did, from having a base there. Barbados tourist investment and New Zealand wine seemed like a good start for 'retirement'.

None of us quite studied the business plan as we would otherwise have done, because the same team of expert advisers used by *Sealife* in Europe was working here. Also, David already had a number of investors and had taken a huge amount of advice on the island from tourism people on the spot.

The freehold of the proposed site (previously a golf driving range) was owned by a number of Barbados investors and I insisted that, for safety, we buy a major stake in the land as well. We did not want to be investing mega-cash in a site owned by someone else.

Barbados residents Ralph Johnson and Peter Chesham owned 35% of the land company, and we UK investors now bought out the other 65% from a mixed group of small shareholders, and both Ralph and Peter were also investors in the *Sealife* company, *Ocean Park*. Safety in local numbers, I thought, and two great people.

Ralph was at that time 'Mr Barbados', with fingers in a lot of pies, and on the Barbados Olympic Committee. He owned *Harris Paints* and knew everyone, so absolutely perfect to have involved. Peter was an Englishman with various business interests, a bit of an entrepreneur like me, and also very experienced in construction.

The construction of the development can only be described as a puzzle from day one, with designers and surveyors by the dozen (one had a nervous breakdown and no one noticed). As we got to the October before the supposed January 2006 opening, both Peter and I started to ask serious questions, but we were warned off because we were 'upsetting' the team there. 'On time and on budget,' was the constant refrain.

However, by January, when we should have been open, the project was completely over budget and nowhere near finished, with disputes everywhere on the site, mostly over money. Looking back, I think David had been terribly let down by his team, and desperately tried to get back on track by cutting costs, but you really cannot do that on a scheme like this. As the investor with previous *Sealife* experience and a substantial amount now invested personally, I was asked to try to sort it with Peter.

We learned that construction spend had been cut to a desperate extent. There was not a scrap of sun cover for either visitors or fish in 10 acres, few hard walkways planned, no catering facilities, and cut-price cooling and filtering – they were to come later from profits. Put that with our having to bring our seawater 5 miles by tanker, and we had a recipe for disaster set up. David's nephew, John, did an enormous job getting fish into tanks and surviving, despite the intense heat.

I hope John will not mind me telling one story about him. John loved the marine side of the park and was very proud to have caught a baby shark, which he displayed in the small touch-pool we had. He was showing if off to a party of schoolchildren, explaining that, at that age, sharks were very safe because their teeth had not developed; whereupon the shark grabbed his leg, giving him a very nasty bite and putting him in Casualty.

John decided to return home to Scotland and we hired Mitchell Hird (Mitch), who had the task of getting the actual attraction on track, and where he did a superb job. Over the years we then tried to make it a success; he introduced other animals to fill the site, the most charming of which was a huge cage of tropical birds, where the public could go inside and feed them. Iguanas were another feature.

Luckily we had already appointed Patricia Affonso-Dass, a local hotel manager, to become our General Manager, and it was Patricia and I who now had to try to sort a way forward, with very sound advice from Peter. Suffice to say that it took two years and another BB\$7m to get the place into shape, and looking like a tourist attraction you might want to visit. Apart from anything else, the scale was so wrong – vast, open areas and no buildings.

We finally opened the partially-complete *Ocean Park* six months late, but there was more than one occasion when Patricia and I said to ourselves that we must advise the Board to pull out. That would have been a terrible failure at that time – closing down before we had even opened. There is no doubt now, that had we at that time been able to see the future, a decision to close would have been absolutely correct and would have saved us all more than a small fortune.

Barbados is a wonderful place for a holiday and a rum punch, and Betty and I certainly enjoyed the Barbados side of our three winters there. But to do business? Not quite the way we know in the rest of the world. As a planning officer there put it to me when I was complaining about planning delays: 'Mr Larter; the British took over this island in 1627 and we never had all the changes from French, to Spanish, to Portuguese that the other islands did; we were British through and through. You taught us bureaucracy.

'When you gave us Independence in 1966, the Government founded a "University of Bureaucracy" and sent all our Civil Servants there. They all qualified! And the golden rule in the civil service ever since has been "If you do not make a decision, then you will not make a mistake".'

We all worked so hard, had super on-site staff, Trish, the hardworking assistant to Patricia was particularly appreciated, and we put in so much money, that we did in the end have a beautiful attraction. It was for all-year and night-time entertainment as well, but the flaw was there from the very start of the park. No way would there ever be enough locals or cruise-ship visitors to make it viable. The tour operators, who were investors, had advised we could look to get 100,000 cruise-ship passengers a year, whereas the maximum we ever got was 4000. They were so overwhelmingly optimistic with their wish… for it all to happen.

At the end, Patricia and I were scrabbling to get any attraction we could there, and I looked into an approval for dolphins. We developed a small 'water-splash' section and a big activity area for children, which they all loved, and had some beautiful weddings and other social events there. However, the day we got a BB\$100,000 bill for electricity **for the month**, we knew we were finished. With Peter (and help from Raymond), I arranged a receivership through *PWC* as we had a possible buyer in the offing, and only an 'official' receivership would ever bring the project to a neat, fast close, even if a very unhappy one.

Unfortunately, the other two Directors and a local lawyer decided they could do better and cancelled what we had arranged. Peter and I (me the Chairman of the company) both resigned as we were no longer needed. Today, years later, the park is still unsold, is derelict, and costs BB\$000s a year in taxes and other costs and, for me, that was the very unhappy end of an association which, after 15 years or so, should have been different.

Betty and I have from Barbados some wonderful memories of occasions and people, of visiting the great houses and some lovely social occasions. We hired a house in Sugar Hill on the west coast each winter, and met up with a great gang of ex-pats.

Patricia and I organized a charity event at *Ocean Park* for two years in aid of the Barbados Heart and Stroke Foundation - maybe with our experiences at *Ocean Park*, one of us was going to need them! The team there taught me about the Chinese Auction system to raise money for the charity – basically you bid and pay in cash of the same value all the time on the spot. Dinner worth $200 for auction; first bidder pays $10, 2nd bidder also pays $10 – with girls running around with baskets to collect the money. It works if the MC knows most of the people at the event.

I decided the second year that I would like to do something extra-special to raise money at the auction, but also something for Betty! On Sugar Hill lived Cliff Richard and also Jackie Monkhouse, the widow of the great comedian, Bob, and who we got to know a little. At one lunchtime, in the clubhouse, I asked her if Cliff was approachable to help an on island charity, and she assured me he was, always, but I would have to approach him myself as she could not.

I duly wrote to Cliff, told him about the Heart and Stroke event, and said I had seen him playing tennis a lot. Could I offer, for auction, a game of tennis with him? My ulterior motive was, of course, to buy the game for Betty. He replied immediately and said: 'Yes, of course!' If we made it a foursome on his own court he would give us some champagne afterwards on his terrace.

I told no one of my coup until the actual charity evening, when I had to ask Peter if he would bid against me until I told him to stop, because I did not want to see such a generous offer only make a few BB dollars. Between six people bidding we raised about BB$4000, with me buying it, of course and, when I reported to Cliff what had happened, I had to tell him there would be five for champagne as I did not play tennis.

Cliff was absolute charm itself. They enjoyed the tennis and we all enjoyed the champagne. On the day they played tennis, by coincidence one of Cliff's sisters was staying – from Dereham, in Norfolk, not a million miles from our own home. So ended the Barbados story for us for the time being, but we will be back for a visit if the project is ever sold.

One lovely side story from trying to get dolphins to *Ocean Park* was that Betty and I had to visit Jamaica to see the dolphin experts and discuss what we had to do. *Dolphin Cove* there is fabulous and very successful, with the cruise visitor in particular, and both Stafford Burrows and his wife fell over themselves to help us with *Ocean Park*. *Dolphin Cove* also has a small unit at the *Half Moon Bay Hotel*, and that is where we stayed on our visit. Stafford told his men there that, as it was slack season, if Mrs Larter (the mermaid) wanted to swim with them at any time, she could do so.

Have you heard of the expression 'A kid let free in the sweet shop'? Betty was in her element. The pool was a fenced-off section of the seashore and they put Betty in with two dolphins. She lay flat on the top of the water and, on command, the dolphins circled and put their noses, one each, against the flat of her feet. On another command, they pushed, and Betty was waterskiing front-first! After that, she held on to one fin of each of the dolphins beside her, and they took her swimming and diving under with them like a member of their family. An absolutely magical experience of which we have a video, and I was convinced this would be the ultimate success of *Ocean Park*; but we were not to last that long.

When I reflect on what was a major disappointment and the huge investment we all lost, *Ocean Park* was also never going to work so far from the actual ocean and spread over 10 acres. It should have been in one of the large, old buildings in Bridgetown, on the shore of the bay, air-conditioned and just like the European *Sealife Centres*, and we would be there today with a very successful business.

Another scheme I designed in Barbados was with the all-time great cricketer, Sir Gary Sobers. Sir Gary is a legend in Barbados, and was going to front *The Barbados Experience* for me. I researched the history of Barbados right back to 1627, and picked out characters and events that, with Bruce Carter (we had seen the *Malta Experience* together in our years there), we would have put into an audio-animatronic show in an old church building we were offered. If we had had success with *Ocean Park*, we would have created this as a second venture and, I think, had great fun.

Chapter Fourteen
India, Russia, Great Yarmouth and Lowestoft, a Death and a Great Wedding Again

This has to be called the LABB era – Life After Barbados, because Barbados is the last disaster I am allowed to have, but here I am, independent again, with what I am good at - property.

2005 brought us a trip across America to see our USA friends, Keith and Tommi Harvey, who also had an apartment at *The Atrium* in Florida. Keith was long-term unwell, but they came out to the New Zealand party, had been to stay with us in Barbados (where we went deep-sea fishing together, oxygen tank and all), and they insisted that we went to stay with them in their home in Lodi, near Sacramento. Keith had made his fortune by inventing a method of repairing helicopter blades, which cost $100,000 each and were otherwise being thrown away. He had sold out for a major sum, and had a *Southfork, Dallas*-style home in the wine country of California, where he now had a major wine holding; hence his interest in New Zealand.

Betty and I had never known such hospitality before, and they would not let us leave when we wanted to get on with a planned trip to Yosemite state park. In the end they agreed, if we took one of their vehicles, did our trip, and then met them up-country at a lodge on the Redding River. When we met, we were told: 'Tomorrow, 4am, we leave to drive to some salmon fishing, and I have a boat with a driver laid on.' This is Keith, approaching 80 years and with emphysema.

Betty, in her traditional Fiji style, soon had a 25lb King Salmon on the end of a line, the only fish we were to catch on the whole trip. That was duly sent home with Keith, to be prepared for lunch on the day we were due to return. We two got delayed and missed the lunch, but had a very memorable trip with two wonderful friends.

2006 brought Betty to 70 and, as I was being financially very careful indeed following *City Star* and Barbados, Betty arranged for us to celebrate her birthday by going on a trip to search for tigers in India – as one does! A private, escorted tour, what a memorable trip it was, not only to see the tigers, but also to visit Jaipur, the palaces and temples, and the Taj Mahal, which is every bit as romantic as it is promoted. Here are some anecdotes from there.

The tigers were way up north, where we had some great treks, saw tigers, and included swimming with an elephant, but came the day when we had to move on to the next section of the trip – by train overnight. We had been told to book a four-berth 1st-class section to ourselves, or there would be no sleep, but on this train you were not allowed to do that.

Consequently, we were allocated two bunk-beds, one above the other but in the corridor of the train, with just a curtain to screen us off. Standing on the platform with the guide who would be travelling with us, I enquired what we did for food that evening, as it was 4pm in the afternoon. 'Food!' he exclaimed, 'did not the hotel give you your evening meal?'

They had not done so, and no way could we eat what was offered on board, because Europeans just get upset tums, so what to do? He and I toured the station and decided the only safe things to buy were bananas. In my bag, because it had been very difficult to obtain up north, I had the remains of a bottle of red wine from the previous night.

I have a lovely picture of Betty on the train that evening in her bunk bed (the lower one – what a gent), with a plastic cup for the wine (cup bought from a chai vendor on the train), and her allocated banana. Lovely memories.

In Jaipur we stayed in the very luxurious palace of the Maharajah, now a beautiful hotel. On arrival there were the traditional rose petals and garlands but, as we checked in, we were told our bags would be taken to our room but we must go immediately to the polo match next door, where we had tickets allocated. There we were given what is known as a 'Royal Welcome', which means two elephants 'guard' the entrance and, as you walk between them, girls in the howdah baskets on their backs throw rose petals on you as a welcome.

We were not able to wait for what we would like to have seen, Elephant Polo. However, we did read the rules of the game, one of which instructs the players that 'The Elephant is not allowed to sit down in the goalmouth.' A fabulous trip all round.

Apart from any personal situation, the world had conspired to make this period of time very tough indeed, so I decided I must now really start to gather in my assets and cash, not least because I had too many projects far-flung and of which, if the current operators were unwell, I would have to take charge. So long as I have a positive plan, I am always fine; and so it was. Having obtained planning approval for the old *Village* site at Fleggburgh, we sold this to *Tredwell* for part cash and part loan and then, in 2011, we sold out completely.

Next, the storage and office property Tom O'Hanlon had been running in Gorleston as his pension from me (he had set nothing up) was closing, as he wanted to retire (at 80!), and we obtained a planning approval there as well, also bought by *Tredwell*. Tom died in late 2012, and thus I lost a man who had been with me longer than any other. I miss him.

In the USA we got a bid for *Collaborate MD*, which is mentioned in Chapter 15, and that came in with a profit. In London, although we had sold York Central in 2004, we had bought an apartment at Spencer Heights in the same year, and now sold that in 2006.

The sale of the Bungay offices in 1999 finally tidied the Holterman connection, and I moved to Main Cross Road in Great Yarmouth, where Bruce Carter and I had our joint ownership. That project now became very important for me over the next three years. I was on site managing the development and had a meaningful property base from which to operate again, and was really enjoying it.

First, a small brewery, *Blackfriars*, wanted to take the ground floor of one of the two buildings we owned. A rent was agreed, which made it more valuable, and shortly afterwards a medical company asked for part of the first floor. I moved into part of the second floor and, within three months, the whole front building was let, with me scrambling like mad to get it all refurbished.

That all made me think on what to do with the second building, where I obtained approval for 4 apartments on the top floor, and other work spaces on the other two floors, now all called *The Courtyard*. I wanted a craft centre and art gallery for tourists, with modest shared rents to help people get small businesses started.

The trouble was that tenants came and, very quickly, we were fully let - but they did not want to help themselves. So long as I did all the marketing, advertising and general work around the place and charged a low rent, they were happy to use it as a rest home! Slight exaggeration, but not much and, in the second year they all left, as I told them they had to look after themselves.

Next we got it fully let as business premises and *Tredwell*, through its pension scheme, bought the *Rex Studios* property next door from Bruce, who now lives mostly in the USA. In addition, the brewery has been taken over in 2013, with the new owners reviving the old *Lacons Brewery*, previously **the** original 1920s and 30s brewery in Great Yarmouth. *Lacons* has taken a lot more of the space, and re-opened on 21 May 2013. In late 2012, *Tredwell* also bought the Bruce Carter share of *The Courtyard*, so I now have a good new partner there with whom to develop.

Great Yarmouth has been allocated one of the five licences for large casinos in the UK, and that has been awarded to an area adjoining our development. We are at the 'wrong' end of town, towards the harbour but, with the casino, the new harbour itself, and the fact that part of the new Enterprise Zone also adjoins, it could mean that we may be in the same situation as I was with *Pleasurewood Hills* (albeit on a much smaller scale), of being a couple of years ahead of Yarmouth, but with an exciting future there.

Another trip I have not had a chance to mention is one Betty also arranged in 2009 - to Russia, travelling from Moscow to St Petersburg by a river cruise. A truly revealing 2 weeks, including the fact that there is not a lot of interest (for tourists anyway) in the areas between Moscow and St Petersburg! A good way to make this trip would be to fly to Moscow and stay for 3 or 4 days, then either fly or take the train to St P and stay another 3 or 4 days.

The actual boat was lovely but, after a week, everyone was screaming: 'I do NOT want to see another Russian church or icon.' We were with two American friends, Bud and Ellie Prude, also from *The Atrium* building, and we should have had Marjorie and TJ Malarney with us, but TJ suffered a stroke just before leaving, which was a great disappointment. However, like the guy who on the death of his father found his shoes and suits fitted, I did inherit TJ's pre-bought drinks plan….

In Moscow, we were moored near an underground railway station by which, with a guide, we went into the centre of the city. London, eat your heart out, the system was immaculate. Red Square in Moscow is every bit as fearsome as when we see the parades on TV, and Moscow is a very clean and safe city – but no sign in any language but Russian. The following day, Betty went off on a bus tour I did not want to join and, left on my own, I was tempted to go back to the city by the underground again, but chickened out because of the language and signs. I regret I did not take courage in my hands.

On to St Petersburg, the city of palaces – and some. I thought that, between England and Paris, we had by far the majority of famous works of art in the world, but St Petersburg has stunning collections; it is almost as if we have nothing! We visited the *Hermitage*, built in 1764 by Catherine the Great, we saw the famous *Amber Room* at the *Catherine Palace* and, for me, the most stunning of all was the array of fountains at *Peterhof Palace*.

Get there in good time and, at 11am, a couple of military maintenance types appear and turn on just two valves, which start water flowing to the most amazing array of fountains and sprays I have ever seen. Acres of them, and on a hill, so an absolutely spectacular sight as they build up one after the other, and all accompanied by spectacular Russian military music. This book is not meant to be a tour guide, but anyone contemplating a visit to Russia would do well to buy a paperback called, simply, *Catherine the Great* – and she was.

When we were in the *Hermitage* museum we did not realize that we were looking at 70 pictures which had previously belonged to Sir Robert Walpole, the first Prime Minister of Great Britain, in the 1700s, and who lived at Houghton Hall in Norfolk. Sir Robert collected all his life, and probably had the best collection in England. Unfortunately, when he died he left substantial debts, of about £6m at today's values, and his heirs decided to sell 70 of his best pictures. You can imagine the effort and the haggling in those days, with simply land and sea transport between Russia and England.

Catherine the Great bought the lot for £40,555, which is about £50m at today's values. The chance discovery at Houghton of an old gallery book showing, in meticulous detail, the position of all the pictures in the house in the 1700s, led to the idea of getting the pictures back for an exhibition. That exhibition was in 2013, and we were delighted to go and see the pictures again.

All through the 80s, 90s and into 2010, I had been looking after Jim Balls, mentioned before as the auditor for *WA Hills*; he died at 93 years in 2010 very lonely, having lost his wife. He once did me a favour by lending me money at a very difficult *Pleasurewood* development time (mortgaging his own house to do so, and I did not know). I felt I owed him, and did my best to look after him. Sainthood comes to mind.

As old people do, in his last two or three years he suffered from dementia (not Alzheimer's), and turned very nasty against me, the only old friend and contact he had. He had no family or other real friends and, if anyone attempted to be nice to him, he snarled them off. I read up on what happens with dementia, to try to understand and accept his extreme moods but, in the end, he actually made me ill. For a period, not only was he constantly telephoning, but he was sending me 20 or 30 unpleasant and threatening emails every day. I stopped that by cutting them off but, although I got him help, which he rejected, there is no way I could ever win in that situation.

He repeatedly told me he was leaving me his estate, but that he would make life as difficult as possible **after** he was dead. Only when he was gone did we find out what he meant – he had hidden his will! I could not find it on searching the property, but his lawyer later found it hidden in his piano music. I actually smiled at what he had done, because that was absolutely in character, and his old self would be laughing with us that we had found it.

2011 saw the marriage of our daughter, Rose, to James Hindle, enabling Betty and me to arrange a great wedding in the grounds of our Hapton home. We had a beautiful August day, a tiny, rarely-used (previous wedding 20 years ago, I think) village church, and our next-door friends, Philip and Rosita Chubb, organizing a couple of their antique cars to collect the bride and groom.

It's not often that anyone has to disguise themselves as church bells, as Rosita did in her car, to make the overall event more realistic by playing a recording of bells from outside the bell-less church. Our friend, Antony Jarrold, played great music on an organ we hauled in, and the ever-popular independent vicar, Richard Collier, kindly held the service for us.

Our perennial student daughter, Alice, always comes up with ideas, Christmas presents or suggestions which are unusual, and always certainly interesting. Therefore, (I suppose like her father in many ways) she did so for the wedding. She took part in the service with a 'reading' for her sister – but not in the way you would expect.

She chose 'I do, I will, I have,' by Ogden Nash, and it is so lovely and amusing I print it for you here:

'How wise I am to have instructed the butler to instruct the first footman to instruct the second footman to instruct the doorman to order my **carriage;** *'I am about to volunteer a definition of* **marriage.**

Just as I know that there are two Hagens, Walter and **Copen,** *I know that marriage is a legal and religious alliance entered into by a man who can't sleep with the window shut and a woman who can't sleep with the window* **open.**

'Moreover, just as I am unsure of the difference between flora and fauna and flotsam and **jetsam,** *I am quite sure that marriage is the alliance of two people one of whom never remembers birthdays and the other never* **forgetsam,**

And he refuses to believe there is a leak in the water pipe or the gas pipe and she is convinced she is about to asphyxiate or **drown,**

'And she says quick get up and get my hairbrushes off the windowsill, it's raining in, and he replies oh they're all right, it's only raining straight **down.**

'That is why marriage is so much more interesting than **divorce,** *because it's the only known example of the happy meeting of the immovable object and the irresistible* **force.**

'So I hope husbands and wives will continue to debate and combat over everything debatable and **combatable,**

Because I believe a little incompatibility is the spice of life, particularly if he has income and she is **pattable.'**

As father of the bride I was not going to be left out so, with Alice as my chief assistant, and in complete secrecy, we arranged a 'surprise' for the wedding breakfast in the form of the *Soprano Bella*. In various guises – we chose police – three top-quality opera singers will attend an event as a surprise. Boy – they certainly were! In authentic uniform and equipment, they 'arrested' the bridegroom, having come in and distributed authentic 'Terrorist WANTED' posters that Alice had printed. James was taken away in handcuffs for a time, and then we had the most delightful half-hour of opera, *Mamma Mia* and, finally, *Nessun Dorma*. Perfect, with a lovely second reception for others the following day.

All those years at Gunton Hall and *Pleasurewood Hills* at Lowestoft had to leave an impression on my soul! In 2011 I spotted an announcement that a group was going to take *The Marina Theatre* at Lowestoft out of the hands of Waveney District Council, and was asking for applications for trustees. On the spur of the moment I applied, and I found that, not only was I to be very welcome, but that Martin Halliday, who had been one of the managers at the *Ripley's Believe It or Not!* that we built at Great Yarmouth, was leading the take-out and was to become Chief Executive.

I duly joined the trust and started to find out what our possibilities were. Martin and I sat in the bay window at the theatre, surveying the other buildings around and observing: 'This one would make a great restaurant, that one would make a new entrance,' etc. We called up various owners and agents, really just to get a feel of the area but, within days, we were into discussing taking over the adjoining building east, as it had just been vacated by *Zenith Windows*, which had 18 months of its lease remaining.

The agent told me that the owner, who lived in Spain, was a Michael Wilson, and that this was his pension fund. Michael Wilson was the man who carried out all the electrical contracts for *Pleasurewood Hills*... Michael and I had not been in touch for over 20 years, but we made contact, emailed each other nearly every other day and between me, him and *Zenith* I made a contract for the trust to take over the lease, with an option to buy in a few years. He is in the Pleasurewood barbecue picture.

I am not embarrassed to say that one or two of the other trustees were pretty surprised (if not frightened) that Martin and I were perhaps, if not bulldozing, at least snow-clearing our way a bit fast. However, we did it and, by the time we signed the lease, we had designed a new box-office and a new link between the buildings, and Andrew had designed us a coffee bar. We made an art gallery, with the help of Michelle Payne of *The Upstairs Gallery* at Beccles, in the link between the old theatre and the new Rotunda building.

With my building experience, I costed the project out at around £100,000 and, of course, wanted to proceed – immediately if we were to keep the momentum up. As part of the original takeover, Martin had negotiated Waveney paying for a complete refurbish of the inside of the main theatre for June to September. He and I resolved that, somehow, I would get the money rolling in a £100k appeal– a very tall order –, and we would try to open the new building at the same time as the refurbished theatre 3 months later.

Astonishing ourselves, we did it. We opened the coffee shop and new box office on 14 Sept, and the new link and art gallery came in on 14 Nov. Phew!! But neither of us would like to have to do it again at that speed.

It was just amazing how we got support so fast, because Waveney, like any local authority, simply does not know how to spell the word 'speed'. We like action, and it has made an amazing difference to the whole theatre operation. Undoubtedly, Martin getting and keeping *The Royal Philharmonic* 'out-of-town' base with us has been the most important ingredient in the whole venture, and our opening on 14 Nov coincided with the start of their tenth year with us. We have pencilled in £25k from a supporter who says he will sponsor the gallery when his cash comes in, and that will tidy the whole project.

I need to record that all these 2005-to-2013 UK ventures could not have been achieved without personal help to me. Laurence King, that amazing jack-of-all-trades I found living at Hapton, and sorting a few problems for me there, and then Ted Masters turned up to build one of the extensions to my house which, in turn, led to a friendship and trust with them both for many other projects. I could not have either constructed *The Courtyard* or completed the work at *The Marina* without them. It is thanks to both, and I hope they will be able to put up with me for many years to come.

Chapter Fifteen
Family Cavalry to the Rescue in the USA, Susan, Mary and Aleks

I have tried to cover the safari of our personal property and other involvement in the USA as we have travelled through the book, from Boca Raton, Deerfield, Melbourne Beach, Vero Beach plot and then the two *Atrium* buildings, but I have given the two USA businesses and Aleks a chapter of their own here, because the story is so interesting (although sad at the start), and *SecureCare* has become such an important part of my life.

In a previous chapter I told you how my younger sister, Susan, had such a difficult time when Father was ill, as she was so young. Looking back, wanting first to train as a nurse was an indication of her nature, although she will not have realized it – to care, but not always very considerate of herself or her own family.

Susan had the Larter 'work ethic', also very much inherited by her son, Aleks and, throughout her life, although often in personal trouble, she was always involved in one scheme or another supporting herself. In 1967 I was home trying to hold the business together, and Susan became very much my responsibility; but no way could I control what she did. Living in Great Yarmouth, she had her own life and, very shortly, I met Aleks Szymanski (now Aleks Sr) and they told me they were getting married.

Aleks was also very young, his family from Poland. He was a jeweller, and he and Susan did actually make an interesting couple, but I think perhaps Aleks did not realize what he was taking on. Susan (my first wife) and I, gave them a lovely reception at Somerton Hall, where we were then living, and I recall some beautiful Polish music and singing on the lawns there at the wedding reception. Although the marriage did not last, one outcome was a son, Aleks Jr, who is now the CEO of *SecureCare* in Austin, Texas and who, for me, has become a very important person indeed, and we love him.

I think Susan must have been a very wild person to live with and, after the break-up, became involved in more than one other partnership and marriage, having another child as well. It was not unusual for me to get telephone calls for money or help – maybe in the middle of the night, asking for a ticket home from Spain or somewhere because whoever she was with had fallen out with/mistreated her, and she was deserted somewhere.

We forever hoped she would settle down and, one day, she turned up with a guy who said he was an accountant in Zimbabwe and the two of them wanted to take over a pub adjoining a tourist attraction near Aylsham. She brought her new daughter, Kelly, who was delightful. They needed to borrow money to take over the pub, where Susan had previous experience. I had a look at it with them and, to my relief, thought maybe at last we had Susan settled, so provided what they wanted.

A few months later, having heard nothing, I called by the pub to find it closed and, on enquiring of neighbours, found that one or both of them had a problem with drinking, rather than selling, the contents. We knew that Aleks Jr was living with his father and his new wife in Norwich, but of Susan we heard very little, other than the odd telephone contact early on until 2006 – maybe a gap of 30 years or so.

In December 2006 she contacted Mary and said she would like to see us, and that she was living in King's Lynn. I arranged to go over to have lunch with her, and immediately realized that she had contacted us because she was dying of cancer, which was in the very late stages. She made no reference to the past, except that she had followed her previous interest in nursing and had been managing a care home in Bury St Edmunds – so near, but so far! We had a lovely lunch and she was very down-to-earth about her situation, and talked just like we had met only the previous week.

She told me a bit about Aleks Jr – that he had married, had two children, and was running his own IT business in Ipswich. She also told me that Kelly now had a partner and a child. I met Susan twice more in January, and each time she was worse. She died a few weeks later. What she told me on the last visit was that I would meet Aleks again at the funeral, and that she knew we would get together.

After the funeral service, we all met as a family in the garden of our old Winterton house for a few minutes of thoughts about her, and then we walked to the beach, where she had asked her ashes be scattered in the sea. A very moving moment for Aleks and Kelly in particular, and then we repaired to *The Fisherman's Return* for lunch. And there, at last, I met again Aleksander Roman Szymanski – little Aleks!

We had a lot of catching up to do and I realized immediately why Susan had said Aleks and I would get together – we have since discovered we are really two peas in a pod, and more like twin brothers than uncle and nephew – but with Aleks having far more built-in common sense than I do. I arranged to meet Aleks for lunch a week or so later, and here's what he did over the next few years, not quite serendipity again, but certainly a very lucky happenstance for me.

My two business relationships in the USA, in Orlando, Florida and in Austin, Texas, stem from meeting Bob Woodrow, a fellow owner in *Atrium I*. He introduced me first to Doug Kegler, a young man who had a fledgling company called *Xgear* in Orlando, later *Collaborate MD*. Doug specialized in enabling efficient medical billing for doctors and medical practices. Bob aimed to raise a few hundred thousand dollars for the expansion of Doug's business. Would I join in?

I met Doug, liked him and duly invested a modest amount. Having returned to the UK and heard nothing for a month or two, I enquired of Doug if they had raised the full amount and he said: 'Nothing at all except your money, as Bob could not get the cash.'

Liking Doug a lot, I felt he had been let down, and so went about raising the cash for him from UK friends and associates, which I managed. We eventually sold out in 2010 – not for mega-bucks, but a useful profit, and Doug has a nice business and we keep in touch. That Woodrow connection led me – astray, Betty and some of my business colleagues would say – into a second USA company, but much more serious.

SecureCare Technologies, Inc., based in Austin, Texas, was a company listed on the NASD Bulletin Board and coming out of 'Chapter 11'. In the USA that is a form of protective bankruptcy, where shareholders and creditors lose most of their cash, but the company is considered worth saving and reviving with a further injection of cash behind a sound business plan and with new investors.

SecureCare enables the secure processing and storing of sensitive documents and data that are exchanged between doctors, healthcare providers and the government, with the aim of grabbing a big chunk of replacing billions (yes billions) of paper documents processed each year. What *SecureCare* does is provide efficient ways to process these files 'electronically' via your computer, tablet or mobile device in a secure and regulatory-compliant way.

I had a look and absolutely loved the idea behind it (and still do), because of the possibly massive scale and its recurring income, and this time there were already substantial new USA investors involved, led by *Gryphon Securities*, a supposedly substantial investment group. So, a much safer start than with Doug, but little did we know!

SecureCare was a very different kettle of fish from *Xgear* and, with poor leadership, they very quickly ran out of cash again. One of the investors alongside me was David McCall, and I will forever be grateful that he took a serious interest in where we were going, and helped me with his much wider business experience.

In March 2006 the company was again out of money, directors gone, all but three executives and employees dismissed, and trying to live on the modest monthly income they had achieved. That income was slowly declining because they could not promote development of products, or keep up a good service.

To be polite to the very hard-working Neil Burley and Gene Fry, trying to keep the company alive, David and I agreed to meet them in Miami in order to agree to close the company down. We asked a couple of USA executives I knew to also be there so we fully understood the position and, to cut a long story short, they all persuaded us to raise another $570k to keep the company going, alongside a complete restructure of ownership.

Neil and Gene hired a new CEO who was, we were told, really experienced in what we needed. That man proceeded to spend all the cash we raised until, at the time of meeting Aleks in 2008, we were about to close down again. With Aleks involved, we discovered that we could get real and serious. Aleks had enormous IT and marketing experience, so here at last I might have found someone who actually understood *SecureCare* and could grasp the opportunity. At that – he may call it 'fateful' - lunch with me after Susan's funeral, Aleks agreed to take a look at *SecureCare*.

He came back saying that, like me, he thought the idea and market had enormous possibilities, but there were some fundamental issues that needed sorting. He offered to make a visit or two, which then turned into two weeks in the USA and two weeks at home for more than 2½ years, running the business in both places - family support way beyond the call of duty.

He later told me that, having thrown his lot in with us, there was a point in the second year when he wondered if he could ever make it. He said: 'You gave me an old Model-T Ford in poor condition and asked me to service it, then make it into a BMW with new wheels, engine and bodywork, but I was not allowed to take it off the road whilst the work was being carried out.' That is a pretty fair description of the job he had.

After running the business since June 2009, with visa H1-B approval, he 'officially' became CEO on 1 October 2010 and then, at the end of 2011, sold up in Ipswich and moved his family over to Austin, where he is now firmly based. In March 2013, he bought a great house there to continue his American adventure. The year 2012 was the first one when he saw all his new systems and hardware really working and, from nothing, he has brought the company to substantial revenue with 17 employees and growing fast.

Looking back, why did we all believe in this and stay so long? I think, obviously, the huge potential of those billions of documents and the fact that IF we got it right, income is recurring and costs would drop dramatically.

Once again, that inbuilt trust I have got us into a lot of trouble but now, in 'entrepreneurial' terms, I would say it was a textbook example of how NOT TO do it – and then how TO do it. Aleks and I do sometimes say to each other: 'What if?' he had been there at the start.

Combined with getting to Florida in the UK cold winter months, it is a pleasure for me to now more frequently go to Austin to see what we are doing. and maybe Susan is looking down on us and wondering where we will go next. I will forever be grateful to Aleks for what he has done, but also to those long-suffering investors, who must have many times wondered if Joe would ever get this one right, and I thank them for their faith in me. They have rarely complained!

And so to my twin sister Mary

Although this is mainly the USA part of my life project it is also about the family, and I think it is a good place to talk about my sister. Different? Twins can be identical or not – and identical we for sure are not!

Mary is one of the most generous-hearted people you will meet, and maybe talks even more than I do. Whereas, when I put my toe in the water of local politics, I really could not stand what I saw as the tediousness of it, Mary has the patience to listen to people and then get on with them, helping wherever she can.

She was the youngest Councillor (at 23) to join the Blofield and Flegg district council (following Father there), became a Norfolk County Councillor, and was also the Chairman of her local Fleggburgh Parish Council for a number of years and, of course, was Lady Mayoress of Great Yarmouth alongside her dear Gordon. Those are all jobs I would never have had the inclination or patience to carry out.

She inherited Mother's skills in both dressmaking and embroidery, starting the local branch of the Embroiderers' Guild and, after training, taught at the Great Yarmouth College of Art, and had various local 'assistance' jobs, such as the St Raphael Club and the James Paget hospital at Gorleston.

In addition, she has been the Chairman of the local district Inner Wheel and its Great Yarmouth President, a long-time Governor of the Great Yarmouth College of Education, Chairman of West Flegg Middle School, Governor of Eastern College and also of Acle High School, the St John Ambulance area President, and a member of the District Health Authority.

She serves on the advisory panel for BBC East and Radio Norfolk, is a Trustee of the *Endeavour Rangers Band* and member of the Friends of Great Yarmouth Hospitals. And in her spare time…. You get the idea. She has had enormous energy to put into all these involvements.

Her first husband, Gordon Chapman, was of the same political 'ilk' and they made a great couple, until the enormous tragedy of him dying the year after he had been Mayor of Great Yarmouth, which stunned us all. Gordon, also a teacher, had the tradition of running in a pancake race at his school and did so that year, dropping dead at the end of the race. I see his portrait every time I go to the Town Hall, and he is sorely missed. Bruno Peek (of Queen's Jubilee fame) has provided me with a lovely picture of Gordon when Mayor, with Mary, at the lighting of the Maritime Britain beacon in 1981. What Gordon would make of politics today, I do not know.

Today, Mary lives happily at Fleggburgh with her second husband, George Lovewell Blake, from the oldest firm of accountants in East Anglia – and, I think, finds her family enough to concentrate on. Two other memories I have of Mary are, first, her dressed as Queen Victoria (a great likeness!) riding in a carriage through Great Yarmouth for the 150th anniversary of *Palmers* store there.

The other occasion, which was charming, was of her meeting Prince Charles on a visit to the Great Yarmouth College of Art in 2012, and him congratulating her on her retirement, which happened to be the same day.

Epilogue – and one Final Story
'A Short Concluding Section at the End of a Literary Work'

That is the dictionary definition : this is my epilogue.

How did I ever do all that which has filled these pages? My answer has to be – 'Occasionally with great difficulty!' In my 74 years to date I really can say I have had a very interesting ball – maybe it should have been a masked ball – sometimes and I might have done a few things differently of course, but then 'serendipity' is not a precise science. I have somehow emerged sane and solvent, after getting into some strange business situations and meeting some amazing people.

Above anything else, I wish to acknowledge that from the time I first set eyes on Betty my heart must have quietly tucked away a message to tell me this was going to be the lady with whom I would spend most of my life. She has brought me immense joy and 40 years on is still one amazing lady. Love story? For sure!

To give weight to my story I asked my sister, Mary, my children and one or two others to express their own thoughts on what I have done and memories they had. My thanks to them all and I wish the likes of Sydney Grapes, Geoffrey Thompson and Keith Sparks were all around to add in their two penny worth.

My character, I believe, was formed by my early years. Living in the simple farm house at Martham, then the freedom of being on the coast at Winterton and then boarding school, gave me a certain way of independence. I am always happy with people, but equally if I have to be on my own I am content. I would say simply, to echo Nelson on his return arrival at Great Yarmouth, 'I am a Norfolk man'.

I would be negligent if I did not here express my appreciation of those few special business friends who have over the years stood by me when others did not, and still stand with me today.

Bob Ludkin unknowingly released a latent talent I had for property when helping me to buy that first piece of land, followed by all the residential and chalet developments arising from that start. Then of course Pleasurewood Hills American Theme Park which has to have been the number one project in my life.

A seminal point of delight for me was attending the Pleasurewood 30th anniversary with Betty and meeting so many who came back for that day. To echo the original opening day, a sky diver dressed as Woody landed and handed me a wooden baton as a memento.

Pleasurewood Hills, followed by two Sealife Centres, the Bure Valley Steam Railway, Ripleys Believe it or Not!, starting Pleasurewood II in Lincolnshire, rescuing the Village development, a vineyard in New Zealand and the two businesses in the USA – I think as they say 'I made a difference'. Many of those projects arose because of that inbuilt autopilot I have mentioned which got me saying 'Yes let's do it' rather than 'Let's think about it'.

There is no doubt that chance moment of serendipity with the broken down taxi in Antigua which brought us the exchange of houses in the Bahamas, in turn leading to our being in the USA for 38 years, possibly had more effect on our lives than any other event. A truly perfect example of Serendipity.

If you ask what we regard as the best special memories, they have to be the delight of various completely surprise events I arranged for Betty and of course that little operatic surprise at the wedding of Rose. And one last story I tell you below which is moving

One couple not already mentioned are David Mellor and his lovely wife Mary, David being the local High Court Judge in Norwich. Not left out because he put me away or anything exciting like that! David and I became friends because he lived in Mulbarton the next village to Hapton. We met at various dinners, parties or events and simply liked each other. One evening at his home he asked what I was doing the next day. 'Nothing if you need some help' I replied and he asked me to come to his chambers at the Court next morning and to sit with him for the day.

I really did not understand what that meant, but had never seen him in action so thought it would be delightful to watch him. However, he really did mean 'sit with him'. An extra chair was placed beside his own and the court rose to receive his Honour Judge David Mellor and Joe Larter! I followed him in or led him out of court all day and we were hearing a murder case.

Two drug dealers, one had murdered the other, or so it was alleged. I could not go to Court for a second day and when I got home I wrote to thank him for the honour he had done me. An absolutely unforgettable day for a simple guy like me with a true friend, but then it all went wrong. David quickly contracted motor neuron disease and within a few months was gone from us. An absolute tragedy to take such a wonderful and good man.

We had him to supper in the very late stages of his illness when he needed a wheelchair and other support, with friends he knew and had a tremendous fun evening with a lot of red wine as was his liking. The following morning Mary his wife telephoned to thank us but also to say David died that night. More than a few tears I can tell you, but with that disease what a great way to go. We buried David in the churchyard at Mulbarton next to the lovely old house where he lived, and I like to think that he is now cared for by the multitude of those Larters of long ago who you have read about here, and are in there with him.

And how are the tribe doing?

Andrew and Jan are happily based with their kitchen design and supply business at Limpenhoe – another couple who love the marshes and Norfolk countryside.

Rebecca is with Mark , developing their business importing and designing heating systems for housing and at this time moving to expanded business premises in Norwich. Their three children thrive, Ben in London teaching music and other things, Imogen teaching in Beccles but really wanting to get into a sailing school in the Isle of Wight, and Abigail now at university in Southampton studying geography.

Rose the Chartered Accountant has taken over the Singapore accounting base of the firm of international lawyers she works for, splitting her time between Singapore, Hong Kong, Shanghai and Australia – with maybe an occasional visit to the UK and we have impressed on her how it is important to have a home large enough to allow elderly parents to visit in some luxury!

Our own perennial student is Alice, now doing a PhD in ancient languages and mediaeval history at Reading University. When she graduated with her second MA at Reading in December 2012 I joked with her that I would be making her a Member of the Institute of Arts – so she could put the letters MAMA MIA after her name.

Other branches of the family?

Mary has her two children Jonathan and Victoria. Jonathan is with his second wife Jenny in the haulage business, and his daughter Samantha has her own daughter Taylor .

Victoria another accountant, is controlling the cash at a firm of Solicitors in Great Yarmouth and is with her second husband Hugh. Her son Brian from first marriage is now an assistant Bank Manager.

In 2013 we heard of Wing Commander Mark Larter being awarded the Bronze Star for Peace by the Americans for his work in Afghanistan. Who he? I have not met him and he lives in Australia, but he is the son of my cousin Paul – son of Harry my father's brother. A great honour and from what I read he seems a remarkable man.

Finally… I do hope as either family or a friend, or just knowing Woody Bear you have enjoyed reading the book, and I thank all of you who have been in touch for your information and kind thoughts. Maybe in 10 years time I will add an update.

Joe Larter

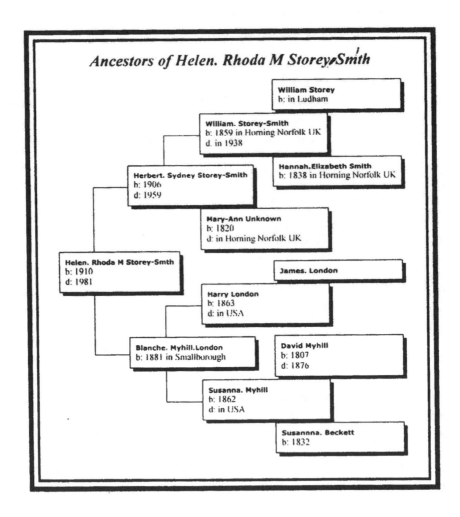

Ancestors of Helen. Rhoda M Storey-Smith

William Storey
b: in Ludham

William. Storey-Smith
b: 1859 in Horning Norfolk UK
d. in 1938

Herbert. Sydney Storey-Smith
b: 1906
d: 1959

Hannah.Elizabeth Smith
b: 1838 in Horning Norfolk UK

Mary-Ann Unknown
b: 1820
d: in Horning Norfolk UK

Helen. Rhoda M Storey-Smth
b: 1910
d: 1981

James. London

Harry London
b: 1863
d: in USA

Blanche. Myhill.London
b: 1881 in Smallborough

David Myhill
b: 1807
d: 1876

Susanna. Myhill
b: 1862
d: in USA

Susannna. Beckett
b: 1832

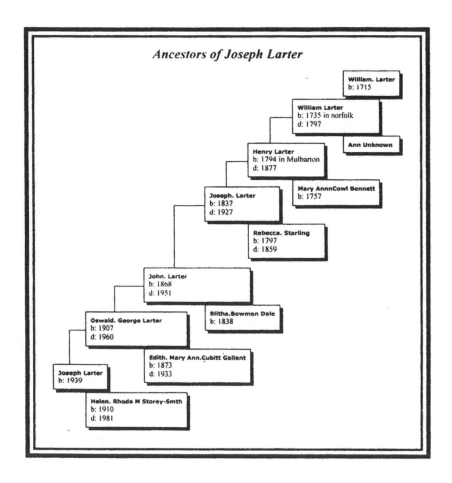

Ancestors of Joseph Larter

William. Larter
b: 1715

William Larter
b: 1735 in norfolk
d: 1797

Ann Unknown

Henry Larter
b: 1794 in Mulbarton
d: 1877

Mary AnnnCowl Bennett
b: 1757

Joseph. Larter
b: 1837
d: 1927

Rebecca. Starling
b: 1797
d: 1859

John. Larter
b: 1868
d: 1951

Blitha.Bowman Dale
b: 1838

Oswald. George Larter
b: 1907
d: 1960

Edith. Mary Ann.Cubitt Gallant
b: 1873
d: 1933

Joseph Larter
b: 1939

Helen. Rhoda M Storey-Smth
b: 1910
d: 1981

Serendipity
The main characters

Joe Larter b 27.7.39
(1) Susan Larter (Baker)
Andrew Michael Larter b 28.4.63
(m1993 Janice Jaworskyj)
Rebecca Jane Larter b 25.7.65
(m August 1986 Mark Tassie)
(Benjamin and Imogen b 28.9.87 Abigail b 2.11.92)

(2) Betty Ann Larter (Rudling) b 7.5.36
Alice Emma Helen Larter b 21.11.74
Rose Sarah Ann Larter b 30.12.77
(13.8.11 married James Hindle)

Mother: Helen Rhoda May Larter (Storey Smith)
(b 1910, m 1938 d 1981)
Father: Oswald George Larter
(b1907 d 1964)
Sisters: Mary (twin) and Susan b 19.9.46 d 18.3.08

Pat Dowsing – secretary and PA to Joe since the Gunton days

Robert (Bob) Ludkin – customer at Somerton Hall, later partner in Larters Estates and various sales and purchases. Mentor.
Freddie Smithson Peter Smithson in London

Alfred Hedges – Winterton friend when father was ill- Gt Yarmouth Librarian
Also wrote The Gunton Story
Reece Hedges, son of Alfred we helped with Caddymatic

Tom Bammant – farmer at Hemsby where Joe obtained planning approvals for the first Holiday chalet developments at Newport
Tom Bammant Jr – son

Jim Crampton and wife Barbara – partners in the Malta investments
Started Air Anglia, Travel Centre in Norwich. Cinema organs.

Jim Parke – owner of Heacham chalet development.
Harry Larter (uncle) owned first piece of land at Martham
Donald Maltman architect for Martham
Maurice Whalley architect at Lowestoft for Gunton and Pleasurewood

WA Hills directors
Alan Hills
Christopher Stowe
George Woodgate

Jim Balls auditor – Looked after him as an old man

Glan Gwna Wales
Jack Enston – sold us Glan Gwna
Derek Moorhouse – agent for sale
Gwylim app Hughes – lawyer
The Jones taxi family
Tom O'Hanlon
John James – both from the Hills building team to help me
Kate Aiken office/sales Manager

The Galliford / Hills deal and buy back
John and Cecil Galliford
John Galliford sold me back the leisure development interests
Jynx Grafftey Smith Wallace Bros Sasoon bank
Peter Deal introduction here, Huw Walters later
Peter Taylor

Keith Sparks – animations company in Colchester
Responsible for Woody and a lot of Pleasurewood Hills – Malta
Bruce carter Rex Sudios and partner in Courtyard
Rodney Scott – Cliff Hotel Gorleston
Tim and Janet Jones– Gunton Hall Lowestoft
Geoffrey Thompson Blackpool Pleasure Beach
John Broom Alton Towers
Andrew Hayworth Booth Windsor Safari Park

Bahamas / Chateau D'Oex swap
Roger Aylen
Julian Snowden
Alan Charlesworth Green Turtle Key Bahamas
Basil and Joyce Bloodworth in Chateau D'Oex Switzerland

Old School Henstead
Ray Gillings 1st Headmaster
Roger Middleditch
Keith Shannon
Derek Walker
Michael Hewitt 2nd Headmaster
Lauri Rimmer Headmaster Framlingham College

Pleasurewood Hills early days
Henk Bembom – rides for Pleasurewood
Andrew Larter catering
Ian Foster – advertising agent
Chris Barnard first Manager
Chris Tooley catering concession BBQs
John Packer Manager

Ronald Toone – Golden Sands rescue

RKF Group takeover
Bob Francis
Brian Bedson
Richard Heron

Pleasurworld plc and buy back
Derek Roll
Gavin Briggs
Tony Shorthose
Peter Haddon
Peter Rowledge
Johnathan Peel
Gareth Pearce
Huw Walters
Dick Williams

John Langford
Gerry McGurke

Priorycraft St Olaves
Wily Stenhild
Vic Martin
Dick Darkins

Major building schemes
Bruce Carter theming studios
Max Milburn – Tesco scheme and home in Stowmarket
David Mace – Sealife Centres
Chris Mitchell
Clive Preston

Seaforths travel
Jenny Mills
Alan Schoenher
Gary Hance

Ripleys and USA
Sylvia Matiko
Bob Masterson
Norm Deska

Fitz Otis – Cine 180

Steam, organs and Bygone Village
Happy Hudson – P wood, BVR, The Village
John Edwards – P wood Bure Valley Railway
Ken Sims Chairman Village
Paul Lovett Director Village
Terry Hepworth – Organs Trust

Fund raising
Noel Edmonds and lottery
Jane and Henry Burke – Playhouse
Martin Halliday Marina Theatre
Paul Bayfield Lowestoft Air Show and Marina Theatre

New Zealand
Andrew Scott
Rex and PJ Brook Taylor Framingham
Barrie and Shelley Mangos vineyard partners
Keith and Tommi Harvey USA

Henry Holterman
Seaforths Travel Reggeborgh
Rivercastle Phonelink   ATP
Barbados Bungay

Graham Ramsey in London
Phonelink
ATP

Securecare and Collaborate MD
Bob Woodrow
Younis Zubchevitch
Doug Kegler
Les Mezaros
Bob Fritzinger
Neil Burley
Dennis Nasto
Aleks Szymanski – my nephew

City Star Airline
Atli Arnesson
Runar Arnesson
Gary Hance
Lee Sharpe

Barbados
Ralph Johnson and Peter Chesham
David Mace Mike Cawser
Patricia Affonso-Dass   Ed Ince
Simon Milligan   Tracy Johnson
Mitchel Hird (Mitch)
Cliff Richard Sir Gary Sobers

Joe Larter